The Cambridge Introduction to
Comedy

'Laughter', says Eric Weitz, 'may be considered one of the most extravagant physical effects one person can have on another without touching them'. Laughter is undeniably connected to the label of comedy for most people in this day and age. But how do we identify something which is meant to be comic, what defines something as 'comedy', and what does this mean for the way we enter the world of a comic text? Addressing these issues, and many more, this is a 'how-to' guide to reading comedy from the pages of a dramatic text, with relevance to anything from novels and newspaper columns to billboards and emails. The book enables you to enhance your grasp of the comic through familiarity with characteristic structures and patterns, referring to comedy in literature, film and television throughout. Perfect for drama and literature students, this *Introduction* explores a genre which affects the everyday lives of us all, and will therefore also capture the interest of anyone who loves to laugh.

Eric Weitz is Lecturer in Drama Studies at the School of Drama, Film and Music, Trinity College Dublin.

The Cambridge Introduction to
Comedy

ERIC WEITZ

CAMBRIDGE
UNIVERSITY PRESS

CAMBRIDGE UNIVERSITY PRESS
Cambridge, New York, Melbourne, Madrid, Cape Town, Singapore, São Paulo, Delhi

Cambridge University Press
The Edinburgh Building, Cambridge CB2 8RU, UK

Published in the United States of America by Cambridge University Press, New York

www.cambridge.org
Information on this title: www.cambridge.org/9780521540261

First published 2009

Printed in the United Kingdom at the University Press, Cambridge

A catalogue record for this publication is available from the British Library

Library of Congress Cataloguing in Publication data
Weitz, Eric.
    The Cambridge introduction to comedy / Eric Weitz.
        p.   cm.
    Includes bibliographical references and index.
    ISBN 978-0-521-83260-1 – ISBN 978-0-521-54026-1 (pbk.)
    1. Comedy–History and criticism–Theory, etc.   2. Comic, The.   I. Title.
    PN1922.C27 2009
    808.8′017–dc22   2009000648

ISBN 978-0-521-83260-1 hardback
ISBN 978-0-521-54026-1 paperback

Contents

Illustrations

Preface

This book is based on the general premise that comedy or the comic requires a vital adjustment to the reading process, through which we elect to take the world playfully. It also advances the idea that knowing something more about the workings of humour, plot and performance can help enhance the mental process of reading comedy. Although I will have cause to discuss some historical contexts and theory along the way, this book is not meant to provide a comprehensive account of either. For those interested in further reading in those areas I have included some suggestions at the end of the book.

One contention of this book is that performance plays an undeniable role in any comic construction – as, arguably, it does in any artistic creation – and such is the case even in a political cartoon, comic novel or email, where the competent performance is crafted for the specific relationship between the author's output on the page and the mind's eye of the reader. A comic text is *intended* toward an audience, consciously fashioned according to the interactive process between a medium's 'writers' and 'readers'. And so, for example, a comic anecdote written to be read in the morning newspaper is likely to be worded at least slightly differently from the same story delivered as part of a late-night television host's opening routine.

Because Western civilization's first formal notions of comedy – indeed, the word itself – derive from ancient Greek drama, the book will retain a primary focus on comedy as it appears in dramatic form. Such an approach also calls attention to the fact that, although a printed dramatic text would appear to be something concrete and unchanging which can be held in the hands and scrutinized long after its original production, it cannot be fully considered without some acknowledgement of the enactment – or at least speaking aloud – for which it is conceived. I have in passing referred to the processing of comedy in other forms, like film, television and literature. I believe that a grasp of comedy and the comic in dramatic texts serves one well for its reading elsewhere, so that the principles found herein can be adapted almost intuitively to the somewhat different processes of reading novels and watching movies.

An anticipation of performance beneath the lines of a dramatic text allows wide-open spaces for the reader's practical engagement with comedy. It is hoped that the reader of this book (and some friends or classmates) will attempt to read aloud some of the cited scenes and texts. There are a variety of things to be learned from gaining a sense of comic practice 'from the inside', the full value of which can never be explained in the words of a book. I also pose questions for reflection along the way, and there is no better spur to lively discussion than one's favourite comic texts, performances and performers.

The land of comedy will always frustrate efforts at precise and consistent mapping. Its boundaries shift with critical perspective; its territories remain ever subject to analytical dispute. One of the things you find out very soon when surveying analytical views on comedy and humour is that they reveal at least as much about the writer as the topic, and sometimes more. I have tried to strike a balance, in choosing sample texts, between those that are 'recognized' (and therefore easy to find in second-hand bookshops) and those that appeal to me. Neither of these criteria is particularly objective, and could well invite disdain from various critical quarters. In the first instance, I have chosen pieces because they *are* easy to find in libraries and stores; if they lead to discussions about the implications of the terms 'literature' or 'art', or invite enquiries into the Western canon and culture, that's not so bad. In the second instance, I think I have fairly broad-ranging tastes in comedy and humour, although it doesn't matter whether you endorse my choices – our differences of opinion may in some way prove instructive, and you can still apply the principles discussed to your *own* favourites.

In terms of a general road map for this book, I have begun with an Introduction to the subject, raising more questions than answers about the topic of comedy in general. Chapter 1 addresses the notion of genre in pragmatic terms, and focuses on the way we recognize that a text requires the crucial adjustment toward reading comedy, as well as on what it tells us in the way it signs off. Chapter 2 returns to comedy's foundations in ancient Greece and Rome, suggesting some ways in which its origins have supplied comic patterns still recognizable today. Chapter 3 looks at the mechanics of humour and how they tend to manifest themselves in the words of a dramatic text. In Chapter 4 I offer an introduction to the *commedia dell'arte*, and call attention to the ways it has shaped some of the texts we read today, particularly with regard to comic character and performance templates. Chapter 5 points out how elements of comedy – primarily humour – have inflected other, more serious stage worlds, especially as any previous dividing line between comedy and tragedy became terminally blurred in the twentieth century. Chapter 6 offers brief discussion first of comedy's relatives, like irony and satire, and then of various theoretical concepts pertaining to the sociopolitical implications of comedy and the comic. Boxes are included throughout the text to provide supplementary food for thought, or to touch upon topics of relevance to the main discussion.

A few housekeeping details, before we begin: I have made my peace with key terms like 'comedy', 'the comic' and 'humour', none of which have standardized, consistent usages in either everyday or analytical terminology, and I have defined them in the Introduction. I use the term 'text' to refer to any artistic object, from novel to film to stage performance. Similarly, we 'read' a text whether it reveals itself through words on a page, images on a screen or actors on a stage. The people who make these texts and those who receive them I call 'writers' and 'readers', even though they may be playwrights, directors and actors in the first instance and spectators in the second. You will notice, however, that I sometimes can't help using compound terms like 'reader/spectator', to make sure that the acts of both reading and watching are held in the mind.

For the sake of tidiness in the supplementary boxes, I have tried to keep citations to a minimum and as unobtrusive as possible. For passages from dramatic texts I have included page numbers in the Notes; they refer to the play's edition in the List of texts. For general quotes the author's name will always be included in the body of the text or in the notes, allowing the reader to find the source in the bibliography; for cases in which I feel obliged to supply a more specific location, I have supplied a page number.

This part of the writing process has come upon me quite abruptly, so I am sure I have forgotten to acknowledge key influences and helpers along the way. By all means let me know who you are and I'll include you next time.

I am grateful to the School of Drama, Film and Music at Trinity College Dublin; to my students, even though they were usually unaware of the things they taught me about comedy; to John McCormick, who supervised the thesis that led to this project; to Dennis Kennedy, who has always had encouraging words; and to Brian Singleton, for his willingness in helping make time in my schedule to work on this book. And, of course, to Ann and Rhona.

I am grateful to the International Society for Humor Studies and its part in my analytical awakening toward the comic, especially by showing it to me through the eyes of other disciplines. International conferences have always challenged my certainty on the subject and sent me away with much to think about. I would also like to thank the Drama League of Ireland, its staff and students, for realizations I have made about comedy during workshops and for forcing me to articulate the workings of the comic in something approaching plain English. I must give special thanks to Jean Buoy, who presided over my birth as a writer and set me on the high road to literary aspiration.

Other people whose help and generosity have contributed in some way include Liz Sheehy and Kristian and Liv Marken. Geraint Lewis has been particularly cooperative in letting me use his photographs; I am grateful to John Cleese and Andrew Sachs for their permission to use the photograph from *Fawlty Towers*.

I am deeply indebted to Vicki Cooper, Becky Jones and Cambridge University Press, all of whom have been endlessly patient and relentlessly supportive throughout this extended writing process. Becky has been particularly helpful in hauling me across the finishing line.

I thank my Weitz and Sheehy families for continued support and understanding. I owe the greatest debt to my parents and their safe haven, where I have written several of the chapters; to Eamonn and Liam, for their constructive distractions; and, of course, to Ann, whose spirit of play is second to none.

Introduction: thinking about comedy

First things

Consider the following series of questions. When you reach for a film in the Comedy section of the local video store, what are the inferred promises which have narrowed your search to this particular category? As you settle in to watch the film, what effect does knowing that it is considered a comedy have on the way you watch it, the way you process information, the way you form expectations about what will happen, and, eventually, how you describe it to other people? Or why, on the other hand, might you have chosen to *avoid* a film which appears in the Comedy section?

In fact, anyone old enough to be reading this book already knows a good deal about comedy. By virtue of being raised somewhere within the force field of Western culture, you have unwittingly acquired a set of guidelines and expectations as to something of the label's connotation in our society and (perhaps more importantly) what it means to you.

This book will attempt to illuminate these things you know without knowing about comedy, and otherwise seek to augment your current level of expertise on the subject. Its overarching project is to assist you in reading comedy from the page – particularly with regard to dramatic texts – more confidently, more knowledgeably, and, should you be so inclined, with a sharper analytical eye. Andy Kempe, who specializes in drama education, offers an interesting comment on reading dramatic texts, by relating it to the way his young daughter might play through a new piece on the guitar (which, apparently, was taking place at the time he wrote the article). She was becoming somewhat adept at playing the actual notes, but, he observes, 'The playing has no "feel" to it and she seems to lack an overall concept of where the piece is going or how it hangs together.'[1] Part of reading any text involves gleaning its instructions as to *how* to read it, what to expect from it, and something of its 'feel'. Identifying a play, novel, or newspaper article as 'comic' in some way calls for a mental adjustment in our processing of its content (see the box on page 2).

Visual genre cues

An exceedingly unscientific experiment may serve to demonstrate something of the reading process that we take for granted. Turn on your television and mute the sound. With remote control firmly in hand, begin to surf the channels, trying to register something of the show's gist before moving on to the next.

It should be interesting to note the cues that 'tell' you the type of television text you are reading. What visual cues, for example, tell you that you are watching a documentary or news programme? What, in the way the actors relate to one another, identifies it as, say, a soap opera? Even if you recognize the show, try to look beneath your familiarity with it – pinpoint the characteristics which would help you identify it if it was the first time you had seen it.

Eventually, limit your search to comedies. Try to spend a few minutes each on situation comedies or film comedies. What, in the use of the actors' bodies or faces, suggests it is comedy? Does the setting, costumes or colour scheme contribute to your assessment? We sometimes read past the 'intended' signals. We may, for example, recognize an actress primarily known for comedy, and endow the show with comic intent, even if the rest of the evidence does not support that. (You may have to cover the markers on the screen supplied by your cable provider or broadcaster to make a fair test of it.)

As we embark on our exploration it may help to explain a few things about the way this book has been written. One of the initial challenges in entering a discussion on comedy stems from the ungainly sprawl, not only of the topic, but of the term's usage. It is difficult to tighten the reins on the meaning of a word most people have long used in their own, personalized fashion. At the same time, 'comedy' necessarily acquires slightly different critical meanings across adjacent domains like drama, literature, film and television. The word 'humour' also bears a number of different connotations, and is sometimes interchanged with 'comedy'. To forestall confusion about a few central terms we will use throughout the book, let us agree upon the following usages:

'Comedy' is a *genre*, a recognizable type or category of artistic creation with characteristic features. Comedy embraces a range of subgenres, like farce and TV sitcom, and cross-pollinates with other genres to form the likes of tragicomedy.

'Humour' is a *social transaction* between at least two people – and, by extension, between a performer or writer and audience – through which one party intends to evoke amusement or laughter. In many cases, it is a telltale characteristic of 'comedy'. A 'joke', for example, is a formal (or even informal) attempt to initiate humour.

'Comic' or 'the comic' refers to the features of comedy, often its humorous inclination, and includes any of its qualities or strategies. A 'bit', 'gag', or 'routine' is a theatrical or visual sequence with humorous intent. These can be considered comic elements and may appear in works which would not wholly be considered comedies.

'Laughter' is a biological *response* to a variety of stimuli including humour. Although laughter may be considered one of the most extravagant physical effects one person can have on another without touching them, it can also be brought about by discomfort and tickling. And though we usually think of laughter as an involuntary reaction, it can be initiated purposefully by the 'laugher' (e.g., to curry favour or to demonstrate ridicule).

Let us get started, then, by laying some groundwork.

Play

In Western culture, it is generally unlikely that a stranger would bid you to undress, expecting casual compliance. There is, however, at least one exception to this 'rule' of social conduct: if the stranger happens to be a doctor in an examining room, there would be nothing untoward about the request. In a similar way, the nature of your transaction with a professor in class probably differs from the way you would relate to her if you run into one another at the local supermarket. You might even carry out a short conversation unrelated to your studies as you both pick through the selection of ice creams.

Sociologist Erving Goffman uses examples like these to describe the way we reach adulthood armed with a complex system for organizing experience, which he calls 'framing'. Through it, we categorize our social interactions, thereby interpreting events and referring to unspoken guidelines for behaviour, expectation and response, like the two examples put forward above. (The term, 'framing', is notoriously inconsistent in literary studies, but in this book will always align with Goffman's usage.) Goffman's concept of 'framing', as the way we gauge what kind of behaviour is called for or permitted and what meanings might be intended for a given situation in everyday life, affects our moment-to-moment engagement in the social world. It can also be applied to the way we make sense of plays, films, novels and any other texts, and so provides a doubly apt introduction to the study of comedy.

In Goffman's system, what we think of as 'real' or original experience is mediated by two kinds of 'primary framework', classified as physical or social. We apply a certain kind of attention to activities like crossing a busy street or interviewing for a job, because it matters to our short- and long-term well-being or social standing. This can also be called taking the world 'seriously' or operating in 'serious mode', because it is somehow connected, even on a mundane level, to our material security.

As you may have realized, we sometimes take time out from serious mode, if only for the length of time it takes to trade wisecracks with a fellow student or co-worker. This amounts to a way of behaving that does *not* take the world or reality at face value, or in some way sidelines the straightforward concerns of serious mode, at least for the moment. Goffman calls this a 'secondary framework', and its behaviour is bracketed from the so-called 'real-world'. In the realm of secondary frameworks, a 'keying' of a secondary framework occurs when we agree to suspend the 'serious' or primary-framework meanings of a strip of experience – e.g., the playing of a game or a sarcastic exchange like the following: I am walking to class one morning, with the rain lashing down and the wind blowing my umbrella inside out. I pass a drenched commuter, waiting for a bus by the side of the road. We catch each other's eye, and I summon as cheery a 'nice day' as I can muster; he responds with a surprisingly game 'glorious day!' In the midst of foul primary-framework conditions – getting to work on time against the fury of the elements – we have, by mutual consent, keyed a brief exchange from a clearly different kind of day for nothing other than shared bemusement at our miserable states.

Similarly, if someone says, 'I have a joke for you', they are keying a divergence from 'serious' conversation (which you would probably accept with an 'OK' or a grin, unless you are in a rush or a particularly bad mood and 'refuse' the invitation). Even without prefacing the joke explicitly, if someone asks you, 'How many English professors does it take to change a light bulb?', you know a 'non-serious' exchange has been keyed because of your sociocultural experience. This kind of implied signalling will have further relevance when we approach humour itself in Chapter 3.

To continue, a 'construction' is brought about when one or more participants fabricate a false primary framework for the benefit of another or others – in other words, one party 'constructs' a secondary, 'non-real' framework, which is meant to be taken by another party as a primary framework. Examples of a construction would include the concoction of a cover story for the purpose of coaxing a friend out of her house so that her surprise birthday party can be readied. An insurance scam or a police sting would also be considered constructions (see the box on page 5).

Goffman's 'keyings' and 'constructions'

A strip of experience from a primary framework might involve two men fighting over a piece of bread; a corresponding 'keying' might see the two men practising together in a martial-arts class; a 'construction' could have the same two men earnestly pretending to fight with each other in a pub, in the hope of getting thrown out to avoid paying their bar bill. Games and sports fall within non-serious or play frames – they amount to secondary-framework enactments of hand-to-hand or army-to-army combat, with rules that stand in for the actualities of physical conflict. You and I may play in a game of football *as if* our lives depended on the outcome, but they don't, in 'reality', and that is the understanding upon which we play. For professional football players, however, their performances may have primary-framework implications for livelihood and physical health, but the game itself remains in a secondary framework.

Goffman awards the 'theatrical frame' its own chapter, describing it as 'something less than a benign construction and something more than a simple keying'.[2] It might be said that any artistic creation invokes some version of this framing balance, in that the readers cooperate in giving it life, yet it maintains interest by continually withholding something of its making.

The realm of secondary frameworks includes a mode of human activity sometimes called 'play', which goes by a number of other names, including 'non-serious mode'. A play frame relieves an event of serious, primary-framework import and meaning. It is usually assumed that all parties to the play frame participate with full knowledge (while a practical joke would be another example of a construction).

Psychoanalyst D. W. Winnicott ascribes to play a universal importance in helping children negotiate a healthy bridge between 'inner psychic reality' and the 'external world', which clearly (and perhaps disturbingly) maintains its own agenda in the face of any given wish by the individual. Later in life, accessibility to this highly personal middle ground may turn into what we call creativity: 'It is assumed that the task of reality-acceptance is never completed, that no human being is free from the strain of relating inner and outer reality, and that relief from that strain is provided by an intermediate area of experience which is not challenged.'[3]

When children play, they do not shift physically to another universe, nor do they lose touch with their actual surroundings. They merely accept (or 'make believe') that, for example, the chair is a throne or a car or a mountaintop, and that they are kings or queens or parents or superheroes (see the box on page 6). It should be apparent that this is exactly what we do in the theatre, and that the spectator is no less involved in the playing just because the involvement appears more passive than the practitioner's. Bruce Wilshire claims that the collective pretending we do in the theatre is not far removed from that which takes place on the fields of childhood: 'Together the audience and the actors engage in incarnated imaginative variation of the meaning of human being and doing.'[4] The play frame operates similarly in film, television and literature. We usually know when to take the images on the screen or the words on the page to represent some 'other' world fashioned by human hands, and we are asked to invest in it as in some way 'real' – although the likes of *Jackass*, Michael Moore and Ali G may have muddied the waters in that regard.

Some views on play

Margaret Lowenfeld (1935) Writing about the importance of play in child development, Lowenfeld observes that 'play has an outer and inner aspect: an outer aspect, which is the form which appears to the playfellow or adult observer, and an inner or psychological aspect, which is the meaning that the type of play has to the child'.[5]

She sets forth four main purposes:

(a) It serves as the child's means for making contact with his environment . . .
(b) It makes the bridge between the child's consciousness and his emotional experience . . .
(c) It represents to the child the externalized expression of his emotional life . . . and
(d) It serves for the child as relaxation and amusement, as enjoyment and as rest . . .

Johan Huizinga (1938) In his well-known study of play, called *Homo Ludens*, Huizinga describes play as 'a stepping out of "real" life into a temporary sphere of activity with a disposition all of its own'.[6] Furthermore, 'it stands outside the immediate satisfaction of wants and appetites', and 'adorns life, amplifies it':[7]

> Summing up the formal characteristics of play we might call it a free activity standing quite consciously outside 'ordinary' life as being 'not serious', but at the same time absorbing the player intensely and utterly. It is an activity connected with no material interest, and no profit can be gained by it. It proceeds within its own proper boundaries of time and space according to fixed rules and in an orderly manner. It promotes the formation of social groupings which tend to surround themselves with secrecy and to stress their difference from the common world by disguise or other means.[8]

Jean-Paul Sartre (1943) Sartre seems to be saying that we come *too much* to terms with the exterior world at the expense of our humanity: 'Seriousness involves taking the world as one's starting point and attributing more reality to the world than to oneself; or reality to oneself only to the extent one belongs to the world . . . It is obvious that the serious man at bottom is hiding from himself the consciousness of his freedom . . . Man is serious when he takes himself for an object . . . What indeed is play if not an activity of which man is the first origin, for which man himself sets the rules, and which has no consequences except according to the rules he has set? . . . The act is not its own goal for itself; neither does its explicit end represent its goal and its profound meaning; but the function of the act is to make manifest and to present to *itself* the absolute freedom which is the very being of the person.'[9]

M. J. Ellis (1973) Ellis outlines fifteen recognized theories of play, including the release of surplus energy and its function as rehearsal for real life. It is not necessary for my purposes to address them all. But Ellis notes at the very start of his study that 'ideologically a human is most human, as defined by our culture, when at play'.[10]

Michael J. Apter (1982) Apter divides subjective activity into 'telic' and 'paratelic' states. The 'telic' state is defined as an orientation by a person toward some essential goal. The goal is real, the course planned, and the pleasure lies in the future, pending the achievement of the goal. In the 'paratelic' state the subject is oriented toward some aspect of behaviour or sensation. It is present-driven, spontaneous and pleasurable in itself.

Richard Schechner (1993) Schechner sees 'playing' as a vital aspect of culture and performance. He says, 'playing is a mood, an attitude, a force',[11] and goes on to suggest the use of the term 'play net' as a more accurate metaphor than 'frame'. He bemoans the fact that the 'multiple realities' of play are always given lesser consideration than serious mode: 'In the West, play is a rotten category, an activity tainted by unreality, inauthenticity, duplicity, make believe, looseness, fooling around, and inconsequentiality. Play's reputation has been a little uplifted by being associated with ritual and game theory. The defense department takes play seriously when it stages war games and simulations.'[12] Schechner concludes, 'The questions we need to ask are: how, when, and why is playing invited and sustained? How, when, and why is playing denied or repressed? Is playing categorically antistructural – that is, does it always take the opposite position or role to whatever is happening at the time it erupts or is invited? Is playing autonomous – that is, will it "just happen" if nothing else blocks, cancels, or represses it?'[13] Although these comments come from his book, *The Future of Ritual*, there is a wide-ranging chapter on Play in his 2002 book, *Performance Studies: An introduction*.

What is comedy?

Thinking back to the series of questions with which the chapter began, it may be instructive to reflect upon some works which in your view typify comedy. Try to isolate those you believe deserve placement at the centre of the classification, then think about *why*. Compare your choices and their justifications with those of other people. For the purposes of this mental exercise, it is important to think in terms of a 'definitive' or even 'perfect' example of comedy rather than your favourite play, film or novel. (After that, go ahead and think about what characterizes forms of 'the comic' most pleasing to you.)

It should not spoil the exercise to suggest in advance that comedy is, at the very least, an unwieldy creature of radically changeable appearance – you would, I suspect, have trouble narrowing your list down to a single entry which presents 'the essence' of comedy, if forced to choose from drama, film, television and literature. It cannot be bad (or unenjoyable) to apply conscientious thought to such a question at the start of our exploration. But, as Alexander Leggatt suggests, we might well be looking at the question the wrong way round: 'There is no such thing as comedy, an abstract transhistorical form; there are only comedies. But they accumulate to create a body of case law, a set of expectations within which writers and audiences operate.'[14] Leggatt's formulation is astute and timely for the practical purposes of this book: we should resist the temptation to become caught up in analytical generalizing for its own sake. It is, rather, worth remembering that we each cultivate our own body of evidence for the framing of genre one text at a time, beginning in the mists of childhood and thereafter redefining our sense of genre with each new text we meet.

Let us reiterate, then, that by early adulthood most people have acquired a considerable range of experience in identifying certain texts as 'comedy' before, during and after they read them (whether from the armchair or spectator's seat). It is surely something most of us do without reflection. And so, if pressed, one might encounter some difficulty in compiling a precise description applicable to *all* texts we intuitively classify as comedy. The works of Aristophanes differ from the plays of Molière, which differ from the television series *The Office*, though it is likely that most people would consider all of them comedies. If we then throw our enquiry open to the performance of a stand-up comic, a novel by Jane Austen, the film, *Bringing Up Baby* (1939), a newspaper column by Dave Barry, and the animated television series, *The Simpsons* (1989–), is there any hope of finding some meaningful, all-embracing characterization?

Something to make us laugh?

The most obvious response to the above paragraph is that all of the texts appear intended to make us laugh or at least amuse us. (They may not all be successful at it, but we usually know when something or someone *means* to be funny). Most of us, at first glance, would consider humorous intent an expected feature of comedy – an identifiable joking attempt within a text's introductory moments would generally guide us toward a comic genre framing, depending on surrounding elements. For those who like to make lists, humorous intent would appear as the most prominent of comedy's 'family traits'.

It might be pointed out, however, that this has not always been the case. In some eras, for example, laughter has been considered morally unseemly, while some theorists have claimed that comedy's sole obligation is to instruct.[15] Although this is no longer the presiding view, it should also be apparent that humour alone does not automatically mark a text as comedy. Recent critics have warned against the superficial definition of comedy as something that makes us laugh. L. J. Potts says, 'I cannot help thinking that to identify comedy with laughter is to begin at the wrong end,' and then goes on to explain, 'The truth is that just as the emotions evoked by tragedy are too complex to be called merely sad, so comedy is too complex to be merely funny'.[16] Surely there *is* something more, both at the heart of comedy and in its surface behaviours.

Susanne K. Langer also contends that, although humour has a habit of appearing in comedy, and may even provide its dominant tone, it 'is not the essence of comedy'.[17] Langer establishes 'foreknowledge of death' as that which distinguishes humans from other animals; their attitudes toward that knowledge inform any drives toward self-realization, and, 'since the instinctive struggle to go on living is bound to meet defeat in the end, they look for as much life as possible between birth and death'.[18] Langer finds this drive manifest in drama's 'comic rhythm', and characterizes the essence of comedy as the 'human life-feeling', a sense of vitality or 'felt life', which lifts us past the awareness of our mortality.

This impression of spirited escape from the harsher realities of corporeal existence recalls the sense of play, discussed above, with which we humans sidestep the serious implications of life on earth, and which I take to underpin the generative feeling of all we take as comedy. This is not to paint comedy as uniformly or even basically escapist, but to characterize the psychic freedom with which it approaches the world, unconstrained by the limits of 'serious' discourse. Humour remains a favourite characteristic of comedy because it embodies the infinite number of playful alternatives to any serious thought or strip of action (snippet of human activity). It is a certain sense of 'taking the world playfully' that generates comedy's affinity for humour, and, I believe, allows us a viable thread through the texts submitted at the end of the previous section, which are widely varied in feeling and form. Humour itself does not exhaust the effect of comedy's impulse to play with the world, yet its intention to amuse is fairly emblematic of that animating force.

Happy endings

Every text comes to an end at some point, and we take as extremely meaningful the intellectual and emotional imprints with which it leaves us. Andrew Bennett and Nicholas Royle, writing about literature in general, note that 'a particularly helpful way of reflecting on the overall force of a literary text is to analyze the nature and impact of its ending'.[19] The last image before blackout in a theatre performance, like the last words of a novel, comprises our final first-hand contact with the world of the text. From a reader's perspective, it is arguable that we cannot know entirely 'what to make' of a text until it is over, that is, until we have its full picture. This is not to suggest that a text ceases to work on us once we part company with it, just that it puts vital finishing touches on its vision of life in the express way that it 'signs off'.

Comedy, of course, has a reputation for ending 'happily' or 'in marriage', sometimes through sudden and unlikely reversals of fortune (which we may come to expect precisely because we 'know' comedy). This sense of comedy's natural shape may survive as a structural echo of the festive upsurge with which Ancient Greek comedy ended. In his well-known work, *The Origin of Attic Comedy* (1914), Francis Cornford posits that standard elements of Aristophanes' comedies follow directly from earlier ritual patterns. He identifies one element as the 'sacred marriage', an ultimate pairing off at the end of any given play. Such an ending may appear tenuously justified to the contemporary sensibility, but, according to Cornford, needed no further substantiation in its historical context, as it remained an insistent remnant from formal comedy's roots in the folk culture's rites of fertility.

Comic resolution is sometimes seen symbolically as an act of rebirth, renewal or reaffirmation. Northrop Frye associates comedy, as one of his four generic literary plots (*mythoi*), with the season of spring. He sees comedy's universal movement as the hero's challenge to existing society in pursuit of the heroine; ultimately they are united, amid a widely inclusive 'new' society. We might collectively be excused for favouring happy endings, even while most of us see through them, as acknowledged by Frye: 'Happy endings do not impress us as true, but as desirable, and they are brought about by manipulation.'[20] He points out that comedy is traditionally based on a string of complications, culminating in a final, fortuitous comic 'recognition' (mirroring the more pitiable tragic version), and which is inevitable only insofar as that is how we expect comedy to end. On the same point, Aristotle seems downright disappointed to note: 'In comedy even people who are the bitterest enemies in the story, like Orestes and Aegisthus, go off reconciled in the end, and no one gets killed by anybody.'[21] Christopher Booker, more recently, sees the action of comedy as the change from ignorance to knowledge: 'The essence of Comedy is always that some redeeming truth has to be brought out of the shadows into the light'.[22]

Having looked beneath the superficial linking of laughter and comedy, we should do the same as regards the happy ending. Once again, it is not to deny some affinity or family association between comedy and final images of fulfilment, but to recognize how such oversimplifications may lead us to underestimate the work that comedy does. Walter Kerr maintains that, 'A happy ending must always be compromised'.[23] Kerr sets aside obvious cases as 'true exceptions', like Molière's *The Misanthrope* (*Le Misanthrope*, 1666), in which the central figure turns his back on the woman he loves and, in fact, all of society; and Shakespeare's *Love's Labour's Lost* (1594–5), in which a death is announced and the four romantic couples agree to defer their marriages for a year. Kerr points out a number of instances in which the surface appearance of the happy ending is either consciously ironized, misapprehended outside of historical context or otherwise called into question.

Despite our yearnings for a world that readily serves up emotional completion and perpetual optimism, most of us will recognize the happy ending as a narrative's convenient stopping place in the lives of people who would surely go on to have fights, bad days and personal disasters. The likes of feminist and Marxist criticisms, however, would dispute the innocence of this narrative pattern, often unpacking the text's underlying assumptions to reveal a self-serving inscription on behalf of society's status quo (e.g., that a woman can only find transcending happiness in heterosexual marriage; or that a man measures true success solely on the basis of monetary wealth and the match it earns him). We would do well to question who defines the conditions of 'happiness' we see represented in any text. It can be interesting – not to mention unsettling – to watch a playwright contrive a finale that follows conventional form while sabotaging it from within: Joe Orton's play, *What the Butler Saw* (1969), concludes with a breathless reconciliation of husband and wife, including a 'happy' reunion with their grown son and daughter, in the process conferring incestuous implications upon previous events.

The comic form itself may be seen to exhibit a certain unease within its own skin, with laughter provocation and happy endings representing contradictory impulses. T. G. A. Nelson launches his study of comedy upon the premise that 'there is a potential for conflict between the subversiveness of comic action and dialogue, full of pratfalls, insults, ridicule, defiance, and irreverence, and the steady movement towards harmony in the comic plot'.[24] It is true that, especially in light of Hollywood's tireless affinity for 'feel-good' comedy, a text may seem to bristle with socially disruptive thoughts and actions before suddenly coming to rest in socially sanctioned balance.

It can be interesting to observe what any text implies – or declines to imply – about life beyond its finishing line. As suggested above, comedy in particular courts scepticism by alleging that human lives can attain a state of suspended perfection. But even the customary curtain laugh with which a play, film or television show might end points to a 'first moment' of real life in which the happy ending has already begun to unravel. As Leggatt observes, 'A comedy that *ends* with a laugh is a comedy that ends not with a solution but with a fresh disaster.'[25] Leggatt offers for example Nikolai Gogol's *The Government Inspector* (1836) and George S. Kaufman and Moss Hart's *The Man Who Came to Dinner* (1939), both of which signal renewed trouble or misadventure in their closing moments.

It may be that comedy became far more knowing in the latter twentieth century. Television comedies like *Absolutely Fabulous* (1992–6; 2001–5) and *Frasier* (1993–2004) frequently aimed their worlds into the future, sometimes implying an impending comic disaster in the final moment. *Absolutely Fabulous* sprinkled several 'extended' endings amid the credits; *Frasier* included a silent 'tag' sequence behind its closing credits, which predicated some visual joke upon a scene from the episode proper.

We will look more studiously at the importance of closings (and openings) in the next chapter, as there is far more range and nuance than I am admitting here. Suffice it for the moment to observe that, in Kerr's words, 'To be comic, the ending must forcefully call into question the issues of "happiness" and "forever after"'.[26]

The world brought down to earth

Another manifestation of the comic impulse may be less apparent than humour and happy endings: comedy habitually seeks to connect with the audience's everyday world. While tragedy typically interrogates the mettle of the human constitution under pressure from life's 'great questions', comedy remains essentially drawn to the more quotidian concerns of the individual as social animal. 'The comic sense', Eric Bentley says, 'tries to cope with the daily, hourly, inescapable difficulty of being. For if everyday life has an undercurrent or cross-current of the tragic, the main current is material for comedy.'[27]

You will already have noted the continued references to tragedy in a book about comedy and there are plenty more to come. This cannot be surprising, as comedy and tragedy arose as major dramatic forms in Ancient Greece, and have since towered over Western literature as prototypical genres. It is, perhaps, inescapable that they are so often seen as inseparable points of reference for one another.

Robert Corrigan tells us that 'we can discuss tragedy (which deals directly with the serious) without reference to comedy, but when talking about comedy . . . we must always refer to the standards of seriousness which give it its essential definition.'[28] It may well be that our life-and-death concerns will always command pride of place in our artistic visions of life – and that all playing in some way refers back to a serious view of the world (see the box below). But it should also be clear that we seem to *require* this other kind of non-serious lens through which to accommodate the fullness of existence, as Potts concludes: 'Athenians found that tragedy was inadequate to express their national life, and in the course of time they included a complementary art-form in their dramatic festivals'.[29]

Defining comedy: beginning with Aristotle

Aristotle's *Poetics* (c. 336 BC) remains a defining document in Western literary criticism, particularly with reference to tragedy. Despite a handful of references to comedy in the surviving sections, it is usually surmised that a 'lost' second book of the *Poetics* contained the kind of detailed treatment and pointed definition of comedy that tragedy receives in the extant passages: 'Tragedy is an imitation of an action that is admirable, complete and possesses magnitude . . . effecting through pity and fear the purification of such emotions.' (For the purposes of highlighting the subject of comedy, I have omitted the middle phrases, which refer to language, form and performance.)

The anonymous manuscript, *Tractatus Coislinianus* ('Treatise on Comedy'), of indeterminate ancient origin, has been backed by some historians and disregarded by others as a key to the missing comments. Some of its supporters claim that it holds a direct connection to Aristotle's intentions toward comedy. In Lane Cooper's attempt at (re)constructing *An Aristotelian Theory of Comedy* (1924), he proposes 'anger' and 'envy' as emotions whose 'catharsis would amount to a form of pleasure as distinct as the catharsis of the tragic emotions [pity and fear]'. He also allows that, as Aristotle would be most occupied by the

> (*cont.*)
>
> 'serious' ends of proper human activity, comedy might be used to control any leanings toward an excess of frivolity: 'By comedy, then, we should be cured of a desire to laugh at the wrong time, and at the wrong things, through being made to laugh at the proper time by the right means.'[30]
>
> In *The Theory of Comedy* (1968), Elder Olson alludes to the *Tractatus*, but wonders why anyone would want to 'purge' such emotions as pleasure and laughter. Olson submits that tragedy 'imitates an action *which it makes serious*; and comparably, comedy imitates an action *which it makes a matter for levity*'. He then extends his postulation: 'Comedy is the imitation of a worthless action, complete and of a certain magnitude . . . effecting a *katastasis* [relaxation] of concern through the absurd. . . . By "worthless" or "valueless" action – the Greek word is *phaulos* – I mean one which is of no account, which comes to nothing, so that, on hindsight at least, it would seem foolish to be concerned about it.'[31]
>
> Richard Janko assembled a projected version of *Poetics II* (1984), justifying a parallel formulation of tragedy's definition: 'A Comedy is a representation of an absurd, complete action, one that lacks magnitude . . . through pleasure and laughter achieving the purgation of the like emotions.'[32]

It is sometimes said that tragedy shows us the universal in the human condition, comedy the particular. Umberto Eco explains this perception as rooted in the frames of reference any given text shares with its audience: 'In a way, a tragic (or dramatic) text is always a lesson in cultural anthropology; it makes even its future readers aware of a certain rule, even though this rule was previously alien to their cultural sensitivity'.[33] Eco emphasizes that the text includes not only a description of the relevant rule of framing, but a sense of the power it possesses for the individual within society.

A Greek tragedy like Sophocles' *Antigone* (date uncertain, though obviously written sometime during the fifth century BC), appears to show us a timeless battle of wills between the two main characters. King Creon pronounces the penalty of death upon anyone who breaks the law against burying a traitor to the state. Antigone stands resolute on the religious frame being broken if her brother, an opposing warrior killed in battle, is denied proper burial rites. This clash of principles is particular to the world of a performance given in Athens over 2,400 years ago. Yet, as Eco says, the rules of their respective framings and the implications attending their breaking are contextualized within the lines of the play to the extent that the play and its human implications remain wholly accessible. The conflict between Antigone and Creon has been employed regularly over the past hundred years to evoke many other specific historical tensions between individual and state, just as Romeo and Juliet have been called upon to represent the innocent victims of hostile tribal framings well removed from their original Elizabethan moorings.

Comedy also hinges upon the rules of social and cultural behaviour in force at a given time and place. The difference, Eco indicates, is that in comedy, 'the broken frame must be *presupposed* but *never spelled out*'.[34] A play like Aristophanes' *The Wasps* (422 BC) can be very difficult for the modern reader to appreciate in any depth, given that its comic motivation lies in the workings of and influences upon the jury system in Athens at the time. The details and implications are not explained during the course of the play, and can only begin to be appreciated intellectually by the reader's diligent and frequent reference to editorial footnotes in a contemporary edition.

Aristophanes' *Lysistrata* (411 BC), offers a prime example of the ways in which a text's comic impact might alter radically from one time or location to another – and that relevance is not necessarily the same as timelessness. By way of introduction to the following passage, from an early part of the play, Lysistrata has called a meeting of women on both sides of the Athenians' war against Sparta, for the purpose of urging them to deny sex to their husbands until a peace is agreed.

LYSISTRATA	Tell me, ladies, if I found a way to end the war,
	Would you do *anything* to help?
MYRRHINE	Oh yes. I'd even pawn this dress,
	If it would pay for a toast to Peace.
KALONIKE	Me too. For Peace, they could fillet me
	Like a turbot, and sell the biggest half.
LAMPITO	If Peace was at the top, I'd climb Taygetos.
	Mountain-range. Where weaklings are exposed.
LYSISTRATA	All right, ladies. It's time to tell my plan.
	If we really want our men to end this war,
	All we have to do is give up. . .
MYRRHINE	What?
LYSISTRATA	I can't. It's too much to ask.
MYRRHINE	Of course you can. Give up what? Our lives?
LYSISTRATA	No. Sex. What's the matter?
	Where are you going? Don't turn away.
	You're frowning. You're pale. You're crying.
	Will you or won't you? It's now or never.[35]

Today's eyes might read this passage as a forerunner of a luncheon chat from *Sex and the City* – and as it happens, one way to access its comic value might be to imagine the show's four central characters in the roles: Carrie as Lysistrata, Miranda as Lampito, Charlotte as Myrrhine, and Samantha as

Kalonike (so go ahead and read it again). Sexual connotations abound in and between the lines, and in Aristophanes are always intended. The sex strike – for which Lysistrata eventually gains support – appears to show ancient Greek women asserting control over their bodies as instruments of political power, made potentially amusing *because* of the conflict with their own physical desires and emotional needs. In a parallel gambit, Lysistrata will oversee the women's occupation of the Acropolis, a symbol of the state and storehouse of its wealth. The revolutionary takeover of a government building is spearheaded by a feisty Chorus of Old Women, in ongoing battle with the cranky and flaccid Chorus of Old Men. Both of these plots are couched clearly in non-serious mode, with the supremely sensible Lysistrata at the centre, allowing the play to give the impression of a bawdy feminist lash at war and sexual politics.

A cursory look at what we think we know of the original conditions of production, however, suggests that the contemporary reader is prone to misjudge the precise nature of the frame breaks upon which some of the comic impact relies. It is generally accepted that Aristophanes was not at all the original liberated man the comic machinations of *Lysistrata* seem to imply. He was, whatever his political inclinations, a savvy writer who knew his society and his audience. Although there may remain disagreement about the possibility of women having attended theatre performances in Athens during the fifth century BC, there is no question that Aristophanes would have been writing for the thousands of male spectators attending the single performance of this play. Women, at the time, were not considered 'full' citizens of Athens. They were presumed by the dominant male framing of female behaviour to be overly fond of wine and sex, and dis-posed toward adultery. Without ever being able to claim precise knowledge of what was going on in the minds of the play's original spectators, we can presume it likely that the sex-strike plot would have sought laughter at the suggestion that women might have been able to conceive, organize, and carry out the plan. It is widely accepted that Aristophanes could not have been advocating a pointedly pacifistic stance, nor that he meant to suggest the Athenian wives should actually take over – as we might read from the play, today – just that they should use whatever means necessary to move the men to a different course of action in the midst of a long, costly and losing military venture.

Douglas MacDowell acknowledges that 'Aristophanes seems to be laughing at women from an external viewpoint, which is what one might expect in a play written by a male author and performed by male actors for a male audience'.[36] He goes on to indicate passages in which women are not ridiculed, and, in fact, appear to be making sensible points that, perhaps, the men in the audience should hear. On the other hand, Lauren Taaffe argues: 'The integrity of male identity is kept whole, while the absurdity of women in public life is played up.' It is a play, she concludes, inspired by the wartime reduction in male population, and which 'highlights the inauthenticity of women and reasserts the power of masculinity'.[37]

Taaffe adds an intriguing implication to our obscured view of the original performance, in pointing out that *Lysistrata* might have been breaking new ground by presenting women in central roles for the first time in a comedy. Such an innovation would have amounted to a formidable frame break in and of itself, with, as Taaffe suggests, the play awarding male actors gilt-edged opportunities to invent ways of portraying women comically.

These considerations and competing views, of which I have merely skimmed the surface, are meant to demonstrate only that we misread the text as necessarily 'universal' just because war and sex do not appear to go out of fashion, nor, it seems, do certain gender stereotypes. In fact, a close reading of *Lysistrata* shows the playwright making jokes along the way about current events of the day, actual Athenians, and theatre practice itself, which can make a reading of the play today a tedious exercise in referring to footnotes, unless an up-to-the-minute translation has sought to replace such references with topical jokes for our own sociocultural moment. The above translator has sought to minimize the disruptive effect of culture-specific references in, for example, the reference to 'Whatsisname', as no contemporary reader would recognize the satirical swipe at a general suspected of collaborating with the enemy. The alert reader may still detect the diminished potency of joking allusions to people and places, severed from the original sociocultural context.

The explicit criticism of individuals characteristic of Aristophanes' so-called Old Comedy changes to social caricature by the time we get to the New Comedy of Menander, an Athenian writing about a hundred years later, and Plautus, the Roman playwright he inspired over a century after that. Their work offers a more plot-oriented comedy of domestic concern and social caricature, which will appear relatively familiar to today's reader. We will, nonetheless, still be able to discuss how the implications of their cultures and theatre conventions inform a contemporary reading in Chapter 2.

In any case, these insights into the 'presupposed' frame breaks mined by a text should give an inkling of the extent to which comedy conducts us beneath the surface of everyday society, because they stand to reveal what 'goes without saying' in a particular time and place (as well as what does not go without saying, here and now).

Summing up before moving on

I have proposed that a human need to take the world playfully lies at the heart of comedy's predilection for humour and upbeat endings. I would extend that contention to embrace its treatment of the audience's immediate, routine world. Our sense of play originates with that which we know so well, even when it serves as springboard for investigation of the exotic or fantastic. In today's culture, a comedy involving aristocrats or Martians is still likely to use the world of the average reader as a central point of reference.

It is this feeling of playfulness that we take to identify comedy, perhaps more so than its individual characteristics. As we have seen, humour and happy endings are common features of comedy, without being definitive measures. Certainly, these two features crop up in texts we would *not* call comedy. Shakespeare's short and brutal tragedy of *Macbeth* (1606), for example, contains obvious humour attempts in the Porter scene, while the cinematic wartime intrigue of *To Have and Have Not* (1945) ends in triumph, with Humphrey Bogart's and Lauren Bacall's characters exiting in what surely qualifies as a symbolic marriage. Neither is observation of life in its on-the-ground pursuits necessarily a signpost to the genre of comedy: James Joyce's novel, *Ulysses* (1922), engages in microscopic description of turn-of-the-century Dublin, Ireland, prompting a 1992 annotated edition with 250 pages of explanatory notes.

The fact remains that the world of comedy will always betray leakage or untidiness when an attempt is made to confine it within consistent parameters, because by nature it cannot resist turning its mischievous gaze even upon the limits of its own framing. The editors of the 1994 collection of essays, titled *English Comedy*, pinpoint the reason: 'For the most part dedicated to flouting norms and frustrating expectations, comedy has an ingrained antagonism to rules.'[38] In fact, comedy can often be seen to test the limits of accepted or acceptable cultural framing, say, in the stand-up routines of Lenny Bruce in the 1960s and Bill Hicks in the 1990s, or television series like *Monty Python's Flying Circus* in the 1970s and *Brass Eye* at the turn of the twenty-first century.

I have characterized comedy as creative expression which takes the world in a particularly playful fashion. Christopher Fry says, 'Comedy is not a drama with the addition of laughs. It is a world of its own',[39] and I would contend further that it illuminates our world from perspectives unattainable by 'serious' means. The mechanics of comedy are embedded in Western culture, having been chiselled into its foundations in Ancient Greek and Roman comedy and the later *commedia dell'arte*. We will investigate some of these building blocks of comedy, after delving a bit further into the ways a reader might enter the world of a comic text.

Chapter 1

Reading comedy

'What kind of world is this?'

When we begin reading a play or novel, we take in much more than the expository information related to Who, What, Where and When. Although we habitually scour any text for the answers to these fundamental questions, we are at the same time searching for cues to anchor the incoming data in a 'kind of world'. This 'kind of world' is based on our own, but carries inferences about the nature of things, which help us gauge not only which facts are likely to be important, but what to do with them, what meanings to assign them; it endows the fictional world with an atmosphere or feeling. We become practised in identifying the characteristics of different 'kinds of worlds'. As discussed provisionally in the Introduction, texts ruled or inflected by comedy tend to give off a sense of playfulness in their blood, although this sense can be manifested in a world of different ways (see Figure 1.1).

As we embark upon any first reading, we attempt to build a contextual scaffold by (consciously or otherwise) referring features and structures of the unfolding world to a matrix of patterns accrued from all our previous reading experiences.[1] In so doing, we begin to compile a version of reality being defined, its rules of engagement, its emotional contours, its projected course and probable outcomes and how it reflects upon the one we inhabit. I call this process, 'genre framing'; it can be approached from the side of the writer/practitioner or from the side of the reader/spectator.

A certain amount of genre theory occupies itself with analysing texts and assigning labels. This sort of treatment can prove interesting for the lay reader, in, say, discovering hidden connections among favourite texts, tracing the evolution of a genre, or noticing the historical conditions under which a particular one sprouted. Most of us, however, do not think about labelling as we process a text – perhaps not even until we try to describe it to someone else. Ordinarily, we respond to genre-framing instructions without conscious reflection, beneath the surface of other sense-making activity.

Figure 1.1 What visual cues in this photo tell you that it is likely to depict a scene from a comedy? *Noises Off*, Lyttleton Theatre, London, 2000.

From a naïve perspective, the reading process would seem to present insurmountable barriers for the reader. We are routinely confronted with multitudes of words, images or other phenomena in coming face to face with a text. How do we know what to make of it all, how to organize it into the kind of sense somehow imagined by the writer? Despite the normalizing tendencies of culture and society, each of us brings a radical individuality to the process of reading. How can we ever know that we are using the same language in the same way as the writer, taking this statement or that action with the intended slant or nuance, so as to make more than superficial meaning? The crux of this theoretical challenge is articulated by John Frow: 'Any text communicated to an *unknown* audience, whether it be a complex aesthetic text or an advertisement, a chain letter or a message in a bottle, must negotiate its relationship with strangers whose response it cannot fully gauge in advance.'[2]

Frow advances a useful analogy for thinking about genre as a personally acquired, culturally driven, ever-evolving master system for selecting and negotiating texts. He likens the notion of genre to a personal awareness of shops in one's culture: we have a strong sense of what 'kind' of shop will best serve a given need, having been inscribed since our school days with a set of cultural basics (like the butcher shop and bakery), upon which we build a more complex and nuanced matrix of shopping knowledge. Times change, of course, and so does retail fashion: a bookshop, nowadays, will surely have books; it may well carry music CDs and DVDs and some stationery; and it might also harbour a coffee shop somewhere on the premises. At the 'edges' of the bookshop genre, further away from its 'core' purpose, as Frow would say, we may find one which also sells concert tickets or hosts stand-up comedy on weekends. We are likely to come across bookshop subgenres, that is, those that specialize in mystery books, theatre books or religious books. We are also likely to know some things about the organizational structures of bookshops (e.g., new releases and best-sellers close to the entrance; fiction and non-fiction stocked in separate sections; bookmarks at the checkout counter).

Because cultures differ, the kinds of shop we know so well in our own sphere of experience may differ from those found elsewhere in the world. Through time, some kinds of shop will no longer be found, while others will come into being, possibly combining features of existing types of shop. This is a broad and sophisticated system of knowledge we probably don't give much thought; we simply draw upon it naturally as the situation arises.

Heather Dubrow offers a slightly different analogy, comparing genre to the unspoken coding of social situations. She refers to the kind of silent understanding which would exist between the host and a guest invited to a formal dinner party. The guest knows that a type of attire is expected, while the host is aware of the quality of dining experience promised. Genre, Dubrow says, 'functions much like a code of behaviour established between the author and his reader'.[3] Breakdowns in communication – mishandling of the code on the one hand, misapprehension on the other – can lead to a sense of annoyance or confusion in the reader.

We make similar kinds of assessments about characters in a play, novel or film, with reference to its genre framing. Say we are introduced to a young woman described as a maid at the start of a text. What level of importance and character attributes might we associate with her if the text is framed as a comedy written by William Shakespeare? A novel by Jane Austen? A French farce? A film melodrama starring Bette Davis? A play titled *The Maid's Tragedy*, or a film called *Maid in Manhattan*? In this regard, genre framing helps us read more efficiently, guiding us toward decisions about which details may or may not be important enough to consider and often what attitude to take toward them.

Both of the preceding comparisons speak to Goffman's notion of framing, introduced in the Introduction, through which we organize and interpret everyday experience (see the box on page 23). They imply a cultural web of associations and differentiations, culturally based and refined through personal experience, which underpins a relationship between two parties, and leads to the cooperative contextualization of a particular shop, occasion or, in our case, text. In the Introduction, I referred to tragedy and comedy in strictly hypothetical – and therefore extremely general – terms. In practice, every *actual* text generates its own 'genre frame', no matter how familiar the writer's approach might seem.

Genre and meaning

The process of 'genre framing', a negotiation between reader and text referred to in this chapter, begins to supply a mood, tone or atmosphere to the world of an unfolding text. It invites us to feel in a certain way toward the characters, to anticipate their actions and fates and, in fact, invokes ready-made systems of morality and meaning. It is widely held that, even while genre facilitates contextualization, its subject matter entwined with its form breeds meaning or ideology. John Frow argues that, 'far from being merely "stylistic" devices, genres create effects of reality and truth which are central to the different ways the world is understood in the writing of history or philosophy or science, or in painting, or in everyday talk'.[4] Tzetvan Todorov explains that these ways of fashioning the world stand to reveal quite a lot about a society's endorsed structures of thinking about reality, that 'a society chooses and codifies the acts that correspond most closely to its ideology; that is why the existence of certain genres in one society, their absence in another, are revelatory of that ideology and allow us to establish it more or less confidently'.[5] What are some of the meanings carried by comedy and the comic in today's Western cultures?

Genre framing, then, comprises an essential part of any reader's engagement with a text. It is carried out largely by habit, with reference to an accumulated experience of reading, interlaced with a practical awareness of living in a particular time, place, and culture. Next time you watch a play or film, you might give a bit of thought to the way your reading antennae detect genre markers, making continual adjustments in your grasp of the world's nature, tone, and organization. Frow offers another instructive comparison: 'Genre cues act rather like context-sensitive drop-down menus in a computer program, directing me to the layers and sub-layers of information that respond to my purposes as a speaker or a reader or a viewer'.[6]

Formal and textual elements

The textual signals from which we construct a genre frame might roughly be divided into 'formal' and 'textual' elements. I take 'textual' signals to refer to components within the body of the text itself, like verbal joking, quick-fire dialogue, and linguistic registers; 'formal' features are inferred from outside the text, like theme, character and structure. In some cases, a genre's formal elements embrace a recognizable set of features. Farce, for example, is a kind of dramatic text, which, formally, includes a roster of two-dimensional character types and a plot based on keeping up appearances amid pursuit of love and/or sex and/or money. Its texts usually contain extreme coincidence, escalating confusion and opportunities for physical humour. In a farcical world all these elements are meant to work in concert with a primary intention of eliciting laughter from an audience. A nineteenth-century French boulevard farce by Georges Feydeau and Maurice Desvallières, like *A Little Hotel on the Side* (*L'Hôtel du libre échange*, 1894), would be considered a quintessential example of this genre.

Kinds and modes

Genre framing, ultimately, proceeds by an unknowable mix of both the highly personal – as we all gain reading competency by means of experiences which are all our own – and the inescapably social – as interaction with culture and other readers gives us a rationale and language for describing texts. The external and internal signals described above relate generally to terms applied by Alistair Fowler, writing from an historical–literary perspective. He advances a theory of genres – or 'kinds', as he calls them – and modes. He defines a kind as 'a type of literary work of a definite size, marked by a complex of substantive and formal features that always include a distinctive (though not usually unique) external structure'.[7] A kind, always expressed as a noun, is considered a work's dominant label, and refers to its 'external embodiment' in form or structure. A 'mode', for Fowler, is always cast as an adjective, and modifies the text's mood through 'distinct signals' from another genre. A most obvious example would also be the most relevant to our discussion: 'comedy' as a kind or genre, describes something of the whole of a work, referring primarily to formal features discussed in the Introduction – for example, 'ending in marriage'. 'Comic', as a mode, designates a tone given to the text through the inclusion of textual elements – such as humorous dialogue – which have been imported without the structure. We then have occasion to resort to labels like Romantic Comedy and Comic Thriller.

This system may serve well for a sort of shorthand in describing texts, but, by limiting the number of generic influences to two, it threatens to oversimplify the composite nature of many a work.

Plautus' plays, such as *The Braggart Soldier* (*Miles Gloriosus*, c. 205 BC), present themselves as prototypes for farce, bearing many of the above features within a different cultural atmosphere; Michael Frayn's *Noises Off* (1982) builds a farce upon the rehearsal and performance of a farce. A reader should be able to identify all three of these worlds as of a type or immediate family. Yet each play will distinguish itself by virtue of other fingerprints particular to its historical, cultural and theatrical circumstances.

We can see across history that forms and components interpenetrate, diverge, recombine and emerge born again within new cultural contexts. One of the keys to tackling texts from outside contemporary writing lies in the ability to handle familiar markers in strange settings, while expanding one's personal generic repertoire to register meanings and subtleties from other times and places. It is not uncommon for texts to bring together signals from more than one genre set, and so we come to recognize that generic cues may be blended to varying degrees (not unlike recipes for well-known dishes made interesting through the use of substituted ingredients or different seasonings). The curious reader will consider the effect of a particular mixture or element upon the meaning and tilt of a world (see the box on page 24).

Again, we make sense of an unfolding text by comparing it to what we know, summoning familiar patterns to instruct us from between the lines how to couch the information in a contextual fabric. At the same time, every text is at least somewhat different, even if it is a comforting variation on a tried-and-true theme – like a romance or detective novel. Such a text usually requires a minimum of conscious effort in decoding (and may well be why someone chooses it for holiday reading), though one assumes that it will offer the reader *some* degree of variation or unpredictability to sustain interest. Some writers will, of course, try to challenge and/or surprise the reader, and in so doing will toy with our genre habits. A text that gives the reader less than the usual amount of traction with regard to genre framing can be considered frustrating or confusing for some readers and provocative or liberating for others. Alistair Fowler maintains that 'literature's true enjoyment must always partly depend on interweaving the strange with the pleasurably familiar',[8] although we might have to note that the preferred balance between the two will always be a matter of individual taste.

As we discuss the process of genre framing – which, in a way, is what this book is all about with regard to comedy – we should be wary of appearing to privilege any position in the constellation of participants as the 'true' site of genre's location. Rick Altman, whose main area of interest is film, none-theless makes many salient points about genre theory at large. He challenges the bulk of genre theorizing (at least up to the publication of his book in 1999), exposing the invisible assumptions and prejudicial perspectives which must be weighed alongside any claims to authority. He emphasizes that academics, media critics and public-relations copywriters all have positional agendas, and can in no way be considered ultimate arbiters. He also reminds us that 'genres look different to different audiences',[9] and even to the same person at different points throughout a life of reading. Notions of genre are always personal formulations, but they are also subject to negotiation and refinement through the ebb and flow of sociocultural influence. Genre is a way of talking about how we communicate through texts (and a necessary one), but, as Altman points out, it is no stable, concrete 'thing' we seek to understand, and 'no isolated part of this process actually *is* the genre; instead, the genre lies somewhere in the overall circulation of meaning constitutive of the process'.[10]

Entering the world of comedy

It is the main order of business of this book to examine how a text speaks to us directly, to explore the process by which we might align it with the features of 'comedy' or 'the comic', and to explore those implications further. We have thus far treated the process of genre framing in general terms, with a few nods in the direction of our chosen subject area. I have tried to give an overall impression of the communicative system by which we, as readers, construe a world for a text, and to highlight how much of this activity goes on without conscious effort.

The process I have referred to as genre framing may relate to Roman Ingarden's concept of 'concretization', a way of describing work done by the reader to actualize words on a page for a mental image of the textual world. This activity becomes a bit more complex, and potentially quite exciting, when we come to dramatic texts. A play, as written, only ever exists as a blueprint for possible performance, so an armchair reading may really be a process by which we defer concretization by sampling provisional stage worlds, rather than completing the experience of the text in our minds.

Arguably the raw materials of words on a page, bodies on a stage or images on a screen remain a collection of signs without cohesive meaning prior to the shape and sense supplied by genre framing. We have often established a provisional substructure for making sense of a text well before we meet it in person. A film has been strongly recommended by a friend for the power of its lead performances; a review of a seldom-seen Jacobean play catches my eye; I pick up a new novel by a favourite mystery writer in the airport bookshop. We cannot help but describe works to friends by referencing genre characteristics, and publicists work overtime to place their wares before us in the most widely appetizing generic terms. In this way, we rarely, if ever, begin first-hand consumption of a text without some sort of generic disposition toward it. In fact, reviews, marketing, dust jackets, titles and subtitles, dedications and the like (called 'paratexts' by Gérard Genette) pre-frame the text from outside the actual work.

I should acknowledge, at this point, a licence I have taken with regard to my explanation of genre framing. I may have given the impression that reading takes the form of a single, pure stream of sense-making, whereas Dubrow is right to remind us that 'the process of reacting to generic signals is seldom a simple and linear one'.[11] To be sure, we may reread a passage in a book, skim a section or flip ahead. We may not complete the actual reading in one sitting, and intervening reflection or experience may affect our processing. We may go back to a text after days, months or years; our framing may be affected by critical opinion, or by a conversation with someone familiar with the work. Similarly, and particularly in these days of the DVD player, we may view a film or television show again and watch a favourite sequence several times. If enough time has elapsed between readings, our relationship to the generic cueing of a text may have altered noticeably. Most people will have had the experience of returning to a novel, play or film after a number of years, and having a decidedly different response to it. A particular production of a play may open our eyes to generic shadings in the text we had not previously noticed.

Furthermore, I appear to have foregrounded the reader's first-time experience of a text. This is not to claim that it is the only, or even the most valid contact we have with it. Subsequent and close readings remain essential to the deeper appreciation and more sophisticated competency for which this book aims, particularly when reading dramatic texts, because of the key ways they differ from reading other texts. I have adopted a necessary idealization of the genre-framing process, without which our discussion would never get anywhere. We might think of it as an 'implied' or 'model reading', a theoretical construct which allows us to explore the means by which a text might bear the *intendedness* of the writer toward a proposed experience for the reader.

The signals we associate with genre framing comprise a sort of infrared map for the reader's navigation through a text, and this signposting is nowhere more crucial than at the point of entrance to a world which asks to be taken in some way as comic. Gerald Mast attributes the name 'comic climate' to a sense of 'fun' (or, in my terms, 'non-seriousness' or 'playfulness') readable through signs planted in the world of the text. Although he is studying film, this notion of a quality or atmosphere endowed by readable signs is valuable for reading other media as well.

Bert O. States refers figuratively to 'the first four seconds'[12] of theatre performance, in which there is a burst of sense-making activity as the spectator attempts to gain purchase on the terrain of the stage world. I would contend that this metaphor applies to all texts, even though the reader of a literary work assimilates the world a word at a time. Such is the difference of burdens, particularly in the realms of comedy and the comic, between the writer of literary works and the writer(s) of dramatic and cinematic texts. Words on a page do not receive the visual/aural support of intonation, facial gesture, physical style and, say, musical cueing which attend the 'first four seconds' of a film or television show (of which the latter may also include a laugh track or studio audience).

Here is the beginning of a short literary piece:

> My Uncle Bertram Twitt was a great man. He told me so himself. One can't argue with facts like that. He was a tall, handsome, cross-eyed man with eczema. He walked with a pronounced limp, L-I-M-P, pronounced 'limp'.[13]

This is the opening passage of a short sketch by Spike Milligan, titled, 'The great man' (1961). Most readers, even if they were not familiar with Milligan's reputation as a master comedian, would recognize the uncle's name as a signal of comic intent, ratified by the undercutting of the second sentence. The fourth sentence begins describing him as 'tall, handsome', an impression deflated by 'cross-eyed man with eczema'. The fifth sentence calls playful attention to a conversational usage of the word 'pronounced'. No reader is likely to take these five sentences as the beginning of a serious biographical reminiscence, the form it lampoons. Milligan cues an overtly comic world – we now know to expect a certain style and tone of gag for the rest of the piece. It is not likely that any of these thoughts would pass consciously through a reader's mind. Indeed, it has taken a full paragraph to talk around several signals the writer has woven into a singularly succinct initiation of genre frame.

Another cunningly crafted opening is also one of literature's best known:

> It is a truth universally acknowledged, that a single man in possession of a good fortune, must be in want of a wife.[14]

This first sentence of Jane Austen's *Pride and Prejudice* (1813) is necessarily less straightforward than Milligan's for a twenty-first-century reader, as our overlap of cultural knowledge is less reliable. We cannot make entirely confident assessments of the linguistic register or cultural assumptions. The utterance takes the form of a philosophical or scientific statement, and, therefore, is slightly out of the league of a claim about social motivations. By invoking the authority implied by the construction of a formal proposition, Austen, like Milligan above, opens a playful gap between form and content, subtly suggesting from behind the words that her statement is not such a straightforward 'truth'. (As far as generic signals go, Austen also has wasted no time in implying comedy's time-honoured move toward marriage.)

Admittedly, I have chosen these openings because I admire their comic dexterity. They both key comic climates from their first sentences by invoking conversational registers somehow out of kilter to their subjects. Susan Purdie, in her book, *Comedy: The Mastery of Discourse*, claims that we find comical

> the use of vocabulary and delivery which entails reference to modes of discourse other than that which would be transparently 'normal' in the context: something is said or done in a manner which registers as intentionally excessive to the situation – 'too much' emotion or 'too high/low' a diction.[15]

This disjunction between the content of an utterance and the register of its conveyance forms a basic mechanism for comic writing as well as comic performing. Also, as observed in the Introduction, the commonality of day-to-day experience remains conventional fodder for comic discourse.

The following example also draws upon these principles:

> I don't care what Aristotle and philosophers say: there's nothing in this world like snuff. All right-minded people adore it; and anyone who is able to live without it is unworthy to draw breath. It not only clears and delights the brain; but it also inclines the heart towards virtue, and helps one to become a gentleman. Haven't you noticed how, as soon as one begins to take it, one becomes uncommonly generous to everybody, ready to present one's box right and left wherever one goes? You don't even wait to be asked, but anticipate the desires of others; and it can even be truly said that snuff inspires all its devotees with the principles of honour and virtue. But enough of that! To go back to what we were saying...[16]

These are the opening lines from Molière's *Don Juan* (*Dom Juan ou Le Festin de pierre*, 1665), spoken by a character named Sganarelle. The subject of snuff is obviously not of our time or culture, but the comic tone is unmistakable. The reader is addressed directly upon a social habit of, it seems, up-to-the-minute interest, couched in terms of worldly importance. The speaker's blithe rejection of such authorities as 'Aristotle and philosophers' establishes a down-to-earth tone, then coupled with the pointed overstatement that 'anyone who is able to live without it is unworthy to draw breath', and then moving on to ecstatic claims about the social and spiritual benefits of snuff. These elements combine to insinuate a conspiratorial relationship with the reader, establishing a comic key by placing a rather inconsequential social habit at the centre of an impassioned and high-minded critique.

I have applied some of the same principles to the *Don Juan* piece as I have to the examples from Milligan and Austen, particularly the use of recognizable conversational framings which inflate or deflate the relative weight of a topic (and this obviously implies a trust in the Molière translation). You may already have realized, however, that the move from literary to dramatic text brings important implications. The two literary texts introduced us to narrative voices as the embodiments of worlds aimed directly at the inside of the reader's head. These comic writers rely on words alone, and the transactions might be deemed more straightforward.

Where a literary text itself might be considered the work's 'performance', that is, the ultimate landing of the work for reception, the dramatic text represents only a step along the way. Although it, too, is comprised of words on a page, it intends itself toward actual production onstage, or what we might call virtual performance on the stage of the reader's mind. The dramatic text presumes much more between – or, more properly, *beneath* – the lines in a fully embodied, three-dimensional stage world in flight. In searching for comedy and the comic in the words of a play text, we must be more open and savvy about our concretizations.

If we look again at Sganarelle's speech, we should note, first, that his voice does not *define* the world in the same way as a literary narrator's might. (That said, Sganarelle's character may indeed be read as a privileged mediator between reader and stage world, as Molière wrote the part for himself.) It may be notable that his is the first voice we meet, but dramatic character occupies a different status in the context of a stage world than does a literary character – its specific sense of authority is always to some degree provisional prior to embodiment in actual performance.

Sganarelle takes the generic position of comic servant, and the reader must realize that his non-serious function would be marked in performance by costume and behaviour – even if we do not recognize the character name as a customary signal of comic intent – well before the actor utters the above string of words. One might imagine the speech delivered by a character actor in a Christmas panto, by a contemporary stand-up comic, or by any number of popular comic film stars.

Having effectively 'warmed up' the audience with his riff on snuff, Sganarelle addresses more expository matters, namely Don Juan's sudden flight from the company of his latest conquest. The point to take here, however, is that even though we can identify cues for comedy on the page, there remains no definitive claim on the play's tone prior to any given embodiment in actual production. The above speech, for example, could be read with passion or analytical detachment, with an undercurrent of sarcasm – or against a backdrop of other action which denies comic disposition.

The playful mismatch of form and content is a common stamp of comic design, and has further implications when we get to the actualization of the words from page to stage (which will become the main order of business in Chapter 4). For now, Molière will assist us a bit further by affording us a few other opportunities for the discussion of comically slanted beginnings. Molière's *Scapin the Schemer* (*Les Fourberies de Scapin*, 1671) plunges us into familiar comic territory. The speakers are a young man and his valet:

OCTAVE	Could there be worse news for a suitor? My case is desperate indeed. You say, Sylvestre, you have just heard at the harbour that my father is coming home?
SYLVESTRE	Yes, Sir.
OCTAVE	He is expected to arrive this morning?
SYLVESTRE	This very morning.
OCTAVE	And he comes for the purpose of finding me a wife?
SYLVESTRE	Yes, Sir.
OCTAVE	A daughter of Seigneur Géronte?
SYLVESTRE	A daughter of Seigneur Géronte.
OCTAVE	That the girl has been sent for from Taranto?
SYLVESTRE	Yes.
OCTAVE	And you heard all this news from my uncle?
SYLVESTRE	From your uncle.
OCTAVE	Who had it from my father in a letter?
SYLVESTRE	In a letter.
OCTAVE	And my uncle knows all about our affairs?
SYLVESTRE	All about our affairs.
OCTAVE	Oh, for Heaven's sake, tell me everything straight out. Don't make me drag it out of you one word at a time.[17]

Here is the traditional young man in pursuit of a young woman. In an amusing reversal, the young master delivers all the information the valet is meant to report. Sylvestre contributes only short affirmative answers or repetitions to the conversation, until Octave's eventual chastisement, 'Oh, for Heaven's sake, tell me everything straight out. Don't make me drag it out of you one word at a time.' The impression might be presumed of a young man thrown into a babbling panic by his father's plans, who loses all self-awareness – and, in passing, supplies the spectator with the usual dramatic exposition. The last line, in fact, might be a common enough plea from an anxious young man with love on his mind, but it reverses upon the actual dynamic of the dialogue – Sylvestre has given short responses because Octave has been filling in all the details.

We should note a craftedness to the dialogue pattern of this scene. It is no exaggeration to say that you can sometimes glean comic purpose from the layout of the lines on the page. A passage that repeats its shape so insistently fairly asks for comic embodiment.

Let's move forward in time to take a look at the opening passage from *The Suicide* (1932), by Nikolai Erdman:

> [*Room at* SEMYON*'s apartment. Night*]
> [SEMYON *and his wife,* MASHA, *asleep in a double bed.*]
> SEMYON Masha? Masha? Masha, are you asleep?
> MASHA [*Screams*] Ahhhhhhh!
> SEMYON What's wrong? What's wrong?
> MASHA What's wrong?
> SEMYON What's wrong? It's me.
> MASHA It's you?
> SEMYON It's me.
> MASHA Oh.
> SEMYON Masha, I wanted to ask you something. There is something I wanted to ask you, Masha. Masha? Masha, are you asleep?
> MASHA [*Screams*] Ahhhhhhh!
> SEMYON What's wrong? What's wrong?
> MASHA What's wrong?
> SEMYON What's wrong? It's me.
> MASHA It's you?
> SEMYON It's me.
> MASHA It's you?
> SEMYON Who else would it be?
> MASHA Oh.
> SEMYON Masha. I wanted to ask you something. Masha? Masha, are you asleep?
> MASHA No.
> SEMYON Good, because there's something I've wanted to ask you, Masha.
> MASHA What, Semyon?
> SEMYON Masha, I wanted to ask if there was any liver sausage left over from dinner.[18]

The stage directions lead one to believe that Semyon has awoken from a distressing dream, which, we might assume, relates to an issue of some gravity connected with the title. There are, however, several textual signals for comedy in this extract. Masha's first scream could suggest comic intent through the actress's portrayal in performance, but the repetitions of 'What's wrong?' virtually assure it from the page. The trivial exchange, 'It's me', 'It's you?', 'It's me', also appears cut from a comic pattern: Semyon is the one who awakens Masha, but is obliged to calm *her* down because of her scream. Semyon fails to tell Masha what is on his mind. She falls back to sleep in the space of two lines, all too suddenly by serious standards. The sequence is repeated, and the new lines – 'It's you?', 'Who else would it be?', 'Oh' – add to an air of vague inanity, despite the weight of Semyon's presumed devastating despair. The repeated textual pattern ensures some degree of comic intent and helps to keep a full identification with Semyon's plight at arm's length.

Semyon finally manages to voice the question, 'Masha, I wanted to ask if there was any liver sausage left over from dinner'. The absurdly mundane request from a man presumed to have suicide on his mind pulls the rug from under our expectations by substituting a ludicrous query about food for some kind of soul-wrenching plea. It invites us to forgo full identification, adopting a playful attitude toward a very serious subject. This genre frame sets the stage for a comic disparity between Semyon's psychic distress and the people around him, who treat his impending suicide not with compassion or concern, but as a grand opportunity to advance their respective personal and political agendas.

In the Introduction, we identified humour and happy endings as common features associated with comedy, as well as a concern with the everyday world of the reader. A world may establish its comic affinity by reference to a corner of familiar contemporary experience and/or a recognizable socio-cultural 'character'. Neil Simon's *Chapter Two* (1977), set in side-by-side New York apartments, begins with a wisecrack to which any latter-day urban-dweller can relate:

> LEO [*coming through the door*] George, you're not going to believe this! I found a place to park right in front of the building. First time in four years . . . I think I'll buy an apartment here – I don't want to give up that space.[19]

The joke and New York character immediately place us in familiar comic territory – the travails of everyday life in the city. Alan Ayckbourn gives us a British variation with the beginning of *Absurd Person Singular* (1973). Again, a domestic space is described in the opening stage directions, this time a kitchen. Jane and Sidney are sketched as a conventional suburban couple in their thirties. Jane '[*is discovered bustling round wiping the floor, cupboard doors, working surfaces – in fact, anything in sight – with a cloth]*'. The dialogue begins:

> SIDNEY   Hallo, hallo. What are we up to out here, eh?
> JANE   [*without pausing in her work*] Just giving it a wipe.
> SIDNEY   Dear oh dear. Good gracious me. Does it need it? Like a
>   battleship. Just like a battleship. They need you in the
>   Royal Navy.
> JANE   [*giggling*] Silly . . .
> SIDNEY   No – the Royal Navy.
> JANE   Silly . . .[20]

Again, it is most likely to be comedy that involves itself in the minutiae of domestic life. This world shows us an ordinary English housewife who is just that bit too obsessive in her cleaning (excess being another trademark of comic character). Words and situation give an immediate inkling of sharply observed life within a stratum of British society. In this world, the quality of joking differs from the 'one-liner' approach in the previous example – many of Simon's gags are aimed past the awareness of the characters to the spectator. In Ayckbourn country, Sidney's humour is more fully accommodated within the stage world. It is inspired by the character's relationship with his wife, and it encapsulates something of what goes on between them in private (though *precisely* what, we can't be sure prior to actual performance). This last extract, though, intimates how comedy can announce itself without the obvious incorporation of usual themes and humour patterns, but with a clear indication of the sharp, localized observation to come.

One can see that it suits comic worlds in particular to establish their genre frames clearly from the outset, *as part of reading comedy effectively means knowing to take it as comedy*. The reader can be guided toward a further triangulation of comic tone by the skilful employment of genre signals, as phrased with disarming bluntness by L. J. Potts: 'The comic writer has to put his work into a form which will make it as difficult as possible for anyone to spoil it in the reading.'[21]

In the way that a car mechanic comes to appreciate the hum of a finely tuned engine, we can look under the hood of a text to see, in these cases, how its comic priming works. And what we require is an overarching grasp that transcends checklists and theories, to prepare us for an appreciation of mixture and subtlety. In dissecting these several opening passages, I have tried to show the quality of attention we can turn upon a text, and a few of the habits and patterns visible to the practised eye. We can say that a disparity between tone and subject will invoke a comic tendency in the framing, as well as an incorporation of humour-related textual patterns and strategies, and a milieu aligned with the everyday world of the reader.

Comedy in the end

Just as the beginning of a text plays a vital part in the process of its genre framing, so does its ending. It may not be until we have a completed picture of a text that we even know what to call it. In the Introduction we established the happy ending or 'ending in marriage' as a primary indicator for what many of us label a comedy. In most cases, with the conflict or quest resolved favourably, a dénouement will tie up loose ends in short order and the text signs off on an upswing.

The Importance of Being Earnest (1895), by Oscar Wilde, ends in a tidy confirmation of generic artifice. Following various deceptions perpetrated by Jack and Algernon, all misunderstandings have been resolved and romantic couplings confirmed. Jack, having grown up without knowledge of his birth and parentage, discovers his given name to be Earnest, a cover name with which he has wooed Gwendolen:

JACK	Gwendolen, it is a terrible thing for a man to find out suddenly that all his life he has been speaking nothing but the truth. Can you forgive me?
GWENDOLEN	I can. For I feel that you are sure to change.
JACK	My own one!
CHASUBLE	[*to* MISS PRISM] Laetitia! [*Embraces her.*]
MISS PRISM	[*enthusiastically*] Frederick! At last!
ALGERNON	Cecily! [*Embraces her.*] At last!
JACK	Gwendolen! [*Embraces her.*] At last!
LADY BRACKNELL	My nephew, you seem to be displaying signs of triviality.
JACK	On the contrary, Aunt Augusta, I've now realized for the first time in my life the vital Importance of Being Earnest.

[*Tableau*]
[*Curtain*][22]

Along with the two young couples, the writer throws in a bonus happy ending for Reverend Chasuble and Miss Prism. All three matches are reaffirmed, in turn, in the above passage, with the final line buttoning the text in the neatest possible fashion. The writer calls for a tableau prior to the curtain's fall, presumably to underscore a lasting image of comic resolution.[23] As mentioned in the Introduction, comedies, although ending 'happily', rarely end on such a note of gracious closure. This makes for a self-consciously idealized finish to the play, the 'perfect' comedy ending, and an appropriate closing to the world of consummate artifice described by many commentators on the text.

Ronald Gaskell says that a play does more than explore and clarify a particular theme: 'It also expresses, and defines, a distinctive vision of human life'.[24] The closing moment of any text places a finalized frame around all that has come before it. A happy ending seems generally to recompose the preceding obstacles and misfortunes in a 'vision of life' which might tell us, for example, that perseverance is rewarded, that true contentment is somehow earned, or that things always come right in the end.

In many a comic world, good and bad are rendered in bold colours. If a villain has been vanquished, it enhances a gratifying vision of life in which selfishness, corruption, hypocrisy or downright evil are sure to lose out in the end. In more textured worlds, comic conflict may breed ill will, disappointment and loss, the effects of which may not so easily be swept aside in final moods of celebration. *Twelfth Night* (1601) is often placed among Shakespeare's lighter comedies. Despite its happy reunion and its multiple pairings at the end, there remains the unrelenting humiliation of Malvolio to consider. With his abasement paraded in front of the gathered celebrants in a final speech by the Clown, Malvolio offers this parting line: 'I'll be revenged on the whole pack of you.' Even though the Duke issues the instruction, 'Pursue him and entreat him to a peace', the imbalance is in no way resolved.[25]

The bad blood between Malvolio and the others remains undeniably embedded in the textual fabric of the play's world, though it may be possible to leaven or try to gloss over it in performance. The treatment of the Malvolio strand in production – from broadly played buffoon to mean-tempered prig to awkward eccentric to many other possibilities – cannot help but resonate within the 'vision of life' it projects. It is, for example, possible for the actor playing Malvolio to deliver the line with a formidable degree of venom or in a way that elicits sympathy, either of which might compromise an unreservedly festive mood. Also, the ultimate joining of Viola and Orsino is pointedly deferred beyond the end of the play as she remains dressed as a man; and the Clown's closing song carries the bittersweet refrain, 'For the rain it raineth every day.'[26] These three points challenge us to read more than simple, escapist shadings into the world as it leaves us.

In *The Playboy of the Western World* (1907), J. M. Synge contrives an ending in the form of a thematic optical illusion. The playwright gives us a young man and a young woman in what appears to be a classic comedy build-up, then sidesteps the 'ending in marriage'. Christy arrives in a Co. Mayo village little more than a young man on the run from the law, thinking he has accidentally killed his overbearing father. He warms to the exotic mystique that surrounds him, growing in stature through interludes with the saloon owner's daughter, Pegeen Mike. When Christy's father arrives and the townspeople turn against him – Pegeen quite actively so – he lives up to the new image he has created for himself. Christy sets out with a triumphant goodbye: 'Ten thousand blessings upon all that's here, for you've turned me a likely gaffer in the end of all, the way I'll go romancing through a romping lifetime from this hour to the dawning of the Judgement Day.'[27] It reads an awful lot like a 'happily ever after' exit line – but he departs without the other half of the traditional happy ending. And it is not the last line of the play.

Pegeen's curtain line seems to seal the world in emotional tragedy: 'Oh, my grief, I've lost him surely. I've lost the only Playboy of the Western World.'[28] These two utterances come only a few lines apart, yet on the page they project a rather ambiguous ground. Christy, ultimately having breathed life into the mythical version of himself that began to take shape upon his arrival, reframes the preceding events as instrumental in the full realization of his new identity, his brush with romance as a stepping stone to self-fulfilment. Pegeen, on the other hand, reframes her interlude with Christy as the opportunity of a lifetime let slip through her fingers. Prior to specific performance, there is no way to suppose a concrete texture to this final movement of the play. We might observe that potentially it is Pegeen's line which hangs in the air as the stage world blinks shut, providing its last bit of seasoning.

Seen from overhead, the ending is certainly anti-romantic, giving us a vision of life in which, for whatever reason or in whatever balance, a man declines the lasting company of a woman with whom he had seemed to find completion. The interesting thing about imagining a text into performance is that we can't ignore the possibility of Pegeen endowing her final statement with a touch of sarcasm, as if assuring us she is well rid of the swaggering lad who emerged from a once endearing shell (though, admittedly, it is likely that this suggestion falls outside the range of what the playwright intended).

Although it is not possible to disentangle a work from a generic anchoring in time and place, a writer shows originality by subverting, varying or extending what the reader expects. As mentioned in the Introduction, Joe Orton's *What the Butler Saw* (1969) resolves in a flurry of discoveries, which reveal Dr and Mrs Prentice as the parents of Geraldine and Nick, both of whom have been on the receiving ends of their parents' respective sexual advances.

Violence and cruelty have propelled this world into the nightmarish side of traditional farcical madness, with its conventionally benign consequences. The writer calls for gunshot wounds that bleed, alcoholic excess and forced drug injections. The play, however, overshoots the subverted happy ending, to conclude with an image of ascension from the hypocrisies of society:

> PRENTICE   Well, sergeant, we have been instrumental in uncovering
>   a number of remarkable peccadilloes today. I'm sure
>   you'll co-operate in keeping them out of the papers?
> MATCH   I will, sir.
> RANCE   I'm glad you don't despise tradition. Let us put our
>   clothes on and face the world.
> [*They pick up their clothes and weary, bleeding, drugged and drunk, climb
>   the rope ladder into the blazing light.*]
> [*Curtain*][29]

Orton expresses his rejection of the culturally approved conditions for a happy ending by exposing the superficiality of its gratification. In the above lines, he offers a parting satiric shot at the civilized 'tradition' of smoothing over uncomfortable truths. He then goes on to propose a vision of life which amounts to nothing short of a literal escape from earthly society. The image as described is striking and adds to an already multi-layered genre frame, pulled in several directions at once: exuberant farce, cynical critique of culture, saturnalian excess, cruelty and verbal affectation.

Every text harbours a unique, lingering imprint in its last moment of direct contact with the reader/spectator, generated by the writer's specific manipulation of generic elements. If a text chooses to situate itself within an identifiable generic scope of feeling, the difference may appear negligible, but the student of comedy (and, for that matter, reading and writing) will always do well to plumb beneath the surfaces. The interested reader might want to look at the endings of the plays whose beginnings we examined above. *The Suicide* and *Absurd Person Singular*, for example, throw up crosscurrents of feeling which should provide ample food for thought and discussion.

It is always informative to go back and examine the first few and last few pages of a text after a completed initial reading. Relieved of first-time sense-making operations, one may come upon subtleties of pitch not previously evident. One can also gain appreciation of cause and effect, efficiency and originality in the manipulation of generic markers. It is, indeed, often an unprecedented variation upon or mingling of generic elements to which a writer's 'originality' can be attributed. Let us now move our investigation to the body of the comic text, beginning with some of the basic building blocks as given to us by Ancient Greek and Roman theatre.

Chapter 2

Comedy's foundations

Back to (what we call) the beginning

I have called attention to the fact that there are things we come to 'know without knowing' about comedy. This happens by virtue of a complex cultural framing system, which we internalize as we grow up and constantly amend throughout a lifetime. In fact, what allows us to understand and appreciate comic texts from other times and other places is owed at least in part to the fact that some patterns can still be seen to betray their roots in past practices. Basic mechanisms of comedy in Western civilization can be traced to theatre practice in Ancient Greece and Rome, and to the prototypical routines and characters of the *commedia dell'arte*, a semi-improvisational, public performance practice which arose in sixteenth-century Italy (and which will be discussed further in Chapter 4).

In this chapter, I will note some of these familiar comic patterns, hopefully inspiring the curious reader to make similar identifications in contemporary texts. I will also regard some of the historical and theatrical conditions surrounding these early comic footprints as a way of reinforcing the equal and opposite pull of comedy between the universal and the localized 'here and now' of any performance or reading.

Take a moment to refer back to the scene from Aristophanes' *Lysistrata*, sampled in the Introduction. Having gathered women from both sides of the Peloponnesian War for the purpose of unveiling her peace plan, Lysistrata has thus far stopped short of describing its precise nature. She has called only for the banding together of women, and up to this point, neither they nor the audience know exactly what Lysistrata has in mind. Of course, the women, seen to be desperate for peace in this scene, have given less than humanitarian reasons for wanting the war to end: the prolonged separation from their husbands exacted by the conflict has brought them to a state of unbearable sexual craving. As Lysistrata signals that she is finally ready to reveal her scheme, each of the other three women strenuously pledges her support, *whatever* the cost. Lysistrata then leads them right up to the precipice ('All we have to do is give up . . .'), before breaking off to stretch the tension a bit further. Her reluctance to continue ('It's too much to ask') prolongs the mystery and builds the expectation that she will be asking for a towering sacrifice, as voiced by Myrrhine ('Give up what? Our lives?').

To be sure, Lysistrata's answer ('Sex') undercuts the life-and-death frame. But the immediate responses of the women implied by Lysistrata's reaction ('Where are you going? Don't turn away. You're frowning. You're pale. You're crying') suggest an active and unified response by the women, which suddenly reverses upon the readiness for any commitment they had promised several lines earlier. The increasing pledge of resolve or allegiance wrested by one character from another (or group), met with sudden, deflating reversal when the actual demand or its price is named, remains a constant in comic writing to this day. It is possible to see this build-and-deflation pattern frequently in contemporary television comedies from *Blackadder* to *Friends*.

It is important to keep in mind that any artist – painters, novelists, and film-makers included – works from a specific time and place, within which personal circumstances are embedded in a social, cultural and historical context. These conditions somehow shape a person's thoughts and perspectives, and engage the individual in a lifelong 'conversation' with the surrounding world. An artist is also born into a matrix of conditions, out of which (or in response to which) creativity emerges. To take nothing from the inspiration of a Shakespeare, for example, there were practical circumstances – for example, a company of strictly male actors and daylight performances – and existing conventions – like the Prologue or Ghost figure, which made unmistakable imprints upon his plays.

To put it simply, *no artist creates in a vacuum*. As we shall see, there were also pragmatic demands of theatre production in Ancient Greece and Rome, which left indelible prints on the dramatic texts. Comparable points can be made about novelists through history – e.g., the practice of serialization or of writing manuscripts by hand – and about film-makers – the advent of sound and colour, the end of the 'studio' system, and the development of computer-generated imagery technology.

Furthermore, *no artist creates from scratch*. Any given historical/cultural moment harbours a collection of possible 'tools', which the artist draws from (consciously or not), rebels against or otherwise interacts with. We have discussed notions of genre and convention, and how they both prompt and provoke the reader/spectator during the course of reception. These formal features supply the artist's framework for imagining; they furnish the contours of a vehicle within which the playwright, for example, exercises emotional insight or comic dexterity. To be sure, a Samuel Beckett may build something which gives the impression of being utterly new. But it is still only ever brought about through an inspired response to his culture's and medium's tools at hand – in *Waiting for Godot*, Beckett appeared to revolutionize drama by expressing a distinctively mid-twentieth-century existentialist view of life, in a theatre work which imports music-hall characters and rhythms to a stage world recalling Luigi Pirandello's previous interrogations of life and art. Let us apply this 'tool-oriented' way of reading to help illuminate features of our earliest dramatic texts and the legacy they left for comic practice.

The dramatic form which emerged officially in competition at the Festival of Dionysus in Athens around 486 BC is referred to as Old Comedy. It is generally assumed that some unverifiable mix of regional folk practices coalesced into tragedy, for which first official mention was made in the late 530s BC. Comedy was legitimized almost fifty years later, and, of course, drew upon somewhat other pre-dramatic activities, the precise nature of which has remained a topic for conjecture since Aristotle.

Alan Sommerstein's summary of drama's forerunners includes choral dancing and extravagantly costumed dancers, 'often grotesquely padded',[1] as would become the practice in Old Comedy. Sommerstein imagines the songs of a *kōmos* (from which comedy derives its name), 'a rowdy, drunken band of revellers moving unsteadily and noisily through the streets',[2] to have led to a form of 'iambic insult-poetry', the influence of which can be seen clearly in the plays of Aristophanes (*c.* 445–*c.* 385 BC). In the Introduction, we noted Cornford's contentions about the origins of comedy in fertility rituals, exemplified in the plot element of the 'sacred marriage'.

Old Comedy today?

It is not easy to find descendants of Old Comedy in contemporary theatre and film, but a play like Dario Fo's *Accidental Death of an Anarchist* (*Morte accidentale di un anarchico*, 1970), incorporates a broad comic sensibility, satiric thrust and undisguised ridicule of real people, in addressing a specific police investigation in twentieth-century Italian society. A film like *Monty Python's Life of Brian* (1979) hangs a mix of vulgarity, highbrow humour and sketch comedy (plus a celebratory closing choral song) loosely upon the backbone of an alternative Christ narrative. *The Simpsons* television show spins a relentless series of topical gags, low humour, cultural satire and even musical interludes upon a loose plot or theme, often veering in unforeseeable directions along the way. A topical revue (the occasional British series, *Bremner, Bird and Fortune*) or satiric magazine (*Private Eye*) may also be seen to carry on the spirit of Aristophanes.

Perhaps now is the time to point out that nine of the eleven plays we have by Aristophanes – out of forty he is known to have written – constitute the basis for all the direct evidence upon which we base our conclusions about Old Comedy (see the box on page 41). By virtue of historical records attesting to Aristophanes' success in festival competitions, it is widely agreed that his received output affords a degree of insight into the standards of comic play-writing from the period (even though we cannot be sure to what extent and in what ways he distinguished himself). Old Comedy is taken to cover roughly the time of its official introduction until the end of the Peloponnesian War in 404 BC, when conditions in Athens changed substantially.

The fingerprints of Old Comedy

Aristophanes' pointed references to culturally specific practices, events and personalities constitute part of the root system of reasons that his plays may at first seem opaque or uncooperative to the contemporary reader. In the Introduction, I proposed how an historical grasp of sociocultural roles and stereotypes in 411 BC might augment a contemporary appreciation of the gender dynamics in *Lysistrata*. It should then be apparent how an on-the-ground insight into the circumstances surrounding Athenian involvement in the Peloponnesian War, as well as the public figures who prosecuted the war and the state mechanisms through which they acted, would constitute further 'inside' information required for an enriched appreciation of the play and its comedy.

Aristophanes' extant plays always begin with some portrayal of an unsatisfactory state of affairs, which a lead character seeks to remedy, often by hatching a fantastic plan. This plan, called by some its 'happy idea' – be it a search for utopia among the birds or a trip to the underworld to remedy the dearth of worthy tragedians by retrieving a dead one – provides the backbone for a loose weave of candid commentary, slapstick, topical satire, bawdy comedy, sketch humour and choral song and dance.

Such a mix would appear, on the surface, to encompass all you could want in a comedy. But a play by Aristophanes is likely to impress a twenty-first-century reader as obtuse and misshapen. Any text remains inescapably a product of its original conditions, and some insight into this web of influences stands to smooth and enhance the reading. While there is insufficient room in this introductory treatment to show how all of the conventions of Ancient Greek theatre reside within the lines – and there are many books, including annotated play texts, which serve this purpose – I would like to show at least a few of the ways in which the reading of a 2,400-year-old comedy can be better appreciated by knowing something more about the conditions of performance. (It is, of course, vital to remember that we read these plays in translation, hence the box below.)

Comedy and translation

Rainer Schulte and John Biguenet take two salient points from their historical collection of essays on translation: '(1) the transferral of the foreign from other languages into our own allows us to explore and formulate emotions and concepts that otherwise we would not have experienced; and (2) the act of translation continuously stretches the linguistic boundaries of one's own language'.[3] These observations speak to an essential and potentially valuable otherness of experience manifested in another language – but they would seem to be going in precisely the wrong direction with regard to the stuff of comedy. As we have seen, comedy and the comic rely on embedding themselves in the everyday experiences and expectations of the target audience, and so translation becomes a make-or-break factor in rendering them in a dramatic text. Slang, jargon or some current catchphrase can prove difficult ground to negotiate for the translator, as can just the right term of endearment or clever insult. Punning is no doubt the translator's greatest challenge, based on the actual sound of the word or phrase and its fortuitously different meanings in the native language. Indeed, a culture's language is so much a manifestation of its history, thought and experience that it is sure to have words or phrases which deny direct expression in another language.

Dialect often serves as a marker of comic or laughable character. A rural accent becomes a pre-emptive signal for a character's naïvety, simplicity or gullibility while upper-class speech becomes shorthand for self-centred or snobbish privilege – both are often presented as likely butts for joking. In Aristophanes' *Lysistrata*, for example, the Spartan character, Lampito, is depicted by Aristophanes as being impressively strong, a reference to the fact that Spartan women were encouraged to be physically fit. I have seen an American translation in which she has been given a sort of hillbilly accent, and an English one in which she is written as Scottish. Another point of comparison for this (and any Aristophanes) play is in the extent to which its obscenity is fully expressed or tidied. The use of poetic forms in Ancient Greek and Roman texts, whose usage would have borne significance for the original audiences, is sometimes suggested in modern translations. The Alexandrine verse used by Molière will have no meaning for a modern-day, English-speaking audience – is it best to translate its twelve-syllable lines into Shakespeare's ten-syllable lines, or some freer form more immediately accessible to a contemporary audience?

In *The Frogs*, Aristophanes parodies the play-writing habits of both Aeschylus and Euripides, two historical writers whose styles anyone would be hard pressed to distinguish even in the most accurate of translations. The classical Greek playwrights became Shakespeare and George Bernard Shaw in the 2004 incarnation of *The Frogs* on Broadway. Think about potential challenges for a translator working on a recent play or novel you have read.

In the age of Old Comedy, Aristophanes' plays would have been written and produced for a one-off performance at one of two yearly state festivals. The larger of these, called the City Dionysia or Great Dionysia, took place in the spring and was a festive occasion of great civic import. The actual demographic composition of the audience remains a matter of inference, but it was probably around 14,000 or 15,000 people, and the largest bloc by far would have been male citizens (although the Chorus addresses 'ten thousand men of sense' in *The Frogs*, 405 BC). The City Dionysia drew some foreign visitors, unlike the Lenaea, which was held in the winter months when travel was more difficult. Although there remains some uncertainty about the order of things, it is generally agreed that during the week-long City Dionysia the audiences saw three tragedies and a satyr play (see the box below) by each of three playwrights, plus five individual comedies. The shorter Lenaea presented two plays each by two tragic writers, plus five comedies. Although there is evidence that some plays were given second chances, they were essentially written for one-off performance, upon a civic-religious occasion. It should be apparent that this contrasts with today's theatre performance, a more socially and economically driven event usually aimed at a widest possible audience.

Aristophanes wrote, then, for a single, relatively knowable group of spectators, without intent to accommodate the possibilities of later productions or future theatregoers. He would be aware of the people, events and attitudes 'in the air' during the past year and the run-up to the festival competition, and appears to have been quite adept at mining this vein of material for comic effect. It can be of no small matter that the plays were written for competition, and, in terms of comedy's generic penchant for humour, the circumstances could not be more favourable. Think of the laughter potential in a skit night for a gathering of workers or classmates, and the room for inside joking at the expense of the boss or teacher.

The satyr play

The satyr play provided a festive postscript to a playwright's three tragedies, by ending with humour and dance. It is so called because of the chorus of satyrs, whose Dionysian pleasure-seeking was used to undercut the psychic weight of the preceding tragic trilogy. The only complete surviving satyr play is Euripides' *Cyclops*, which spins its own irreverent variation on the well-known chapter of the Ulysses myth.

In the course of Aristophanes' *The Wasps* (422 BC), the Leader of the Chorus launches into a speech which begins:

> Now once again, spectators, if you love
> To hear plain speaking, pay attention, please!
> The author has a bone to pick with you
> For treating him unfairly, when, he says,
> You've had so many splendid things from him.

Here, the Leader of the Chorus serves as a mouthpiece for the playwright himself, who appears to blame the audience for an unsatisfying result with *The Clouds* in the previous year's competition. Several lines later he says:

> Yet he did not rest
> Upon his laurels, suffer from swelled head
> Or flounce about the wrestling-schools, like some
> Successful poets we have known, nor yet
> Would he consent to prostitute the Muse
> And hold some simpering stripling up to scorn
> To satisfy a lover's jealous whim.[4]

By 'calling out' these rivals in such familiar, knowing terms, Aristophanes adopts a stance not, perhaps, unlike the drunken band of revellers imagined by Sommerstein, relying on highly localized knowledge of events and their social undercurrents. *The Wasps* was performed at the Lenaea, which would have drawn a more strictly Athenian audience. These references are essentially 'private jokes' for the citizenry of Athens.

Interlaced with these *cultural* fingerprints from another historical context, Aristophanic texts leave *formal* fingerprints from Ancient Greek theatre practice. Plays like *Lysistrata* and *The Wasps* display familiar enough signs of character and humour to a contemporary reader. They remain, at the same time, somewhat alien in their plot structures, rhythms and choral passages.

Some knowledge of historical performance practices, for example, helps to explain the limited number of speaking roles in any scene. Three principal actors were employed for each comedy in the competition, with some historians allowing for a fourth. It is hard to imagine the passage from *Lysistrata* in the Introduction being acted with fewer than four speakers, and one historian assigns the minor role of Lampito to an 'amateur actor'.

All actors and Chorus members wore masks, which facilitated the doubling of roles. A modern-day reader might imagine the masks for gods – for example, Dionysos in *The Frogs* – or real-life Athenians, such as Euripides in *Thesmophoriazousae*, displaying comically pitched identifying features. A reader might also suspect that a line like the following, delivered by Kalonike to Lysistrata at the start of the play, was intended to call attention to the character's mask: 'Good heavens, Lysistrata, / What's the matter? What *are* you scowling at? / Your eyebrows look as though they're taking off.'[5] It is impossible for us to know for certain the precise culture-specific resonance such a mask would have sought to exploit (an impression of an ill-humoured or exceedingly serious Athenian wife?); but comic wisdom strongly suggests there must have been one.

Built into a hillside to avail itself of the natural slope for raked seating, the Theatre of Dionysus hosted both the tragedy and comedy competitions in the fifth century BC. The main dramatic action took place in front of a wooden building, called the *skene*, which could have been painted with a scenic backdrop and whose double doors constituted a main entrance. Most historians allow for the possibility of a slightly raised 'stage' in front of the *skene*. The Chorus performed primarily in the *orchestra* in front of this principal playing area. Side passages, or *paradoi*, led to the *orchestra* from the right or left. The Chorus would enter along one of these passageways. Two stage devices were employed: the *ekkyklema*, a platform which could be rolled out from the central doors of the *skene*; and the *mechane*, or crane, which could 'fly' characters onto (or off) the stage.

It is possible to detect in the hypothesized staging practices of Old Comedy something of a response to and release from tragedy's 'serious mode'. Comic playwrights were given a twenty-four-strong Chorus – as opposed to tragedy's twelve to fifteen – and allowed secondary Choruses, as well as small or non-speaking roles. Comic playwrights might avail themselves of an extra door or two and a window. The aforementioned stage devices were also used in comedy. The *ekkyklema*, for example, was often used in tragedy to display a tableau of death following an offstage murder or suicide, such as the revealing of Eurydice's corpse in *Antigone*. An under-cutting of this weighty practice must always have been at least part of the fun when Aristophanes enlisted the rolling platform. In *Acharnians* (425 BC), he takes a satiric jab at a well-known tragic playwright who may be overly reliant on this particular 'stage effect', *and* has the character make use of it for a laughably unworthy purpose:

DIKAIOPOLIS	Euripides! Eur-ee!
	Pray lend an ear. God knows I need one. Oo-oo!
	It's Dikaiopolis, your neighbour. Me.
EURIPIDES	I'm busy.
DIKAIOPOLIS	Use a stage effect.
EURIPIDES	I can't.

DIKAIOPOLIS	Of course you can. You always do.
EURIPIDES	All right.
	If it gets it over quicker. Just a mo.
DIKAIOPOLIS	High tragedy. So this is how it's done.[6]

The inference is that Euripides rolls out on the *ekkyklema*. Aristophanes offers a critique of Euripides' dramatic technique while generally mocking the senior form itself.

In Western culture, theatre and comedy have long moved away from their initial civic and spiritual moorings. But, as the festivals were once held in the name of religious celebration, it should not be surprising to find such references in the plays. Gods, odes and religious practices appear in Aristophanes' plays, both earnestly and in a spirit of mischief (though not disrespect). *Lysistrata* ends, for example, with a series of lyrical odes to the gods. Earlier, however, Lysistrata and her sisters-in-arms swear an oath to their cause over a mock sacrifice replacing the customary blood with wine.

Two elements noted by Douglas MacDowell as expected components of a comedy at the time[7] – obscenity and personal ridicule – can be fairly self-evident to the reader, depending on the translation. An experienced reader comes to note the extent to which any given translator attempts to 'tone down' lewdness and genericize jokes about specific Athenians. Obscenity or its intimation, of course, opens itself to emphasis (or lack thereof) in production. Scatological references to penises, bums, flatulence and excrement abound in Aristophanes, as do unsubtle jokes about sex. The old rascal Procleon says to the Flute Girl in *The Wasps*, 'Come on up here, my little ladybird. Hold on to this rope. Be careful, it's a bit old and worn: but you'd be surprised what it'll stand up to.'[8] According to some historians, a non-speaking, walk-on character, like the Flute Girl in this example or Reconciliation in *Lysistrata*, would have been the one role in any play to be cast with an actual young woman, possibly appearing unclothed. Imagine the effect of the preceding comment on the all- or mostly male audience.

Old Comedy's costumes were close-fitting leotards or body suits, padded around the belly and buttocks for comic effect; older men would be rendered as particularly decrepit and past sexual potency. A formidable leather phallus would have been sewn to the basic costume. Although most sources describe them as hanging flaccidly, it is easy to imagine the potential for adult humour in a well-known scene from *Lysistrata*. Myrrhine's husband, Kinesias, has returned from battle, in the agonizingly unfulfilled state of arousal the sex strike has exacted upon Athenian and Spartan combatants. As Kinesias approaches the Acropolis, Lysistrata spots him from a lookout post: 'Look, a man! Look at the state he's in.'[9] If it was customary for the phallus to be limp, this scene would suggest to the watchful reader an anatomically correct variation on the oversized costume piece.

The element of personal ridicule, noted in the above Leader of the Chorus speech from *The Wasps*, might be expanded for our purposes to include all topical jokes. This feature, which so roots the text in its social context, presents a challenge for the contemporary translator and reader, and necessitates continued reference to footnotes in a faithful translation. In the opening page of the play, for example, jokes are made at the expense of the Corybants (a sect known for its orgiastic rites) and Cleonymus (one of Cleon's followers, who must have dropped his shield in battle), two obscure allusions for even the most widely versed reader. (Then again, even some episodes of *The Simpsons* are old enough, by now, for some of the more subtle topical references to have slipped into obscurity.)

Historians have identified certain formal elements in Old Comedy, which Aristophanes would have been obliged to include – or at least consider – in the writing of his plays. The contemporary reader, unaware of these elements, will naturally try to process the unfolding text according to reception techniques that don't really apply.

A reader, for example, could be forgiven for wondering what, if anything, the above choral passage from *The Wasps* has to do with the previous two-thirds of the play. Thus far we have been introduced to Procleon, a comically irrepressible old man, addicted (like many of his peers) to serving on juries in an Athenian court system which rewards them with a monetary allowance and the crotchety pleasure of condemning defendants. The man's adult son, Anticleon, has tried to break his father of the habit by sequestering him at home and foiling his various farcical attempts at escape. Anticleon has argued in a mock legal battle with his father that these 'waspish' jurors, rather than simply indulging in a harmless diversion, play an unwitting part in a cycle of political corruption. Contemporary structure would not ordinarily countenance a gratuitous and formal halt in the proceedings seemingly unrelated to plot, character or theme. A modern-day reader aware of some of the structural elements of Old Comedy, however, expects something in the form of the above passage called the *parabasis* (and might even notice that it appears relatively late in this play). The *parabasis* is a conventional 'stepping aside' from the play's narrative course for direct address of the audience – sometimes in the author's own voice – on matters which may have nothing to do with the play's events. In the case noted above, Aristophanes used the first part of the *parabasis* to vent his spleen on those responsible for his previous entry's lack of success in the competition, and to renew the attack on Cleon, one of his favourite targets.

The *parabasis* is one of several structural elements in Old Comedy. Aristophanes conventionally begins with a prologue, in which the first characters to appear deliver exposition. It can therefore be interesting to observe the various ways in which Aristophanes furnishes the necessary information via humorous means. The Chorus then enters with a song, called the *parados* (the singular form of the side entrances). There is a central debate between two characters called the *agon*, and a final scene of revelry, called the *exodos*.[10]

The Greek Chorus presents a particular challenge for contemporary readers. Although integrated into the plots of Classical Tragedy and Old Comedy, it was usually placed in the *orchestra*, with the main action going on behind. Thematically, the Chorus became a play-writing device for guiding the spectator's attitude toward the central character(s). With its singing and dancing, the Chorus promised a certain degree of entertainment value as well.

For Aristophanes, the conventional Chorus of twenty-four became a springboard for variation, for example, splitting the Chorus in *Lysistrata*, so as to increase the comic potency of engaging a bunch of Old Women and Old Men in a battle of the sexes. *The Wasps* includes a secondary chorus of boys, who may have doubled later as puppies. It should be pointed out, as well, that the Chorus would have been dressed in a manner appropriate to the characters. In *Lysistrata*, this might have meant comically grotesque exaggerations of Old Men and Old Women. In *The Wasps*, the Chorus of old men would have been costumed as wasps, perhaps taking full advantage of the possibilities the stinger might pose as a symbol of waning manhood.

Aristophanes' plays are written in various lyric metres, another element whose significance can never be fully appreciated by a contemporary reader/spectator. Some translators attempt a semblance of poetic rhythm throughout – even though we would have no grasp of the original significance of the metres – while others render only the choral sections in verse. The contemporary reader may take account of the poetic setting for a choral ode, but fail to realize that it would have been sung and danced. Performance was accompanied by a musician playing the *aulos*, described by David Wiles as 'a double pipe made of wood or bone' akin to the oboe.[11] This is another way in which application of our own cultural reading strategies skews reception of the text. It might be tempting to compare the choral passage from Old Comedy to the 'production number' in American musical comedy, but the religious connections and structural obligations of the ancient form render a direct substitution superficial at best. It remains an interesting challenge, then, for the individual reader (or stage director) to imagine this feature in cultural translation. For some of us, part of the fun of reading texts from other times and places lies in just this consideration of how other sensibilities under other circumstances generated these collections of words, and how one might reread these words through our own contextual prisms. Hopefully, this brief introduction will serve to suggest how a more informed awareness of historical and theatrical conditions supports a more enriched reading of a text – especially a comic one – as we move on to New Comedy.

Our old friend, New Comedy

To the extent that Old Comedy continually reminds us of its otherness, New Comedy may appear so familiar as to seem hackneyed. Many a student has responded tepidly to the assigned reading of a Menander or Plautus text, reporting, for example, that it was interesting from an historical perspective, but that the play seems ordinary. Not everyone, of course, will be taken by any given text, regardless of its historical value. What should be emphasized, however, is that these playwrights cut the original pattern for a popular genre whose edges may have been worn flat by endless recycling.

New Comedy's setting in an everyday milieu familiar to the audience, its reliance on misunderstandings or hidden information, its negotiation of obstacles toward romantic fulfilment, even its staple diet of stock character types can be found at will in today's cinema listings and the popular-fiction section of any bookshop. We should, of course, realize that these general-izations mask the subtle identifying marks of another culture's contextual details, as a more informed reading revealed in the preceding section. But a play by Menander or Plautus looks like an old friend compared to Aris-tophanes, because it retains archetypal fingerprints we recognize, including its structure and social observation. Erich Segal does not overstate the case by writing, 'from the point of view of influence, Menander is arguably the most influential figure in the history of Western comedy'.[12]

New Comedy is generally assigned a starting date of around 323 BC – the year Alexander the Great died, having vastly increased the size of the Greek world through military conquest. The period some call Middle Comedy essentially bridges the time from the end of the Peloponnesian War in 404 BC to the rise of New Comedy. Such clear-cut demarcations may provide handy guideposts for historians, but they belie a more gradual development due to changes in the sociocultural landscape. Alas, we have even less original material from the single extant proponent of Greek New Comedy, Menander (*c.* 342–*c.* 291 BC), than we have of Aristophanes.

Menander's plays were entered into the same competitions as were Aristophanes' many years before. The Greek world had changed, however, and two main factors shaped New Comedy: first, Sparta's eventual defeat of Athens began a move away from the democratic openness of the fifth century BC, and an atmosphere which no longer tolerated the candid satiric references to people and institutions – playwrights were wise to watch what they said, on pain of death. Second, theatre performance began to spread beyond the two Athenian festival competitions, and so needed to position itself for a far more general audience. By Menander's time, theatres could be found in many a Greek community outside Athens, providing a new kind of occupation in the form of touring companies of actors.

Importantly, the theatre stage became standardized, based on a permanent stone theatre built in Athens around 330 BC, with three onstage entrances along with the two side entrances; the stage itself was eventually raised above the *orchestra* area. Masks were still used, but they came to represent standard character types, and costumes came to reflect more closely the clothes of everyday Athenians (without the comically grotesque padding and phalluses). There are never more than three speaking characters in a scene at any given time, and in some passages it is possible to detect the playwright's need to shuffle entrances and exits to allow his three actors to populate the entire stage world.

As much as any given Old Comedy text was aimed at a single, specific audience, New Comedy sought a far greater geographical reach, to attract and please the individual spectator, rather than to criticize or instruct him on state issues – for Greek New Comedy was still aimed at male citizens. New Comedy came to occupy itself with the vicissitudes of middle-class life in the Hellenistic world. As characterized by Segal, 'the transition from Old to New may be epitomized as a journey from the topical to the typical'.[13] R. L. Hunter distils an underlying difference between Aristophanes and Menander, which saw the beginning of a socially conservative inclination: 'New Comedy offers no grand vision of a new world; the plays offer rather the comforting spectacle of the restoration of the status quo after disturbance caused by folly or ignorance.'[14] To this day, the New Comedy template, in the guise of drama, film or literature, offers the same reassurance of society's basic goodwill and underlying wisdom. Such soothing reinforcement of culturally inscribed values raises fair questions from the likes of feminist, Marxist and postcolonial critics (which we will address in Chapter 6).

New Comedy centred its intrigue upon the plight of a young man in pursuit of a young woman, amid various possible complications of a society which had become increasingly mobile. Obstacles usually took the form of disapproving fathers, competing suitors, and/or the inappropriate status of the desired young woman. (It can be unsettling for a contemporary reader to discover how easily rape was used as an expository justification for the young man to set his cap upon a young woman originally thought beyond his reach.)

Fragments of nineteen of Menander's estimated one hundred plays exist in all, though, until relatively recently, his reputation was taken on trust from the opinions of ancient critics. Only two plays by Menander have survived in anything approaching full texts, and the bulk of that material has only been unearthed in the past hundred years. *Dyskolos* (316 BC), translated in J. Michael Walton's version as *The Malcontent* (and in others as *Old Cantankerous* and *The Grouch*), is the most complete Greek New Comedy play we have, and so will serve as a model for discussion of key characteristics.

The play is set on a village street, with the three standard entrances representing doors to two of the characters' houses, and one to a religious shrine in between. Unlike Aristophanes' worlds, which might shift locations, the New Comedy stage represents this same place throughout, and always stands for a street in front of at least two houses. It is believed that the side entrance to the audience's right was taken conventionally as leading toward the city, with the one to the audience's left leading to the countryside or harbour.

The Malcontent opens with a monologue by the minor god, Pan, the beginning of which follows:

> PAN We are in Attica. Suppose it so for now.
> The village of Phyle, and for all Phylesians,
> This shrine from which I entered is sacred to the Nymphs.
> The locals farm this stony waste somehow, and it's a holy place.
> Here to my right, your left, lives Knemon,
> A malcontent, if ever there was one,
> Hostile to all comers, cranky in all company.
> 'In all company' did I say? Never in his life
> Has this Knemon volunteered a friendly word
> To anyone, never made overtures to a living soul.[15]

Pan will go on to inform the audience that he has made Sostratos, 'a young man, son of a local farmer', fall in love with the crotchety Knemon's daughter. We can, however, observe several things in addition to the actual information imparted. We are introduced to the stage world by a minor deity, who gives an omniscient account of the circumstances. He explains that he is helping the young woman because of her dutiful attention to him, confirming that a religious connection is still taken for granted, though not held to dominate the proceedings. The tone is informal and agreeable, as the character literally sets the scene, by labelling each of the three entrances (e.g., 'Here to my right, your left, lives Knemon'). Compare the vernacular language of this speaker with the lofty register of any opening speech from a tragedy, and you have observed a rather telling indicator of a text's generic intentions. (As sometimes happens, here and in the Roman comedy to come, this character will not appear again in the play, having served his purpose.)

The contemporary reader will find this text much easier going than the Old Comedy of Aristophanes. The thematic territory – a young man in love and human foibles embodied in a social 'type' – is entirely familiar, as is the sense of a plot and dramatic arc. Despite the incorporation of elements foreign to our experience, there remains a familiar sense of ordinary life. In *The Malcontent*, the young, smitten Sostratos seeks to overcome the formidable obstacle of Knemon's ill-humoured misanthropy to wed his daughter. Knemon has driven his stepson, Gorgias, from under his roof, and the hard-working young man now occupies the house represented by the third of the onstage doors, with Pan's shrine in the centre. Over the course of the play, Sostratos convinces Gorgias that his intentions toward Knemon's daughter (Gorgias' stepsister) are honourable. When Knemon accidentally falls down a well, Gorgias leads the rescue effort, thereby earning a significant admission from the old man, if not a full-blown change of character:

> KNEMON . . . I was wrong about one thing, I suppose. I thought I was the only person in the world who was self-sufficient. I thought that I didn't need people. Now I've stared death in the face and know he can turn up when you least expect him. My mistake and I admit it. Everyone needs a helping hand sometime. You see, I'd lost my faith in human nature. I'd watched how friendship had become no more than a commodity with a calculated profit margin. And I assumed that the same was true for all relationships everywhere.[16]

Knemon then puts Gorgias in charge of his affairs, including the arrangement of a proper marriage for his daughter. Gorgias sanctions the match Sostratos has been pursing throughout the play, who, in turn, arranges a reciprocal marriage between his new friend and his own sister.

One can easily glean from the above passage the sense of a 'serious' moral utterance, which we must assume was inspired by social trends of Menander's time. Although Knemon explains how he was driven to anti-social behaviour, and even goes on to defend it to some extent ('If everyone behaved as I do, the law court would be redundant; we wouldn't need prisons; and there'd be an end to war. Every man would be content with his lot'),[17] it is clear that the play ultimately argues against widespread adoption of such an attitude. Menander's play does not teem with formal jokes; it would appear primarily to serve as a vehicle for gentle lessons in civilized conduct.

There are several other such social commentaries sprinkled throughout the dialogue in *The Malcontent*, supporting this notion of Menandrian comedy seeking to 'normalize' society, by finding tempered amusement at the expense of extreme deviations from behaviour threatening to the social unit (see the box on page 55). A look at the last speech of Act I, delivered by Gorgias' slave, Daos, emphasizes this and other noteworthy points:

> DAOS This doesn't smell right. What's going on? Very fishy. A young chap running errands for a girl. That can't be right. As for you, Knemon, God rot you for letting an innocent young girl wander about on her own without any sort of a chaperon. I expect this chancer found out and thought he was onto a good thing. I ought to let her brother know about this so we can arrange to keep an eye on the girl. In fact, I'd better do that right now. Look, here's a group of drunks heading for the shrine. I don't think I want to get involved with that lot.[18]

Slaves became stock characters in New Comedy, given integral parts to play with regard to the machinations of plot and humour. Daos adopts a chatty relationship with the audience, and would seem to be afforded a degree of authority by the playwright. He lends the weight of his disapproval toward Knemon's antisocial ways.

We also gain an insight into the culturally approved treatment of a young woman in Daos' fairly harsh condemnation, 'As for you, Knemon, God rot you for letting an innocent young girl wander about on her own without any sort of a chaperon.' It appears to have been improper for an honourable woman to be seen in public unescorted, let alone for her to talk to a man who wasn't related to her. In *The Malcontent*, the female romantic interest is unnamed, and two other 'respectable' citizen women do have names and do appear, but never speak. Although the consummation of romantic love ostensibly drives every plot, one can see even in the short passage above the studiously decorous position and tone adopted by the playwright's mouthpiece (in stark contrast to the regular diet of crude humour seen in Aristophanes).

By this point in New Comedy, the breaks between acts had become the single remaining province of the Chorus, which was now totally disengaged physically and thematically from the action of the play. The Chorus appears essentially to be charged with providing singing and dancing entertainment between 'acts'.

Theophrastus' characters

The Greek philosopher Theophrastus (371–287 BC) could well have been writing material for a stand-up comedian when he sketched a series of thirty portraits and behavioural descriptions, striking for the degree to which they can still be recognized in our marketplaces and at our parties. See if you recognize this guy, labelled 'the Talker': 'The talker is the sort of man who, when you meet him, if you make any remark to him, will tell you that you are quite wrong; that he himself knows all the facts, and if you listen to him you shall learn what they are.'[19] Theophrastus' caustic eye settled also upon types like 'the Toady, or Flatterer', 'the Boaster' and 'the Skinflint', all of whom recall stock characters in ancient drama and the later *commedia dell'arte*.

The observation of sociocultural types, recognizable for their quirks and excesses, has long constituted a staple of comic drama. It is remarkable that, despite the specificity of behaviour in historical time and place, there seems to be some continuity with regard to the social animal in Western society. In recent times, performers like Lily Tomlin, Whoopi Goldberg and Eric Bogosian have built solo performance pieces around a diverse cast of keenly observed characters, all of which they portray themselves.

We find its arrival loosely justified in the context of the play, right before the first act break and in the general manner above as spoken by Daos: 'Look, here's a group of drunks heading for the shrine. I don't think I want to get involved with that lot.' Although it appears during all four breaks in the action, it is not subsequently mentioned in the dialogue.

Menander adopted a five-act structure, which, in the wrong hands, could impede continuity or dramatic momentum through repeated interruption of the narrative. E. W. Handley points out the fact that the conventional pattern 'of introducing a new development towards the end of an act is a recurrent one in Menander, and, naturally enough, the development is often brought by the arrival of a character new to the play, or new at least to the preceding sequence'.[20] Menander uses this technique in each of the first four acts in *The Malcontent*. In every case, the character not only provides an addition to the population of the stage world, but justifies some manner of quickening momentum, and projects the action toward the following act. The introduction of Knemon's daughter at the end of Act I re-inflames Sostratos' passion, which, in turn leads to the above speech by Daos. The reader's confidence that Daos has misapprehended the lad's intentions – 'I expect this chancer found out and thought he was onto a good thing' – promises further intrigue in the next act. This method of tautening the line between text and reader before an act break or the end of an episode may now seem so natural to Western reading processes as to be invisible.

It is worth remarking upon a few other textual features, which might otherwise escape the contemporary reader's notice:

The ekkyklema

Having been rescued from the well, Knemon is apparently too injured (or hoping to appear so) to make his way out of the house under his own power. Sostratos says, 'Lord, what a sight', and the translator includes the stage direction, '*Enter Gorgias and Knemon, probably on a couch*'.[21] The knowing reader will suspect this refers to the *ekkyklema*, or rolling platform, discussed above. Again, it is not clear as to what tone of reaction it might have been intended to provoke, but it is inescapably a citation of Classical Tragedy, and at least a subtle lampooning of the character's distress.

The 'running slave' and 'slave whacking'

In the midst of an early expository scene between a sponger named Chaereas and Sostratos, the young man's slave Pyrrhias enters:

PYRRHIAS	Gangway. Mind your backs. I'm coming through. There's a loony after me.
SOSTRATOS	What the hell...? Pyrrhias...
PYRRHIAS	Scatter.
SOSTRATOS	What is it?
PYRRHIAS	Clods of earth. Slinging them at me. Stones. I'm all in.
SOSTRATOS	Slinging them at you? Now where are you off to, you little devil?
PYRRHIAS	What? Whew. Maybe he's called off the chase.
SOSTRATOS	Nobody's after you, for God's sake.
PYRRHIAS	I could have sworn he was.
SOSTRATOS	What are you talking about?
PYRRHIAS	We've got to get out of here. Please.
SOSTRATOS	And go where?
PYRRHIAS	As far as possible from that front door. That man you sent me to see. He's a psychopath, out of his tree. What a business. I've broken half my toes.[22]

The playing space on the Greek stage had become standardized as wide and shallow, allowing for plenty of room from left to right and not much from back to front. The 'running slave' comic convention would have made good use of this lateral space, as, in the manner of the above passage, a slave character burst onto the scene in apparent fear for his life. As you can see, the text supports ample opportunity for the physical embodiment of fear and panic, which fails to diminish over a page of dialogue, even though it is quite apparent that the actual threat has evaporated. This is a stock feature of New Comedy, and has survived to this day wherever broad comedy appears (e.g., cartoons and sitcoms).

This routine finds its justification in a summary threat of violence by certain characters toward their slaves. Pyrrhias describes Knemon as having flung stones and clumps of earth at him and having 'picked up a piece of fencing and belted me with it'.[23] Knemon later inflicts a whipping upon Sikon for pounding on his door. This tradition of what I call 'slave whacking' – the act, description, or threat of violence against slaves – continues in Roman New Comedy and up through twentieth-century master–slave relationships like those of Baldrick and Blackadder (in the *Blackadder* series) as well as Manuel and Basil Fawlty (in *Fawlty Towers*, see Figure 2.1). It might be said that this strain of gag, based around the infliction of physical punishment which is only painful for comic purposes and never truly life-threatening, led to what we have come to think of as 'slapstick' (described a bit further at the end of Chapter 4).

Figure 2.1 In the popular BBC comedy series, *Fawlty Towers*, Basil Fawlty (John Cleese) and his employee Manuel (Andrew Sachs) echo the comic master–slave relationship born in Ancient Greek and Roman comedy.

Entering while talking back to someone offstage

It was apparently conventional for a character to enter while talking back to someone offstage. Here is one example from *The Malcontent*:

> GETAS What now, blast it? I've only one pair of hands, haven't I, not
> thirty? I've got the oven going. I've fetched, I've carried. I washed
> up while I was chopping the liver. I baked a cake. I've set the table and
> blinded myself with the smoke. The beast at the feast, that's me.[24]

This technique constitutes a clever way of preventing the dramatic momentum from dropping while a new scene gets underway. The character arrives with a certain emotional momentum, boosting vocal energy. It can impart a bit of information and indicate something of the character's frame of mind, prior to being confronted with some new impetus onstage.

Many of these New Comedy conventions carried through to Roman Comedy as we have received it in the plays of Plautus and Terence. In fact, Roman Comedy drew heavily upon Greek New Comedy – and Menander in particular, according to the texts we have received – for plot and context. Having looked at defining features for New Comedy in Ancient Greece, I will give brief introductions to our extant Roman playwrights, Plautus and Terence, and try to impart some sense of their distinctive takes on the form.

New Comedy in Roman hands

By the time Plautus (254–184 BC) was writing plays, sometime after 215 BC, Roman civilization was in the ascendancy. Wars and conquests had given Romans a taste for things Greek. In fact, all the plays we have received from this period are of a type called *fabula palliata* ('plays in Greek dress'), drawing upon the likes of Menander, reworking and mixing plots or characters, while giving the plays a Greek context so the audience might have rein to laugh at things the stricter Roman society would never condone.

Other conditions now differed from those surrounding Greek comedy. All Roman theatres of this period were temporary – it was not deemed morally acceptable to sanction such a structure permanently – featuring a raised wooden stage backed by a scene building, the front of which had three doors. The stage, like Greek New Comedy of the previous century, was wide and shallow, raised above the orchestra area.

Plays were performed at religious festivals, which might number up to seventeen a year,[25] as well as state occasions. At these so-called 'scenic games', plays competed with many other forms of entertainment, including boxing matches, gladiatorial contests, athletic displays and wild-animal fights. Far from having captive audiences, the players would have to win and hold the attention of a group of spectators who could at any moment decide to move on to another entertainment. Amid this fairground atmosphere a playwright knew he had to compete for his audience and retain their attention all the way through the performance.

As entertainment value had become of primary import, we can read in Plautus' plays a more concerted attempt to keep the spectator laughing. The narrative focus changes from the fortunes of starry-eyed young men to the deceptions woven by their nimble-minded servants, the stock 'witty slave' character at the centre of many a Roman Comedy.[26] There is no longer a Chorus, nor are there any act breaks. It appears that Plautus increased the musical element of his plays over the course of his career, crafting certain sections of text to be accompanied by *tibia* (the Roman version of the Greek *aulos* or reed pipes).

It was more incumbent upon Plautus than it had been on Aristophanes and Menander to cultivate crowd-pleasing techniques – he was writing plays for financial gain. It is uniformly held that earlier in his life Plautus had been an actor in a travelling troupe, taking the name of Maccius. The name refers to one of the stock characters in Atellan farces, considered a popular form of comic performance which led to Roman New Comedy. It is further surmised that, having somehow squandered his earnings, Plautus turned to play-writing to make a living – and there can be no mistaking his comic savvy in writing for performance.

The Braggart Soldier (*Miles Gloriosus*, c. 205 BC) is among the earliest of Plautus' extant plays. It starts with a duologue between the title character and his 'parasite' or professional flatterer. Pyrgopolynices is the boastful, preening coward, a personage who must have lampooned a certain type of Roman soldier at the time, and who has come down to us in endless variations since. Artotrogus is his resident Yes-Man, and we pick up the dialogue a few speeches into the scene:

> PYRGOPOLYNICES Tell me – who was that chap I saved at Field-of-Roaches, Where the supreme commander was Crash-Bang-Razzle-Dazzle
> Son of Mighty-Mercenary-Messup, you know, Neptune's nephew?
>
> ARTOTROGUS Ah yes, the man with golden armour, I recall.
> You puffed away his legions with a single breath
> Like wind blows autumn leaves, or straw from thatch-roofed huts.

PYRGOPOLYNICES   A snap – a nothing, really.
ARTOTROGUS   Nothing, indeed – that is
                   Compared to other feats I could recount –
                     [*Aside*] as false as this.
                   [*To the audience, as he hides behind the soldier's
                     shield*]
                   If any of you knows a man more full of bull
                   Or empty boastings, you can have me – free of
                     tax.
                   But I'll say this: I'm crazy for his olive salad![27]

Most readers will have the wherewithal to recognize the well-wrought comic potential of this exchange, especially once they've identified it as a kind of double-act model we still have occasion to meet in film and television. We can read the overblown, posturing modesty in the language of Pyrgopolynices (as well as the translator's attempt to simulate Plautus' linguistic invention in the naming of the alleged battle site and commanders). Artotrogus takes every cue and embellishes upon it – ideally we can imagine the character's fully invested admiration of the soldier's accomplishments, suddenly undercut by his confidential remark to the audience ('as false as this'). We might further incorporate in our imaginings the conventional comic wisdom of casting two actors who contrast physically.

The character then initiates a relationship with the audience across the imaginary barrier between stage world and real world, pressing the point with a direct and immediate offer ('you can have me – free of tax'). He then reverses the tone suddenly, puncturing his own sense of exasperation with an admiring remark about the olive salad. The scene, in its entirety, represents the skilled exploitation of a stock comic set-up. No exposition is attempted or needed; the audience's attention can be grabbed immediately via an entertaining variation on a familiar pattern, based on two character types who require no introduction.

With the audience duly enticed, these two characters leave the stage for the entrance of Palaestrio, the slave who orchestrates all the plotting to come. He delivers the prologue, which begins like this:

> Now, folks, if you'll be kind enough to hear me out,
> Then I'll be kind and tell you what our play's about.
> Whoever doesn't want to listen, let him beat it
> And give a seat to one of those in back who need it.[28]

Here the audience is addressed as a gathering of actual people, any one of whom has the real-life option of taking the speaker at his word. The aim, of course, is to disarm the audience with plain speaking, enough to capture their attention and goodwill. It is suspected that the actor had licence to supply improvised interjections, in the manner of a stand-up comic, to deal spontaneously with crowd reactions.

These opening snippets should give a provisional sense of Plautus' spirit of attack, privileging entertainment value and adopting a strikingly candid attitude toward the audience. His text is rigged with particular shrewdness for comic embodiment, as anyone who takes the time to read this opening scene on their feet will discover.

Our other piece of the Roman comedy puzzle comes in the form of six plays by Terence (*c.* 185–159 BC). Terence was a slave who was brought from Africa to Rome, where he was educated and freed. (We find regular reference in Roman comedy to the possibility of a slave being awarded his freedom.) He is thought to have died in a boating accident, on his way to unearth more of Menander's plays for future adaptation.

Terence, whose relatively short life may or may not have overlapped the tail end of Plautus', had loftier aims than his popular predecessor. His plays show an almost defiant effort to do more than entertain, emphasizing the human element amid the plots he combined and adapted from the Greeks. Terence uses the same Greek source material as Plautus, but exploits for his own purposes the customary plot complications generated by trickery, coincidence, and mistaken identity. At one point in *Andria* (*The Girl from Andros, c.* 166 BC) a character labours through the implications of his next course of action in the kind of soul-searching way that a Plautus character would never consider:

> As it is, what can I set about first? So many worries block my path, pull me opposite ways; my love and pity for Glycerium, anxiety over this wedding, respect for my father who has been so indulgent up till now and let me do anything I liked. How can I think of going against him? Oh, it's terrible! What can I do? I just don't know.[29]

This bespeaks a more thoughtful treatment of farcical plot construction, encouraging the spectator to consider the real-life consequences of behaviour which is conventionally a function of comic convenience.

We have now sampled wares by Aristophanes, Menander, Plautus and Terence, our only viable representatives of Greek and Roman comedy in the Classical period, and none of whom wrote concurrently. We can see in all of them distinctive comic visions: Aristophanes' blend of high and low comedy, a freewheeling approach to political and cultural criticism; Menander's concentration on the affairs of the common man, replete with standardized roster of social types; Plautus' privileging of entertainment value, with an emphasis on the comic exploitation of popular tastes; and Terence's more thoughtful approach, using comic form to inquire into the subtleties of human behaviour.

This chapter's summaries of individual styles notwithstanding, there remain a number of headings under which we can comment upon devices used by some or all of the playwrights discussed thus far. The recognition of these elements in Classical texts and ever after provides a strong basis for a summary improvement of reading comedy, and will form the basis for exploration in the next chapter.

Chapter 3

Comedy's devices

Towards a study of comic traits

Our treatments of Old and New Comedy sought to illuminate the conditions under which comic form as we know it coalesced. This earliest recorded evidence of 'writing comedy' shows the extent to which a text bears traces of the conditions surrounding its original creation. It should be remembered, however, that the *dramatic* text represents a cultural artefact notable for its defining element of incompleteness. The words are only ever the tip of a virtual iceberg, and their concretization in performance remains subject to the constant flux of theatre practice. We can make suppositions about the ways in which a textual pattern from Classical Greek comedy 'asks' to be performed, but it is important to remember that we cannot help reading it through the prism of our own theatre-making and theatre-viewing experiences. As we have seen, a contemporary reader may be quite unaware of meanings, resonances and implications which are owing to theatre practices or sociocultural circumstances of the time.

While acknowledging what might appear to be an unbridgeable gap of time and culture, it is, however, remarkable that comic form and content appear in key ways to transcend the experiential expanse separating a modern reader (and practitioner) from a text's historic origins. Characters, situations, human impulses and social dynamics are capable of giving an impression of timeless relevance despite their localized details. Labels like City Comedy, Elizabethan Comedy, Restoration Comedy and Sentimental Comedy, for example, identify subgeneric guises of comedy through a particular stretch of English theatre history. While they all bear distinct features of their own social and theatrical conditions, all these texts tend to exhibit traits which mark them as part of a family for which classical forms supply key genetic markers.

Humour and its mechanics

A general intention to elicit laughter or amusement remains the signature element of what we consider a comic text (see the box on page 64). As established in the Introduction, such an utterance – whether between friends or between performer and audience – is what I call humour, with 'jokes', 'bits', 'gags' and 'routines' referring to instances of humour in a performed or performable text. It is true that we sometimes find amusement where none is intended, and that lies outside the boundaries of the *intention* to joke which I consider a defining element of humour. Our main interest in humour for the purposes of this book lies in the strategies by which writers seek to incorporate humour into their texts, and, more specifically, attempt to weave its potential into the words, characters and situations of a play.

Laughter

When reflecting upon laughter, we should remain mindful of the one aspect easiest to overlook: it feels good. Jonathan Miller, among others, has supposed in it an 'evolutionary pay-off' for the species, comparable to the way sexual pleasure ensures continued procreation.

Along these lines, laughter can be seen to encourage psychic flexibility through bodily reward which, in effect, aims toward keeping humans adaptable. This perspective has been ventured more lyrically by Sean O'Casey, who wrote, in an essay titled 'The power of laughter': 'Man is always hopeful of, always pushing towards, better things; and to bring this about, a change must be made in the actual way of life; so laughter is brought in to mock at things as they are so that they may topple down, and make room for better things to come.'[1]

In this way, laughter simulates a sort of bodied earthquake, often brought about by humour's successful attempt to topple, at least momentarily, our petrified psychic patterns.

Comedy can lead an audience to humour but cannot force them to laugh. For any given humorous moment in the theatre, someone may laugh or bristle against laughter or laugh privately at friends in the cast or even seek to disrupt performance through laughter, and all these reactions are owing to exceedingly private contributions to joking material and performance. These are reasons beyond the scope of the practitioner's artistic intentions, usually unshared by other spectators, although possibly having an effect on audience dynamics.

Henri Bergson points out that, 'laughter is always the laughter of the group' and that 'laughter always implies a kind of secret freemasonry, or even complicity, with other laughers, real or imaginary'.[2] What happens to our laughter when we find ourselves amid a group of laughers at a cinema or party? What happens when we find ourselves in the presence of humour, the prejudice of which we do not endorse, especially when these sentiments appear at odds with the group?

It must be said that laughter, although always perceived as an explicit validation of humour, is a decidedly unreliable gauge of its 'competence', owing to the great number of variables attending every circumstance. We should also note psychologist Nico Frijda's observation that laughter is typified by a psycho-physical feature found also in weeping and vomiting called 'surrender', reminding us that issues of power and its wielding always come into play when trying to make someone laugh.

In Chapter 1 I showed how the formal beginning of a text might establish some manner of humorous intent. In passing, we sampled some introductory evidence of how the dramatic writer foresees humour in performance by invoking the textual traces of conventional comic strategies. Interestingly, we can recognize consistencies upon the page across historical subgenres, and an ability to spot them in an unfamiliar text enriches one's competency in reading comedy. A brief look at the way humour works, shall we say its mechanism, will illuminate some of the patterns we have observed thus far and equip us for a further survey of some of comedy's textual traits.

Although no two people will always agree on what constitutes 'successful' humour (and probably not even the same person at two different times), we can note the conditions generally present when someone *does* find something funny. This allows us to sketch a general image of what I term the 'humour transaction', a phrasing which refers to the fact that a humorous utterance always solicits a kind of active engagement by a reader/listener, which might then lead to laughter, a smile, quiet amusement or, alas, none of the above. When a joke does hit the mark it will be indebted to a fortuitous confluence of joking material, its performance and the psychic disposition of the reader/viewer/listener.[3]

Simon Critchley provides as good an oversimplification as any at the start of his book, *On Humour*: 'Jokes tear holes in our usual predictions about the empirical world.'[4] A good joke punctures the brittle shell of experience as characterized by serious mode, thereby advancing a truth about things from deeper within the realm of our worldly experience. It suspends gravity (pun intended) to show us an unlikely perspective we hadn't considered, or, indeed, one we know quite well and haven't acknowledged. Our closely held systems of personal/social/cultural framing give way to new and unlikely connections, sponsoring an unorthodox kind of sense-making with a definitively human accuracy (what Jerry Palmer calls 'the logic of the absurd'). Humour reminds us that, for humans, there is more than one way to make sense. Furthermore, it involves a feeling *about* that sense, which sometimes makes a truth told by humorous means seem *truer* than one conveyed through serious discourse.

The structure of the humorous transaction in a text can best be approached by looking at what happens when one person tells a joke to another in everyday life. Arthur Koestler, in *The Act of Creation*, supplies us with an image of two geometric planes suddenly perceived as intersecting, even though the point of contact is not explicitly illustrated. In humour terms, someone relates the body of a joke, what I call the *set-up*, establishing one of the planes. The punchline, or what I call the *reversal*, suddenly reveals a divergent plane of reference, the connection of which cannot be reconciled by serious or logical means. By applying a non-serious form of sense-making to *bridge the gap* between planes, we recognize how they can be seen to intersect via application of unspoken, shared knowledge with the joker – we call this 'getting the joke'.

Koestler coins the word, 'bisociation' to emphasize the psychic leap required in recognizing what connects the divergent frames.[5] The construction of a joke, then, sees the cultivation of a frame of knowledge or experience, which clashes with another, incompatible frame. The explicit point of contact between the two planes is left unspecified, inviting the receiver to make the connection privately. In a good joke there is an efficiency and cleverness to the gap delineated by the divergent planes, which is why attempts to explain in serious mode why it is funny are doomed to fall short of the actual experience. It might be suggested that, because any joke presents a sort of challenge to make sense of nonsense, a spark of mastery at having succeeded in bridging the gap contributes to the ignition of laughter.

Importantly, the gap to be bridged also implies a prejudice or disposition toward one of the frames. This is most famously postulated by the philosopher Thomas Hobbes as 'sudden glory' over another person or one's former self (see the box below). It instructs us that there is no humour without a complicit attitude, no joke without a 'butt', even if it is the fairly negligible ridicule of language's inefficiency in a gratuitous pun. It is possible to 'get the joke' *without* approving its prejudice, which is why I can successfully bridge the gap of a racist joke and not laugh at it. At the other end of the scale, think of the extra charge to your laughter in response to the deft put-down of a disliked public figure.

Classic approaches to humour

There are three broad strands of classic thought on humour, to which most individual theories belong or respond:

The Incongruity Theory was proposed by Arthur Schopenhauer, among others, positing the cause of laughter as 'simply the sudden perception of the incongruity between a concept and the real objects which have been thought through it in some relation'.[6] More recently, the theory has undergone a certain refinement with the claim that the incongruity must then be resolved as making sense in some way. As described more fully in the body of this chapter, Koestler says that a joke builds upon the 'bisociation' of two incongruent frames; the listener is invited to make sense of the 'nonsense' in order to 'get' the joke.

The Relief Theory, proposed in the nineteenth century by Herbert Spencer, claims that laughter comes as a release of nervous energy. It was formulated, perhaps more famously by Sigmund Freud, as a sudden 'economy' of psychic expenditure. Freud connected 'humour' directly to feeling – as opposed to 'jokes' with inhibition, and 'the comic' with ideas. This strand embraces physiological effect as well. Daniel Berlyne describes an 'arousal jag', whereby a kind of stimulation or expectation escalates past the point of comfort during the build-up of a joke. Its sudden decrease, following the punchline, causes pleasure; the sharper the easement, the more the pleasure.

The Superiority Theory is best captured by Thomas Hobbes's sense of 'sudden glory' over another person or one's former self. The effect has, at other times, been described in terms of 'diminishment' of value or status, 'debasement', 'deflation' or 'triumph'.

Let us draw upon a simple joke to illustrate the model: 'Two cannibals eating a clown. One turns to the other and says, "Does this taste funny to you?" '[7] Even without my announcement that a joke would follow, the bizarre image constructed by this short text's first sentence would be taken by most readers to signal joking intent. We might say that the first sentence and a half comprise the *set-up* frame. 'Does this taste funny to you?' provides a simultaneously sensible and bizarre conclusion to the utterance – it is a common conversational usage implying that there is something odd or unsavoury about the food. As the text has clearly ended – it is the written-narrative version of a joke teller using voice and expression to let us know that the punchline has been delivered – we treat the line as a *reversal*. It directs us to look for an alternative, co-present framing thrown up by the last line. Through the application of shared, unspoken knowledge, we bridge the *gap* by recognizing the semantic alternative to 'funny' as 'laughable'. A pun is one of the most straightforward examples of humour form. The joker contrives a clash of frames for two or more words that sound alike but mean different things, or as in this case, a word that bears more than one meaning.

A humorous transaction is always 'about' the loaded contents of the gap to be bridged and the silent affirmation it implies between joker and listener. It might at first glance seem that our individual experiences are too much our own to find concurrence with anyone else's; we can never really know what it is like to be inside someone else's life, let alone everyone else's. We are, indeed, forever trapped within our given bodies, with our own genetic imprints and specific experiences and inscriptions shaping our perspectives, feelings, and the ways we engage the world. Norman Holland claims, from a psychoanalytic perspective, that, 'In laughing, we suddenly and playfully recreate our identities.'[8] Our identities, like our lives, are radically our own.

Yet humour may provide a fleeting sense of oneness with others' perceptions of and feelings toward experience. Anthropologist Mahadev Apte observes, 'Humor provides the best evidence of the psychic unity of mankind.'[9] If there is a yearning to validate our experiences of life with others, it may account for some part of the spark of recognition which attends the response to a successful joke, a sudden revelation of, 'Yes, I've felt that way, too!' or, 'That's absolutely true!' Our senses of life and humour are individually constructed, but jokes would never succeed if they didn't also attest to shared experience of the world.

A popular joke tells us quite a bit about a culture or subculture – more, in a way, than many a social scientist's questionnaire, because so much of its activity reveals what is taken for granted among the participants. Observe the efficiency with which the above joke draws upon cultural inscription to build and trigger itself. The initial image of two cannibals constructed in the mind of a Western reader probably owes more to cartoons or old Hollywood films than any genuine familiarity with cannibalistic societies. The word 'clown' also conjures an all-purpose representation of a red-nose, baggy-pants cultural icon with oversized shoes. The joke counts upon the mismatch of these stereotypes, internalized culturally by Western society.

A phrase along the lines of 'one turns to the other and says' – a common joking cue for 'here comes the punchline' – in this case redefines the cannibals with an incongruous sense of domesticity. Cannibals and clowns come from grossly incompatible sectors of our cultural knowledge wells: one eats humans, the other entertains children. The joke's most obvious prejudice would be directed toward the inefficiency of the English language as spoken every day. There may, however, be an undercurrent for some readers: it is likely that most will have had more direct experience of clowns, usually held as the epitome of innocence or laughter-giving. The cartoonish image of a clown's demise in the name of wordplay might serve up a harmless enough chuckle for many. But for some of us, the clown's comic misfortune may also stir a (blatant or latent) bonus amusement at the expense of a type of entertainer we have had occasion to find cloying, frightening or otherwise worthy of ridicule. It is also possible – perhaps if you are or know a clown – that you don't find it funny at all.

Admittedly, this attempt at the rational explanation of a joke is the kind of exercise that gives books on comedy a bad name. It is, however, important to impart a glimpse of what a humorous utterance tries to do, the breadth and depth of its covert operations and the sheer impossibility of quantifying its comic formula for all listeners.

Humour and the dramatic text

The transaction becomes far more open-ended for a writer casting the net of a joke into the wide-open future of a published novel or play. Let us now pull back our focus to see how this model applies to the humorous transaction between writer and reader. Bisociation and some configuration of set-up and reversal still underwrite the transaction. But what if the above joke appeared as a line in a dramatic text? How would it change the process of its reading? And, by inference, how would it have changed the process of its writing? For Jerry Palmer, 'the principle is beyond doubt: all jokes, and much humour, are dependent upon performance skills'.[10] The writer for the ad that included the cannibal/clown joke contrived its performance for the newspaper reader. We might say that the writer settled upon a precise wording, reproduced above, to plant and trigger the humorous mechanism (what we have called set-up and reversal) for maximum effect, given the known process of newspaper reading. I have not here reproduced the full advertisement, but the graphic artist's choice of typeface and the actual arrangement of the words on the page also contributed to the performance.

The humorous transaction follows much the same model wherever it goes, but joking from the page of a dramatic text complicates matters. Trevor Griffiths's *Comedians* (1975) shows us a handful of would-be stand-up comics both in the classroom and onstage, and so it is a dramatic text filled with jokes made consciously by the characters. Each comic performs part of his stand-up routine in the second act, with the real audience standing in for the fictional one. The characters also make 'spontaneous' jokes, as they attempt to sharpen their wits and calm their nerves in the run-up to their moments in the spotlight.

The play, in fact, exposes some of the more jagged social impulses upon which joking and laughter predicate themselves. At one point the class mentor, named Waters, enters upon an unannounced demonstration meant to warn against the shoddy laughter wrought by jokes built on mere pejorative cultural stereotypes. Following a paragraph denigrating the Irish, Waters moves on to the Jews:

> They have this *greasy* quality, do Jews. Stick to their own. Grafters. Fixers. Money. Always money. Say Jew, say gold. Moneylenders, pawnbrokers, usurers. They have the nose for it, you might say. Hitler put it more bluntly: 'If we do not take steps to maintain the purity of blood, the Jew will destroy civilization by poisoning us all.' The effluent of history. Scarcely human. Grubs.[11]

The class member named Samuels then says: 'He must've met my wife's family.' The line's implications in the context of reading a dramatic text are far from straightforward. Technically, the passage and Samuels's quip offers the standard set-up and reversal of a joke, and, given the context of a roomful of comedians, we can assume that it is made consciously by the character. But this passage suggests a growing discomfort in the onstage audience, as Waters appears to transgress any boundaries of what might be excused under the banner of 'only joking'. He reels off a catalogue of stock anti-Jewish attributes, culminating in a quotation from Hitler, the twentieth century's anti-Semite *par excellence*. The diatribe, though, remains a prime set-up for Samuels's reversal. 'He must've met my wife's family' offers a kind of relief from the tendentious attack, undercutting the sweeping 'ideal' of a simmering neo-Nazi bigotry with a mundanely personal pseudo-explanation. The punchline includes a swipe at wives and in-laws, one of those all-purpose target areas for derision in Western culture.

Although built like a humorous utterance, this extract emphasizes a salient difference between reading dramatic texts and literary texts. There is no all-seeing or first-person narrator to delineate the atmosphere or mood, to tell us how to take things, or to provide a reliable (or unreliable) point of reference. The comedians in the classroom, however, supply an inner audience through which to refract Waters's rant and Samuels's reversal. We might say that Samuels, being Jewish, is in some way 'entitled' to make the joke, but even he may not be so sure. Deprived of a certain amount of control over a text's eventual realization, a playwright sometimes offers side coaching to the reader or actor through a stage direction (e.g., '[*sarcastically*]'), and in this case, he instructs delivery of the line as '[*unfunnily*]'. The playwright is trying to steer the mood, perhaps by suggesting that the speaker's heart does not completely support a joking utterance he can't help making. It might also imply that the onstage listeners do not laugh, and, as Susan Purdie observes in a comparable instance, 'The other characters' response is probably the more critical factor in determining how seriously or comically an audience treats represented emotions.'[12]

The effect for a given theatre audience (and, of course, a given spectator within that audience) will be less predictable, as palpable discomfort can give way to a certain type of laughter courted by contemporary television shows like *Curb Your Enthusiasm* and *The Office* (see the box on page 71). It is possible that the character's inability to refrain from making a joke, even in the most inappropriate circumstances, might somehow spur a kind of downbeat amusement. Indeed, a character consciously making a joke in a dramatic text always tells us more than he or she realizes – about the world of the characters, the character who makes it and joking itself.

Comic distance

The terms 'distance' or 'comic distance' are usually taken to refer to a detachment from emotion, particularly necessary for adopting a playful attitude toward any given subject. Bergson says, 'The comic, we said, appeals to the intelligence pure and simple; laughter is incompatible with emotion',[13] but this is an oversimplification. We do not laugh at things we don't care about, and the subjects toward which we have the strongest feelings (e.g., a pet peeve or despised politician) stand to elicit the sharpest humorous response. What is required is not necessarily a stepping back so much as a *leaning sideways*, momentarily out of the reach of serious mode's high beams. Emotional attachment to the real-life material of a joke remains essential to its success, insofar as it exists co-presently with a temporary setting aside of first-order implications. For the most troubling topics, this amounts to a daring psychic trick, as it is the spectator's steadfast knowledge of the serious implications which makes the joke.

Comedian Ricky Gervais has become a master purveyor of what we might call 'cringe humour', in his British television series, *The Office* (2001–3), and more recently, *Extras* (2005–7). Larry David's *Curb Your Enthusiasm* (2000–) is another comedy series which some people have trouble watching, so psychically painful are some of the social situations portrayed. These comic worlds seek to mine a relieved amusement in the spectator by rubbing salt in the wounds of someone else's social discomfort. They produce, in effect, jokes about transgressing the boundaries of social framing, i.e., acceptable or approved behaviour in given interpersonal situations. Embedded in such contexts, a racist or sexist joke becomes outlined in pathos and pointedly unfunny (or laughable for an entirely other reason).

In many cases humour is directed by the playwright 'over the heads' of the characters, especially in unabashedly comic stage worlds. Tom Stoppard's *On the Razzle* (1981) is a farcical romp through Old Vienna, and is filled with the kind of wordplay for which the playwright is renowned. This snippet comes from an early scene in which Zangler, a prosperous shop owner, hires a young man named Melchior as his new servant:

> MELCHIOR When do you want me to start?
> ZANGLER Just a moment, aren't you forgetting the interview?
> MELCHIOR So I am – how much are you paying?[14]

It should be easy to identify the set-up, through Zangler's question and then Melchior's, 'So I am.' The reversal, 'how much are you paying?', reveals an alternative reading, which turns the power dynamic on its head. We would assume that Zangler means, 'Aren't you forgetting that I am supposed to interview you?', but Melchior appears to be the one assessing the suitability of the arrangement. Zangler, rather than asserting his authority, appears to be drawn into a vaguely defensive posture over the ensuing dialogue, as if he has to prove his employment conditions worthy of the applicant. The point, once again, is that the mechanism of set-up and reversal can apply to interaction between or among characters who are not consciously joking – and they appear to persist in their discussion unaware of any comic effect.

Mine the gap: the reader's view

In the passage from which the above exchange is taken, a job candidate, rather than adopting the compliant posture of a traditional interviewee, gives his would-be master a polite grilling. We learn in comedy not to ask certain questions, such as, in the above case, why Zangler doesn't simply dismiss Melchior as impertinent. On a larger scale we know not to ask why, in *Lysistrata*, neither the men nor the women simply seek out alternative outlets for their sexual urges. Comedy disarranges the systems of relevance we know so well from real life. It is part of our contract with comedy that we go along with its conceits, or, as Olson puts it, 'every comedy proper, in short, requires us to take certain things seriously so that we may see something else as not to be taken so'.[15] These discrepancies construct a sort of subtending gap to be bridged, upon which individual humour attempts base themselves. These comic plotting strategies 'mine' or exploit this gap, opened by the reader/spectator's awareness of circumstances beyond the awareness of the characters.

In many cases, what enables the humour is the fact that the stage world treats the situation with a level of seriousness which reads as 'too little' or 'too much', relative to how much it would warrant in real life. A couple of texts from 1894 suggest each of these approaches. In George Bernard Shaw's *Arms and the Man*, a young Bulgarian woman's bedchamber is entered by a Serbian soldier, but through their language and engagement we perceive that the construction of their world is such that she is not quite as afraid nor he quite as threatening as the situation would warrant. In Georges Feydeau and Maurice Desvallières's *A Little Hotel on the Side*, a married man pursues an amorous assignation with the beautiful wife next door, applying himself with heroic fervour. In one case, we are asked to accept that the threat of wartime violence remains a secondary concern – in the other, that the fulfilment of adulterous sexual desire merits life-and-death urgency. These two comic conceits, which remain in widespread use to this day, can be seen as the bisociation of framing that breeds humour: a register or matrix of response from one kind of situation (too serious or not serious enough, in many a case) is imposed disjunctively upon the outward conditions of another situation, resulting, as Purdie puts it, in 'a lapse of normal implication'.[16]

Classic comic plotting takes further responsibility for humour creation in the ways it constructs its fictional worlds. By orchestrating character, relationship and situation in proven patterns, the writer generates another level of shared knowledge with which to prime joking attempts for the reader/spectator. Key to this enhanced comic capability is the reader/spectator's wide-angle perspective upon events.

Booker, in *The Seven Basic Plots*, observes the extent to which comic worlds thrive on the confusions, disorientations or misconceptions of their characters. He notes several 'familiar sources of misunderstanding':

- characters donning disguises or swapping identities;
- men dressing up as women, or vice versa;
- secret assignations when the 'wrong person' turns up;
- scenes in which characters are hastily concealed in cupboards or behind furniture, only for their presence to be inevitably and embarrassingly discovered.[17]

These and other common comic plot devices tend to generate competing or alternative readings to dialogue, behaviour and events, by awarding the reader a privileged view upon the fictional proceedings. Knowledge hidden from one or more of the characters then becomes the linchpin for humorous set-ups. The clever playwright contrives the conditions under which the participating characters' divergent interpretations provide a series of stepping stones for multiple frames of reference, which also harbour situational implications. The reader/spectator need only sit back and enjoy, especially if one of the parties is of a character whose discomfort or outrage pleases us. Let us look a bit closer, now, at some of the textual motifs the above situations tend to produce.

Crossed conversations and double meanings

A prototype for the crossed conversation – in which each of two characters believe they are discussing different subjects – crops up in Plautus' *The Pot of Gold* (*Aulularia*, *c.*195 BC). The crotchety miser, Euclio, has developed a paranoiac obsession over his hidden pot of gold, presuming that everyone is out to take it from him. Young Lyconides, who has no knowledge of the stolen cache, has come to ask for Euclio's daughter's hand in marriage. He hopes to earn the man's good will by owning up to the fact that he had sex with her in a moment of weakness, and declaring his decent intentions:

EUCLIO	Who is that?
LYCONIDES	A very unhappy man, sir.
EUCLIO	Are you? So am I, utterly ruined, the victim of every misery and misfortune.
LYCONIDES	You can take comfort, though.
EUCLIO	How the devil can I take comfort?
LYCONIDES	Because the wicked deed that causes you all this distress was my doing; I confess it.[18]

We can see how Plautus arranged this straightforward misunderstanding: The 'wicked deed that causes you all this distress' is interpreted by Euclio as a confession that the young man has stolen his gold, rather than violated his daughter. Further exchanges, such as the following, are phrased in ways that enable the misunderstanding to continue while supplying the reader/spectator with a bird's-eye view of crossed wires:

EUCLIO	What induced you to touch my property without my leave?
LYCONIDES	Love – and drink.
EUCLIO	Impudent rascal! . . .

We can imagine that Lyconides takes Euclio's outrage as an understandable paternal response to his indiscretion, while Euclio finds the alleged thief's candour increasingly infuriating:

LYCONIDES	But I have come of my own free will to beg your pardon for my foolishness.
EUCLIO	I've no use for people who when they've done wrong come whining with apologies. You knew you were taking what you had no right to take; you should have kept your hands off.
LYCONIDES	But having touched, my only plea is that I may possess entirely.
EUCLIO	What!! Do you think you're going to keep something that is mine, with my leave or without it?

Lyconides' last phrasing, above, makes for a neat bisociation of the competing frames. The young man, in the throes of romantic feeling, enters an honourable plea, which, from Euclio's position tops a string of presumptions in its audacity. We should take time to note how much the actual playing of the sequence contributes to the humour value, Lyconides' naïve ardour contrasting with and exacerbating Euclio's growing ire. It is always worth remembering to imagine how the incongruity between the *embodiment* of characters' emotional framings might support the integrity of the misunderstanding while augmenting the gap to be bridged.

It is, perhaps, part of the joke that Euclio's parsimony is such that he applies a degree of outrage to the loss of his money one would think better reserved for his daughter's virtue and (in our day) psycho-physical safety. This leads us to look closer at the part character plays in these types of comic mechanisms. Booker claims as the generic basis for comic plotting 'a coming to light of things not previously recognized',[19] if not for all the characters, at least for those of us watching. There is generally what he calls a 'dark figure', who somehow blocks or impedes this recognition. Comedy, he argues, centres on 'a contrast between the self-regarding delusion of someone who is in some way blinded by egotism, and our capacity to see from outside what he is unable to see'.[20] Other theorists have referred to a lack of awareness or psychic stiffness, which comedy and humour seek to relieve through ridicule. As we can see in the above section, the fact that one of the characters, trapped in misapprehension, reacts out of such narrow-minded self-interest should incline the spectator to enjoy his distress all the more. By applying a bit of comic wisdom derived from our dissection of the humorous transaction, a contrasting character in mood or energy (like Lyconides' most earnest intentions) tends to emphasize the incongruity between competing frames.

There have been myriad versions and variations on the preceding pattern through Western dramatic history. For the student of comedy it is always worth unravelling the crossed wires to inspect beneath the surface of clever contrivance: how do character, relationship, and circumstance support humorous effect, and what possibilities are created for performance? It is not *any* misunderstanding which stands to amuse us, but one which somehow hooks into an emotional disposition we might take toward situation or personality.

Comedy is endlessly resourceful, and so the device's configuration remains ever open to innovation. The following extract, from more recent times, represents an opportune incorporation of theatrical circumstance and the spectator's real-life cultural knowledge. In Terry Johnson's *Hysteria* (1993), the character of Freud has awoken, disoriented, in the middle of the night. Here he is speaking to his daughter, who is obviously responding from elsewhere in the house, over an intercom:

> FREUD   . . . What's this thing?
> [*In front of his face hangs an electric light pull; a four-foot cord with a brass knob on the end.*]
> ANNA   What thing?
> FREUD   This thing hanging here in front of me. This thing in my hand.

> ANNA   Um...
> FREUD   It's just dangling here. It's got a knob on the end.
> ANNA   Mmm hmm?
> FREUD   What is it?
> ANNA   I've...no idea.
> FREUD   What am I supposed to do with it?
> ANNA   Shall I call the nurse?
> FREUD   Shall I give it a pull?
> ANNA   No, just...leave it alone, father.[21]

The character of Freud is clearly intended through name, dialect and appearance as an embodiment of the psychiatric personage, Sigmund Freud (1856–1939). Unsure of his bearings, he is confronted with an object new to his surroundings – an electric light pull, which has just been installed that afternoon. His daughter cannot see what he is talking about. The spectator is placed fortuitously to recognize that, as Freud earnestly tries to figure out the purpose of this unfamiliar accoutrement, Anna comes to suspect he has woken up with his penis in his hands. Freud's questions are shrewdly phrased to allow the misunderstanding to persist, and, as he becomes more insistent on some sort of an answer, Anna tries a few different ways to skirt the subject, no doubt attributing the problem to an old man's deteriorating mental state. Artfully configured and executed according to the crossed-conversation model, the playwright draws for an extra dash of amusement upon a scrap of unspoken but widely shared cultural knowledge. The character of Freud is not just any absent-minded, randy old man – he is the 'father of psychoanalysis', whose theoretical approach famously centred on the genitalia and sexual development. This sort of stage-world confusion so pleasing to comedy can also be brought about by other sorts of all-too-perfect coincidences.

Mistaken identities

A mirror image of the crossed-conversation mechanism arises when characters are drawn to mistake or misapprehend someone's identity, thereby treating them somehow inappropriately. Here, again, the configuration provides ample opportunity for humour: within the stage world, a character may be taken as someone other than who he or she is, possessing various attributes and experiences. The mistaken character may or may not be aware of the error, but the spectator's privileged view supports the bisociation of the character's actual framing and the framing misattributed to him or her. For maximum humour effect, it is not simply an error of identification, but one loaded with amusing inferences for both parties.

Identical twins and lookalikes lend themselves most obviously to the plotting of mistaken identities. As Harry Levin puts it, 'a twin is regarded as a kind of human pun, where an imperceptible substitute unexpectedly switches the continuities'.[22] They may also tap into an innately human fascination with the possibility of nature producing an exact copy of itself, as well as our beliefs in the profound individuality of one's life and experience. *The Comedy of Errors* (1594), by William Shakespeare, remains potently laugh-provoking in its manipulation of situation, while at the same time explicitly inviting us to contemplate the stuff of which we fancy ourselves made.

Drawing from Plautus' *The Brothers Menachmi* (*Menaechmi*, pre-201 BC), Shakespeare increases the confusion exponentially by supplying the twin brothers with twin servants. A shipwreck, years prior to the start of the play, separated the twin boys of a young family as well as the twins who were being groomed as their respective attendants. Antipholus and Dromio of Syracuse were renamed after their lost 'other halves'. Now a young man, Antipholus of Syracuse, in search of his brother, arrives in the city of Ephesus along with his Dromio. His character bespeaks a sensitivity that will not allow him contentedness until he finds his brother. The other Antipholus, who has grown into a well-established merchant in Ephesus, possesses a jealous wife, a hotter disposition, and, of course, his own Dromio (see Figure 3.1).

Upon separating, Antipholus and Dromio of Syracuse become mistaken for their twins in Ephesus, finding themselves treated with mystifying familiarity by complete strangers. Antipholus of Syracuse unwittingly carries on a conversation with Dromio of Ephesus, who has tried to urge his master home for dinner and warn him of his wife's ill humour. He departs and Dromio of Syracuse returns, whereupon Adriana, Antipholus of Ephesus' wife, and her sister, Luciana, happen upon them:

> ADRIANA   Ay, ay, Antipholus, look strange and frown,
> Some other mistress hath thy sweet aspects;
> I am not Adriana, nor thy wife.[23]

Adriana observes a husband who appears not to know her and addresses him with wilful irony, already suspicious that he has of late preferred the favours of other women. She goes on to bemoan at length his distant behaviour. He responds:

> SYR. ANT.   Plead you to me fair dame? I know you not.
> In Ephesus I am but two hours old,
> As strange unto your town as to your talk,
> Who, every word by all my wit being scann'd,
> Wants wit in all one word to understand.

Figure 3.1 This production of Shakespeare's *The Comedy of Errors* enhanced the twin effect of the Dromios with unmistakable hair styling. Swann Theatre, Stratford-upon-Avon, 2005.

LUCIANA	Fie, brother, how the world is chang'd with you.
	When were you wont to use my sister thus?
	She sent for you by Dromio home to dinner.
SYR. ANT.	By Dromio?
SYR. DRO.	By me?[24]

As with Euclio in the example of *The Pot of Gold*, above, Adriana's inflamed possessiveness, supplemented by her sister's disapproval, throws into comic – which is to say, incongruous – relief the Syracusans' bewilderment. We should try to imagine an incarnation of Antipholus' question, 'By Dromio?'; his reality is suddenly disengaged from his servant's, *and* he may already show signs of love at first sight toward Luciana. A second gap is quickly opened through the abject innocence of Dromio's, 'By me?', which may be aimed at his master as well as the women.

Inherent in any textual world is an invitation to place yourself in its circumstances. In this case, as in many a comic world before and since, the gaps to be bridged are lined with the relief that we observe these predicaments from a safe distance. Once again, though, notice how the reader/ spectator window upon the textual world affords a sort of 'inner' band of experience through which our knowledge of the outside world can be channelled. There can be no humour in the stage world without a link to the thoughts and feelings about misunderstanding and confusion which we bring to the text from our own fields of experience.

We take for granted a spirit of cosmic contrivance in comic worlds, which we would not accept in others. It allows us to accept outlandish coincidences like those that lead to the confusion or misapprehension arising from crossed conversations and mistaken identities. Comedy tugs at the beard of a natural world devoid of straight lines and exact copies. It wreaks mischief upon the endlessly differentiated fabric of real existence by offering up improbable meetings, progressions and patterns. Now let's look at some consistencies that arise from characters operating consciously within these worlds.

Scheming and evasion

'The best tragedies, like the Oedipus story, are extremely simple',[25] says Maurice Charney, and, indeed, there is a sense that their protagonists undertake an unbending dedication to a chosen goal or principle, turning aside all obstacles with a profound inner resolve. By thematic inference, the rest of us are not possessed of such spiritual steel. The comic protagonist's projects are of a more commonplace quality, entered upon somewhat less heroically, though perhaps more artfully.

For Aristophanes, the 'happy idea' was essentially a fantastic scheme for, say, ending the Peloponnesian War or restoring the erstwhile standard of tragic play-writing. New Comedy and its descendants are generally driven by a desire for money, sex or social standing, with society's strictures, blocking figures or individual biases to be circumvented. Comedy, therefore, usually identifies itself with the hatching of schemes and the opportunistic disguise of true motives. These intrigues may be conceived by one or more characters in advance, but they are also subject to revision or redirection on the spot, as plans go awry or unforeseen circumstances arise.

Evasion provides an engine for many a play as a whole, very often when illicit liaisons are involved. The tactics of avoidance often throw up passages of dialogue in which characters are required to extemporize explanations – either they have assumed roles within which they do not possess the required knowledge, or they must fabricate explanations to avoid exposure.

Early examples of this dialogue feature can be found in *Lysistrata*. The women of Athens have taken over the Acropolis as part of their two-pronged plot to end the war, denying men access both to sex and to the funding sources contained in the stronghold of state power. After a few days some of the women begin to weaken, attempting to sneak away to satisfy their sexual needs. Lysistrata is aware of their intentions, and meets one of them pretending to be in the midst of birth pains:

MYRRHINE	. . . The pains have started. Look.
LYSISTRATA	You weren't even pregnant yesterday.
MYRRHINE	I am today.
	Oh, please, Lysistrata, I must get home.
	The midwife's waiting. There it goes again!
LYSISTRATA	What nonsense! Just a minute. What *is* that bulge?
MYRRHINE	A darling baby boy.
LYSISTRATA	What d'you mean? It's hard.
	It's hollow. It's Athene's golden helmet.
	You said you were pregnant.
MYRRHINE	I am, I am.
LYSISTRATA	So why the helmet?
MYRRHINE	In case the baby comes too soon. Before I get home. A cradle. That's what it is. A holy cradle.[26]

Lysistrata presents the figure of a sceptical inquisitor. Each objection forces Myrrhine to come back with something else even more far-fetched, though in some way clever. A variation on this pattern occurs shortly thereafter, when Myrrhine is sent out to meet her husband with the brief to secure his commitment to peace before submitting to his advances. The passage is still based on avoidance, but with a slightly different slant. With her husband in an advanced state of arousal from the start, Myrrhine tries to increase the pressure on him to capitulate by 'remembering' a series of accoutrements she needs to get from inside the Acropolis every time they reach the verge of sexual contact. This inclines toward another common comic structure based on interruption or frustration of an urgent (though sometimes secret) goal-oriented action, to which the protoganist may get closer and closer without ever quite reaching completion.

In Act I, Scene ii of Terry Johnson's *Hysteria*, Freud's doctor, Yahuda, has entered upon a scene which finds a barely clad young woman stuffed in the closet and the surrealist painter, Salvador Dali, unconscious on the floor. Yahuda has begun to examine Dali, when Jessica, the young woman, emerges from the closet prematurely:

[FREUD *steers her back in and closes the door, stubbing her elbow.*]	
JESSICA	Ow.
FREUD	Ow. That was the sound he made, just before he collapsed.
[YAHUDA *rises.*]	
DALI	Owwww.
YAHUDA	This man has suffered a blow to the head.

FREUD	Yes. He was going into the garden and hit his head on the door frame.
YAHUDA	As he fainted?
FREUD	Yes.
YAHUDA	Which?
FREUD	Both.
YAHUDA	That's not possible.
FREUD	Yes it is. He was standing on the filing cabinet, fainted, and hit his head on the way down.
YAHUDA	What was he doing on the filing cabinet?
FREUD	I don't know. I wasn't here. I was already in the garden.
YAHUDA	Doing what?
FREUD	Chasing a swan.
YAHUDA	Where did that come from?
FREUD	I haven't the faintest idea. But it could have been the swan that entered the room very aggressively and forced Dali to retreat to the filing cabinet where he fainted in terror.[27]

In many an avoidance situation, a 'hidden character' makes a noise, which the onstage speaker is required to explain in order to maintain the pretence. Yahuda, here, is convinced the psychoanalyst has finally descended into dementia. Yahuda is sharp enough to pick up the least inconsistency in Freud's explanation, forcing him to ever greater heights of spontaneous invention. Once again, we should observe how a passage like this becomes more than a series of discreet reversals, based on our 'private knowledge' that Freud is making up each increasingly ridiculous detail to cover up the fact that Dali has been knocked out after trying to interfere with the young woman hidden in the closet. Yahuda's question, 'Where did that come from?', allows for a degree of ambiguity that could mean, 'How did you just come up with such an irrelevant explanation?' Rather than give up by confessing his duplicity, Freud supplies a final reversal by turning the answer into a tidy and even more unlikely explanation.

A comic conceit underpins the sequence: that of the iconic psychoanalyst, renowned for his thoughts on sexual repression, having to justify himself amid the undignified conditions of a sex farce. We can also try to anticipate the performance value of a passage like this as a world-class ping-pong match between players of contrasting inner states: the long-suffering sceptic versus the man on the spot, who sometimes can't be sure of what he's come up with until after it leaves his mouth.

We might pause to notice that many of these extracts base themselves on a question-and-answer pattern. Stock plot configurations involving evasion and confusion would lead naturally to questioning dialogue. The construction supplies a humour-friendly pattern, in which any given question 'sets up' the opportunity for a joking response (whether or not the respondent is aware of the reversal). In Shakespeare's *Twelfth Night*, Viola, disguised as a man, meets Feste the clown:

> VIOLA   Save thee, friend, and thy music. Dost thou live by thy tabor?
> CLOWN   No, sir, I live by the church.
> VIOLA   Art thou a churchman?
> CLOWN   No such matter, sir. I do live by the church; for I do live at
>   my house, and my house doth stand by the church.[28]

The clown plays once and then again on the meaning of the phrase, 'to live by'. A question by definition incurs expectation (of *some* answer, if not a specific answer), making for a predictable pattern of set-up and reversal. Walter Nash has catalogued the 'Question and answer' as one of our age-old joking formulations. 'The classic two-line form embraces riddles, comedian-and-straight-man jokes, and the whole schoolyard gallimaufry of bananas, elephants, waiters, what-do-you-dos and how-can-you-tells'[29], says Nash, referring to several popular incarnations of the question-and-answer joke through the years. He notes that the 'question element is the immediately recognized signal of intent' in everyday joking. In a stage world we come to anticipate an oncoming reversal, given our acquired internalization of the two-line rhythm.

Let us dig just a bit deeper beneath the pattern. If, as Purdie says, 'power in discourse belongs most obviously to the speaker',[30] the questioner presumes a sort of authority in many of the extracts in this chapter. It is usually a 'serious' character, blocking figure, or other authoritarian who conducts the interrogation. The person on the spot often manages to parry the question, as in the passage from *Hysteria*, and sometimes overturns the power balance with wit, as in the extract from *Twelfth Night*.

Role-playing and disguises

With scheming and avoidance so endemic to comedy, characters often choose or are forced to assume artificial demeanours or take on other guises, a type of situation which provides a sort of flip side to the inadvertent confusions of twins and lookalikes.

Once again we need look no further than Aristophanes for an instructive example of a basic comic device. *The Frogs* (405 BC) sees Dionysos, god of drama (among other things), in such despair at the inferior state of Greek tragedy, that he embarks upon a journey to the Underworld to bring back one of the late, great poets of the Athenian Golden Age. With Xanthias, his slave, in tow, Dionysos dresses up as Herakles, the only person (demi-god that he is) ever to have been to the netherworld and back. Aristophanes mines the audience's knowledge and perception of the hero first by having Dionysos knock on Herakles' door to seek advice. Aristophanes depicts Dionysos as made of far less heroic stuff than Herakles, but he arrives outfitted iconically with lion skin, yellow costume and club. Herakles finds the image so funny he has to retreat indoors to recover. Dionysos' pale copy of the Greek superman standing face to face with the original supplies a bass-note punchline to underline the entire scene (which clearly tapped directly into the original audience's psychic reservoir – imagine, say, Woody Allen as Dionysos and Dwayne 'The Rock' Johnson as Herakles).

Later Dionysos and Xanthias meet Aiakos, gatekeeper of the Underworld. Dionysos introduces himself as 'Herakles the Strong'. As previously suggested, we should imagine this announcement as contrasting wildly with Dionysos' appearance and bearing. Aristophanes reverses on the earlier reception by having Aiakos readily accept this laughable imitation of Herakles for the original:

> AIAKOS   *Ho. You* again.
> Bastard. Conman. Bum.
> Cheating, lowlife scum.
> Ere before, weren't you? [31]

Aiakos goes on to enumerate the forms of extravagant revenge to be taken on Herakles, then adds, 'Oh, we've been waiting, mate. Don't go away'. Sporting the cowardly mantle of the traditional comic hero, Dionysos decides it would be better if Xanthias, his slave, put on the Herakles disguise to receive any forthcoming punishment. He does, and a Servant Girl comes out, promising the 'new' Herakles a feast and quite a lot more than mere gastronomic pleasure. In a double-act clowning pattern which would be familiar to fans of Laurel and Hardy or Abbott and Costello, Dionysos then suddenly chooses to reclaim the disguise – whereupon the Landlady comes to the door to present the *faux*-Herakles with a whopping bill for his previous stay. Dionysos forces Xanthias to don the disguise once more. Aiakos returns and, confronted with the vengeance-seeking gatekeeper's advancing minions, the slave says:

> XANTHIAS   Look, I've never been here before.
> I've never stolen a hair off your head.
> If I have, may I go to Hell. Here's a fair offer:
> Take my slave, and torture him. *Then,*
> If you find I'm guilty, do what you like to me. [32]

The quick-thinking slave turns the tables on his master and saves his own neck (at least for the moment). Comic practice trades so often on evasion that the adoption of an honest explanation effects a reversal of sorts. Xanthias' devilishly clever 'fair offer' supplies a crowning reversal to the series of alternating impersonations.

In plainly pragmatic terms, the astute comic writer incorporates elements like mistaken identity and role-playing, not simply to pledge allegiance to the time-honoured patterns of comedy, but *because of their potency in generating possibilities for humour*. The challenge reaches well beyond having engineered the conditions for a juicy misunderstanding or inventive scheme, to how effectively they can be 'cashed in'. We should recall the extent to which humour thrives on a cunning sleight of hand between expectation and surprise. The comic writers we remember work from the same recipes as other novelists and dramatists, but spin their own resourceful variations to stay a step ahead of the reader/spectator.

Hidden characters

Another classic comic arrangement worth mentioning is a natural product of evasion-related plotting, coupled with dramatic circumstances in which the spectator possesses a privileged view of the stage world. A character may hide, be hidden from, or go unrecognized by one or more characters onstage. It puts an amusing spin on an utterance because of the potentially undesirable revelation of information or attitude that it brings. There is great comic value to be gained from the reactions of hidden characters who cannot afford to disclose their presence. In *Twelfth Night*, the haughty Malvolio has been falsely led to believe that his mistress, Olivia, fancies him. Sir Toby, Sir Andrew and Fabian observe him from a place of hiding. Malvolio swaggers upon the scene, having jumped head first into the trap. He takes to fantasizing how he will conduct his affairs at Olivia's side. He goes on to enact for his own pleasure a future scenario in which he calls the carousing knight, Sir Toby, to account:

MALVOLIO	Saying, 'Cousin Toby, my fortunes having cast me on your niece, give me this prerogative of speech'.
TOBY	What, what?
MALVOLIO	'You must amend your drunkenness'.
TOBY	Out, scab!
FABIAN	Nay, patience, or we break the sinews of our plot.[33]

There is potentially a triple delight, here, given the knowledge about these people previously acquired by the spectator. Malvolio, previously established as a rigid killjoy, indulges in a preening rehearsal of the higher station he envisages. There is both an uncharacteristic playfulness to it as well as a confirmation of his stiff-necked arrogance. Sir Andrew, hardly a menacing figure, is pleased to threaten Malvolio from the safety of their concealment: 'Slight, I could so beat the rogue.' His false bravado contrasts with the rough-and-ready Sir Toby, whose default state of inebriation denies any last vestige of self-control. We might imagine him finally breaking cover with, 'Out, scab!', and Fabian desperately trying to reel him back in on the next line. It is a common performance convention for comic worlds that the character in Malvolio's position remains oblivious to the commotion going on behind him.

It can also become a fertile source of amusement when we see characters engaged in the foreground of the scene made uncomfortable by the turn of the conversation, because they know who's listening. In Richard Brinsley Sheridan's *The School for Scandal* (1777), the scheming Joseph Surface has invited Lady Teazle into the library of his house, counting upon a flirtation with her to further his pursuit of another young woman. Her husband Sir Peter arrives unexpectedly, and she takes cover behind a dressing screen, a useful set piece favoured by Restoration and eighteenth-century comedy for just these set-ups.

Sir Peter has thus far approved of Joseph over his rascally brother Charles. He is in the midst of confiding various apprehensions and resolutions regarding his much younger wife – and he is particularly suspicious of Charles's intentions toward her. When Charles's arrival is announced, Sir Peter implores Joseph to draw out his brother upon the nature of his relationship with Lady Teazle. He then hides in a closet.

Not only does Charles pass the 'test' with honour, he turns the spotlight back upon Joseph:

> CHARLES   ...But brother, do you know now that you surprise me exceedingly by naming *me* with Lady Teazle; for, faith, I always understood *you* were her favourite.
>
> JOSEPH   Oh, for shame, Charles! This retort is foolish.
>
> CHARLES   Nay, I swear I have seen you exchange such significant glances –
>
> JOSEPH   Nay, nay, sir, this is no jest –
>
> CHARLES   Egad, I'm serious. Don't you remember, one day, when I called here –
>
> JOSEPH   Nay, prithee, Charles –
>
> CHARLES   And found you together –
>
> JOSEPH   Zounds, sir, I insist –
>
> CHARLES   And another time, when your servant –
>
> JOSEPH   Brother, brother, a word with you.[34]

We can see Charles, in a robust spirit of fraternal banter and unaware of the eavesdropper, turn the screws on Joseph, who does his best to squirm away from the topic until he simply has to pull his brother aside and tell him who is listening.

For all these comic habits, the spectator occupies a position at a safe and opportune remove. We can see human foibles and egotism lay the conditions for their own undoing, even as the cosmos conspires in its own ways to spring the traps. Supplied with a better vantage point than we have in real life, the gaps of these reversals would not to this day bear such comic fruits if the situations failed to speak directly to our own experiences of deception and embarrassing utterances.

Mine the gap: the spectator's access

By virtue of the shared experience and feeling that humour seeks to validate between joker and laughers, comedy will always conduct its affairs with a conspiratorial gleam in its eye. It 'mines' or exploits the gap opened between the realities of stage and audience. This winking relationship is manifested in comedy's habitual acknowledgement of its art and contrivance, which can be observed in a few general behaviours.

Comedy often calls attention to itself

Comedy is often pleased to expose habits and pretences we come to take for granted – beginning with its own.

Aristophanes' *The Frogs* begins with the following exchange:

> XANTHIAS   Hey, sir, shall I start with one of the old routines?
> They never fail.
> DIONYSUS   Yes, if you must
> So long as it's not 'I've had this up to here'.
> Not that again. I've had that up to here.
> XANTHIAS   Something more upmarket?
> DIONYSUS   'I'm knackered'? No.
> XANTHIAS   The Mother of all Funnies?
> DIONYSUS   Good idea –
> Unless it's the one I think it is.
> XANTHIAS   Which one?
> DIONYSUS   When you shift your bags about, and shout
> 'I've got to dump my load'.[35]

Here we can see Aristophanes laying bare a handful of the 'old routines' to which his audience had become accustomed in comic performance. The line, 'They never fail', along with the subsequent remarks, implies criticism of those playwrights who continue to rely on such routines; it also carries a veiled swipe at the audience for so predictably lapping up these hackneyed jokes. It would appear that 'I've got to dump my load' had become a catchphrase which, no doubt because of its bathroom connotation, garnered laughter out of all proportion to the situation. Think of similar catchphrases from recent and contemporary television characters, which simply become a signal for laughter, rather than a spontaneous spur. In the second season of *Extras*, its fictional series-within-a-series, *When the Whistle Blows*, stands in for a long line of sitcoms with shameless milking of cookie-cutter gags. In it, Andy Millman (played by Ricky Gervais), as writer and actor in the make-believe series, stops the show every time he finds an excuse to insert his catchphrase, 'Ya havin' a laff? Is he havin' a laff?'

Think also of late twentieth-century films like *Airplane!* (1980) and *Scary Movie* (2000), which were based entirely on the comic deflation of popular movie genres and their clichéd habits. *Blazing Saddles* (1974) sends up the conventions of the Hollywood Western, seeking additional comic mileage at the expense of the racial and homophobic prejudices inherent in the rigidly white/macho ethos of the target genre. Director Mel Brooks smashes cinematic pretence in the movie's finale by showing his brawling cowboys crash an adjacent Hollywood soundstage, within which a vintage musical is filming, replete with mincing chorus men. The two stars, Gene Wilder and Cleavon Little, ultimately arrive at the opening of their own film and join the audience watching themselves on the screen.

We can find humorous forays across the footlights throughout the history of dramatic comedy. Through the mouths of the characters, the writer delivers glancing blows to the fourth wall, which will always resonate more immediately given the actual co-presence of stage world and spectator. It is a tap on the shoulder favoured by comedy, and it reminds the spectator with a winking honesty of the artistic artifice we all agree to ignore. Prior to the resolution of William Congreve's *The Way of the World* (1700), for example, one of the characters asks, 'Hey-day! what, are you all got together, like players at the end of the last act?'[36]

Johnson again offers a version of a classic comic device at the opening of *Hysteria*, treated earlier in this chapter. A single onstage character, meant to be Sigmund Freud, sleeps in his chair on a rainy night. The stage directions continue, 'Wakes and looks at his watch. A long silence.' The dialogue begins:

> FREUD   If you are waiting for me to break the silence you will be deeply disappointed. The silence is yours alone, and is far more eloquent than you imagine.[37]

This first utterance of the play stands to place the reader (in the audience) as the intended target. The character's sentiments are at once provocative, especially the second sentence, and, perhaps, humorously self-contradicting, given that he has indeed 'broken the silence' with his remark. Lest the reader/spectator dwell too long upon it, though, the stage directions instruct: '[*He turns in his chair and looks towards the couch. Double-takes when he sees there is no one on it. Looks around the room. Opens the door peers out, closes the door.*]' The writer has invited the reader/spectator into a brief misunderstanding, which might be seen as a first joking reversal. He then reverses again by explaining it away within the context of the fictional world. This inclination toward a disarming candour between text/perform-ance and reader/spectator will always court a laughter response, while defining that special collusion upon which comedy bases its conversation with an audience.

The 'aside'

Comedy is often disposed to acknowledge the actual presence of the audience in the here-and-now, indeed to use it as a sea of confidants. In the previous chapter, we observed the direct address in the prologue to Menander's *The Malcontent*, and commented that the character's familiar, solicitous disposition is particularly indicative of comic worlds. The pro-logue aims to give the spectator an insider introduction to the stage world. One can also find soliloquies in classical and Elizabethan drama, in which a character alone onstage voices an opinion or works aloud through a prob-lem. It is possible, in these cases, to say that the character is talking to him- or herself, or that the audience serves the character as a sounding board. The spectator, from a corresponding point of view, becomes privy to feelings, information and a hidden quality of character which would be inaccessible in 'realistically' rendered social interaction.

A subset of this inclusion of the reader/spectator in the fictional world is the 'aside', which refers to the theatrical practice of a character turning to make a comment to the audience, unnoticed and unheard by anyone else onstage. It implies a momentary break from the fictional reality, and thereby invokes a conventional 'disattention' from the other characters, who remain unaware both of the character's action and the content of the utterance. The aside represents a device found in dramatic texts for which a mere reading of words threatens to undervalue the full comic potential in performance (see the box on page 89).

Selective disattention

The aside in performance calls upon other onstage characters to ignore the substance of the momentary timeout, if not remain altogether unaware that it happened. This 'selective disattention' to events which would ordinarily be plainly evident is sometimes extended to short utterances or interludes between characters.

Toward the end of *The Braggart Soldier*, the young woman, Philocomasium, and the young man, Pleusicles, are thrust together, with the title character, Pyrgopolynices, still deceived about their true relationship. Philocomasium has pretended to faint and is being held up by Pleusicles. She suddenly 'revives':

> PHILOCOMASIUM   What? Where am I? What's been going on? Who are
> you? [*Aside*] Hello, darling!
> PLEUSICLES   Ah, you have revived, [*Aside*] my darling.
> PHILOCOMASIUM   Goodness! Who am I embracing?
> Who's this man? I'm lost – I must have fainted.[38]

Here the two characters are able to switch quickly in and out of a private space, to which no one else onstage (with the possible exception of Palaestrio, the witty slave) has access. Their two 'states' are diametrically opposed: they pretend to be complete strangers, while furtively allowing glimpses of their intimacy. Philocomasium apparently then catches herself hugging her beloved and, for Pyrgopolynices' sake, wonders aloud how she has come to embrace a stranger. Again, the effect is based on the comic principle of sudden change between opposing emotional states or energies. The convention remains popular in theatre stagecraft, and shows up frequently in film and television comedy.

Although a furtive word in the ear of a stage world's inferred audience is not the private domain of comedy, blunt honesty and glimpses behind the masks we wear for each other (and ourselves) in social interaction remain pillars of humour principle, and therefore of comic worlds. States has written about the phenomenology of theatre, an analytic stance which seeks to address the actual experience of theatre-making and theatre-viewing, and the ineffable connection between them: '[T]he comic aside, together with the conventional prologue and epilogue, suggests a generic liberty that most comedy takes with its audience. The current of this liberty is not simply reference to the audience, but the comic project itself: the production of laughter.'[39] A character may speak aside to make or emphasize a plot point or to confide an opinion or assessment of the situation. There are, however, further implications when we read potential performance into the dramatic text. In *The Braggart Soldier*, Palaestrio, the 'witty slave', uses an aside to forestall confusion on the part of the audience. He engineers a plot to bring together a young woman, abducted and held in close quarters by the title character, and a young man. The woman is in the process of describing to the soldier's servant a dream she had, the details of which have been fabricated to gain her the freedom to meet her beloved. Palaestrio turns aside to assure the audience, 'Palaestrio dreamed all this up', then he readdresses the young woman: 'Go on – continue please.'[40] One can imagine the general opportunity for performance inherent in the 'aside' construction, as given by this specific example: Palaestrio plays at listening curiously to the young woman's story. He suddenly turns to the audience to apprise us privately of the stratagem, possibly betraying a degree of pride in his own cleverness. Just as suddenly he returns to his attitude of rapt attention. Rapid switches between incompatible emotional bearings always invite amusement, and remain a prime element of comic performance technique.

The quality of the aside sequence changes from one of 'laughing with' the confiding character to 'laughing at' him when it involves someone like Euclio in Plautus' *The Pot of Gold*. Euclio is a *senex*, or 'old man', in terms of Ancient Roman character types.[41] He is a citizen of modest means and tight fists when it comes to money. Megadorus, a wealthy neighbour, has come to ask for Euclio's daughter in marriage, and the old man's irrational suspicions supply the impetus for many an aside:

> MEGADORUS   How are you keeping? In the best of health, I hope?
> EUCLIO   [*aside*] A rich man doesn't pay compliments to a poor man for nothing. He knows I've got money; that's why he's so smarmy.[42]

Megadorus, in fact, has quite honest intentions, and no expectations of a dowry, despite Euclio's fears. Comic value derives from the gap between the innocence of Megadorus' questions and Euclio's outlandishly paranoid response to them. One can imagine a comic disjunction between Megadorus' genuine interest and Euclio's rabid suspicion, given vent through the aside.

Of course, every convention stands ripe for subversion, even (or especially) comedy's own favourites. This variation on the aside is from Terence's *The Eunuch* (*Eunuchus*, 161 BC). All one really needs to know is that Parmeno is the scheming slave and Gnatho a professional flatterer. The two serve rival masters; Gnatho is pleased to believe he has had the better of Parmeno:

> GNATHO   [*aside*] That annoyed him.
> PARMENO   [*aside*] That's what he thinks.[43]

With the spectator presuming that Gnatho's comment goes unheard, Parmeno breaks convention by responding to it. As the 'witty slave' figure in the play, he possesses the capability to trump any other character, by whatever means, up to and including the reordering of theatrical metaphysics.

Restoration Comedy made ample use of the aside, taking advantage of its shallow staging area and compact playhouse to support its confidences. In *The Pot of Gold*, the aside underscores the comic excess of suspicion shown by the miserly Euclio, who assumes everyone is angling to lay hands on his money – in Restoration Comedy the subject on (or not far from) everyone's mind is sex. Ageing men in William Wycherley's *The Country Wife* (1675) serve as central comic butts in one of the more recognizable traditions of the *senex*. Pinchwife has married a young woman from the country on the assumption that her simplicity will spare him the cuckoldry for which London wives are renowned. He displays a bad-natured desperation toward the possession of his wife, comparable to that of Euclio and his pot of gold. Horner is the young rogue-about-town, who has cleverly advertised himself as having contracted a disease which rendered him impotent. Considered a safe pair of hands by husbands, he is allowed the unchaperoned company of their wives. He has, of course, set his sights on the new bride of Pinchwife, who, as a countermeasure, has had her dress up as her own young brother from the country.

The restoration of Charles II to his throne saw women allowed on the English stage for the first time, playing female roles previously taken by men. The 'breeches part' – in which dramatic necessity dictated that a female character should dress as a man – became a popular feature of Restoration Comedy, in no small part, notes J. L. Styan, due to the titillation it provided male theatregoers in seeing 'as much of the female anatomy below the waist as a man's dress would allow'.[44]

This scene represents a masterpiece of comic contrivance. It is, as Styan observes at length, 'an inverted game of hide-and-seek',[45] during which the ingenuous Mrs Pinchwife becomes less and less committed to disguising herself from the dashing Horner. Here Horner comments provocatively upon Mrs Pinchwife's appearance:

> HORNER   Methinks he is so handsome, he should not be a man.
> PINCHWIFE [*aside*] Oh, there 'tis out, he has discovered her. I am
>   not able to suffer any longer. [*To his wife*] Come,
>   come away, I say.[46]

The scene is peppered with increasingly panicked asides by Pinchwife, as he attempts to keep his cool while desperately trying to pry his wife from Horner's insistent attentions. In this case, it is not Horner's innocence which drives the humour. He is well aware of the disguise, and mercilessly plays the situation to maximize the husband's torture. Again, when reading an aside off the page, comic wisdom would advise us to imagine opposing inner and outer states in performance. In this case, we might picture Pinchwife trying to maintain an authoritative veneer, perhaps approaching a patriarchal impatience. His aside, though, betrays fear, loathing and a gathering exasperation. As a husband who is easy to read as mean-spirited and unloving, Pinchwife's unleashed discomfort provides for delicious comic retribution.

It is easy to overlook the bodied aspect of *any* aside when reading from the page. But our new familiarity with the notion of *reversal* as a succession of incompatible frames should shed new light on the workings of the aside for performance: the tone, emotional weight or urgency of the aside enables two *reversals*, one from 'scene reality' to 'private confidence', and another in the return to 'scene reality'. The side-by-side embodiment of contradictory emotional states within a single human psyche will always court comic effect, because the perceiving body sees such complete and sudden changes in states of being as anathema to the natural fluidity of human life. The device, perhaps, implies a timeless swipe at the way our social manners cause us to play false with our real feelings.

I hope, with this chapter, to have engendered a fundamental understanding of comic construction as regards some of its favourite dramatic devices and textual inclinations. My list is not exhaustive, nor would such a list benefit a reader as much as an acquired ability to apprehend the comic impulse at large through the textual traces of its incompatible or transposed framings. Let us now carry forward our insights into the mechanics of humour in performance of a dramatic text.

Chapter 4

Comedy in the flesh

Comedy for the stage of the mind

We enter the many possible worlds of comedy by reading its ultraviolet signals, urging us from behind the words of a text toward some playful vision of the world we know. We have discerned some prototypical features that tend to confirm our presence in these types of worlds, and noted some of the patterns, devices and configurations that serve one of their prized purposes: to make us laugh. We have seen in particular how a clever reassignment of a situation, event or utterance to a relative but teasingly inappropriate framing marks many a comic construction. And we have inspected the humour gadgetry of set-up and reversal, with its resulting gap to be bridged always drawing from deeper down the well of experience than we can articulate.

With this chapter, we embark on a vital next step in learning to feel at home in comic territories: now that we know more of what comedy looks like on the page, we shall shift our attention to what it looks like in the mind. As observed previously, this act of concretization, or filling in the blanks generated by a written text, carries different implications for dramatic reading and for literary.

We saw in Chapter 1 some approaches taken by writers of literary texts, in which comic tones feed upon a disparity between the narrative register and the strip of experience being described. In literary humour the narrator's 'voice' often establishes a subtending 'gap to bridged' – to use our terminology from the previous chapter – between the linguistic frame and that of the action, feeling, thought or character it describes. The voice tells us quite a bit about the fictional world and its relationship to ours in terms of characters and events.

Here is a short passage from the first chapter of *Candide* (1759), by Voltaire:

> One day, while Cunégonde was walking near the castle in the little woods that they called a park, she saw Dr. Pangloss in the underbrush; he was giving a lesson in experimental physics to her mother's maid, a very attractive and obedient brunette. As Miss Cunégonde had a

natural bent for the sciences, she watched breathlessly the repeated experiments which were going on.[1]

Even with the extract severed from its proper context, most of us would form a fair enough picture in our minds as to what Cunégonde observed. Therein lies the humour: despite the narrator's description somewhere between the idyllic and scientific we can picture primal activities going on in the bushes. Without putting too fine a point on it, whatever images of sexual congress may pass through the reader's mind provide a serviceable enough end product, in terms of plot and character information, and the establishment of a light and reasoned narrative tone for conveyance of humanity's most animal impulses. Importantly, the literary writer knows that the next stop for words on the page is in the mind of the reader (unless, of course, mediated for a listener by a spoken-word performance or recording).

Playwrights, as we've established, write under a more complex contract. They aim past the armchair reader toward some future spectator, by way of a potential performance whose matrix of possible meanings lies in those words on a page.[2] The informed reader learns to take in a dramatic text with different eyes from those that would be cast upon a literary text. This factor can place sophisticated demands upon the reader trying to glean joking intentions. Quite simply, we have less recourse to explicit cues when imagining a comic text on the stages of our minds.

Let me offer a glimpse of what I mean. Here are the first two lines of Georges Feydeau and Maurice Desvallières' *A Little Hotel on the Side*, a play visited briefly in the preceding chapter:

> PINGLET   [singing as he works] Comes my love, with little fairy footsteps
>   Comes my love, tiptoeing o'er the grass...
> MME PINGLET   [off] Pinglet![3]

As pointed out in Chapter 1, there is no narrator to shepherd us toward the desirable realization of this world. In fact, much of what we do with this exchange will draw upon what we already know about French farce and its potential embodiment. Pinglet is poring over some architectural plans, '[*singing as he works*]', when his wife calls him from the next room. Even though we expect humorous intent in a play from Georges Feydeau (his name remaining synonymous with nineteenth-century French farce), the potential for comic embodiment in this opening snippet might slip by unnoticed. It may be only when we imagine the slightly broader acting style usually applied to farce, while recalling the humour pattern of the puncturing reversal, that we realize the possibilities for humour in performance.

The alert reader might imagine some mode of light or lilting delivery of the song by Pinglet as a set-up for an offstage vocal blast from a character whose utterance invites reversal by conveying much the antithesis of the 'fairy footsteps' and 'tiptoeing' sprite enshrined in the song. We can 'hear a body' – a phrase borrowed from Roland Barthes[4] – and so picture Mme Pinglet supplying a laughable demolition of her husband's airy depiction.

The ability to perceive comic potential in performance still leaves quite a bit of room for the range of specific embodiment. For example, despite the sharpest of practical instincts, playing with the voices of the two characters warrants exploration in rehearsal, as does Pinglet's attitude toward the song and the precise manner of its rendition. Any given actor brings something unique to the enactment, as well, and we should remain wary of claiming too clear a picture of comic concretization in the abstract.

Herein lies the double-edged challenge of reading drama in general and comedy in particular: few (if any) theatre practitioners would contend that there is a single authorized or 'perfect' actualization of any given textual moment – that's the fun and adventure of rehearsing, the intangible effect of cast and director upon text and the joy of viewing different productions of the same play. We will discuss in a later chapter ways in which comic tone is subject to adjustment, and how it affects the fabric of a text from one production to the next. For now, let's look further into the reader's capacity to generate mental images of provisional comic performance as generated by a dramatic text.

Performance fabric and outlining

The phrase 'performance fabric' can be used to refer to the fullness of theatre enactment in progress. The complex interweaving of performance phenomena – set, props, space, light, costumes and actors – all co-mingle to give an atmosphere or feeling to the real-life engagement with a stage world in flight. This aspect of the spectator's actual experience, so difficult to put into words yet impossible to ignore, is addressed by what has been called a phenomenological approach to performance. The philosophical movement called phenomenology attempts to address the actuality of experience, not simply our thought processes and sense-making, but the parts our bodies and senses play in engagement with the world. Simon Shepherd, in his book *Theatre, Body and Pleasure*, pinpoints a central motivation for such an approach to the act of theatre: 'Effects are produced in the spectator simply as a result of materially sharing the space with the performance. Many of these effects, bypassing the intellect, are felt in the body and work powerfully to shape a spectator's sense of performance.'[5] The preceding extract from *A Little Hotel on the Side* suggests the extent to which an informed reckoning of performance fabric stands to enhance one's ability to read comic potential into a seemingly inconsequential exchange.

I would like to introduce one other term to facilitate discussion of comic performance (and which can be extended to other media). I have derived a usage for the concept of 'outlining' from the work of the French philosopher, Maurice Merleau-Ponty (1908–61).[6] In his essays on painting, Merleau-Ponty refers to the artist's use of line to mark the outer contours of objects in space and the meeting of one texture with another, even though 'there are no lines visible in themselves'[7] for someone perceiving the same object(s) in the real world. The line as outline has become a conventional technique for transposing the apple from perceivable space to the flatness of the canvas, a way of 'lifting' the apple to meet reception.

I contend that what we call practical theatrical technique involves a similar outlining of behaviour, word, action, image and other phenomena, the better to pry it from that free-flowing morass of the lived-through world and position it with a particular boldness, softness, tone or pitch. I am talking about the actor's gesture or vocal delivery, the director's pacing or visual image and the playwright's linguistic delineation of character. The actress outlines her voice through volume and articulation, possibly through dialect or register – it is the way a practitioner seeks to etch signs as cogent and readable.

Outlining is also beholden to practical convention in culture and genre. Shepherd relates how the studio audience of *Whose Line is it Anyway?*, a 1990s television show in which actors engaged in improvisational games, could immediately identify a Restoration performance style by the actresses' upper-body carriage and imaginary fluttering of fans: 'The corporeal stereotype of Restoration comedy appeared in an instant and was instantly recognised by its studio audience.'[8] Most of us would recognize caricatures of other outlining styles from stage, screen and television without a word being uttered, including, for example, melodrama, the Hollywood Western and silent film comedy. One might anticipate how outlining plays a vital role in practical humour technique, which is highly dependent on precise frame renderings leading to crisp reversals.

Reading comic bodies and voices

As I have acknowledged, it is not possible (nor, perhaps, even desirable) for the armchair reader of a dramatic text to anticipate the fullness of production with any great specificity. Surely the richness of a good play lies in its wealth of possible nuance, and for a good comedy, in its 'laughs' being actualized owing to the individual sensibilities and talents of actor and director. As readers, though, we can improve our ability to spot comic opportunities in a text by gaining familiarity with performance pragmatics and conventions.

I sometimes use the phrase 'thinking in theatre' to refer to an awareness of the ways that voice, body, design and space have palpable effects upon the spectator. It is meant to remind us of the living and breathing conceptualization wanted for reading of dramatic texts. This may involve, to some extent, an intuition about performance fabric, something of its feel and outlining. It should be emphasized that, although we have seen how a play's time and place of writing help explain things about it, those of us who are not historians need not try to imagine some notion of its 'original' production. Theatre remains particularly attached to the 'here-and-now' of performance, regardless of its age and origin, and nowhere more explicitly for an audience than in the realms of comedy.

We as armchair readers should try to become adept at reading comic bodies and voices into those words on a page, by means of looking out for the comic splash enabled in advance by clever writing. Despite the fact that we assemble the world of a play a line at a time in its reading, it behoves us to remember that an actual spectator will have ongoing access to a full perceptual field. In reading comedy it can help to remain on the lookout for costumes, props or, indeed, people, which, once mentioned or inferred by the text, are left simply to 'be there' in performance, and upon whose presence humorous effect may come to rely. Farcical misfortune often places an inopportune or embarrassing prop in the hands of a hapless character or somewhere in precarious proximity to discovery by the one character who shouldn't see it.

In the first act of *What the Butler Saw*, the lascivious Dr Prentice has manoeuvred Geraldine, an astoundingly naïve young secretarial applicant, into a state of scanty dress. Mrs Prentice arrives unannounced, and Geraldine remains hidden behind a curtain for several pages of dialogue. Although her status may recede into the background of the reader's awareness, her inferred presence behind the curtains is likely to retain a bearing on the comic values of the scene. Could she pop out unbidden at any moment? To what extent might Mrs Prentice unknowingly skirt the possibility of discovering her? And what discomforts might Mr Prentice be forced to endure, what subtle emergency measures might he be forced to take? This is not to say that we should try to imagine what *will* happen, but that we should be aware of the kinds of comedy-related implications for a scene in which her presence disappears from the actual lines.

Let's look at a few examples of how a simple inference of three characters placed more or less side by side by side have been scripted for comic value on the stage of the mind. In Ben Jonson's *Volpone* (1606), the wily title character seeks to increase his own fortune by preying upon the unscrupulous greed of others. With the help of his crafty servant, Mosca, he feigns deathbed illness in order to pit three greedy men against one another in competition to be made his sole beneficiary. The business of the play's first act centres around a series of three scenes, wherein the candidates arrive in turn bearing gifts as they try to ingratiate themselves with Volpone.

Volpone is necessarily confined to his bed. Recalling our wisdom about comic contrast, an actor would likely make a show of the character's health and vigour in the opening scenes, so as to highlight his feigned languishment at death's door. The dialogue suggests that Mosca leads each candidate into the room, acting as agent for each of them even as he fans their avarice on his master's behalf:

VOLPONE	I cannot now last long –
MOSCA	You are his heir, sir.
VOLTORE	Am I?
VOLPONE	I feel me going, uh! uh! uh! uh!
	I am sailing to my port, uh! uh! uh! uh!
	And I am glad, I am so near my haven.
MOSCA	Alas, kind gentleman; well, we must all go –
VOLTORE	But, Mosca –
MOSCA	Age will conquer.
VOLTORE	Pray thee hear me.
	Am I inscribed his heir, for certain?[9]

The staging is necessarily straightforward and simple, with Mosca for the most part mediating between master and mark. (The one short passage in which Volpone beckons Voltore to him leaves Mosca space to deliver a cynical aside.) This configuration, carried forward through the next two scenes, allows Volpone the possibility of exchanges with Mosca or the audience, unacknowledged by the third character. Voltore leaps willingly into the pretence which the other two play to the hilt. This, of course, represents a prime area for exercise in reading comedy: envisaging Volpone's ability to outline debilitating illness – think, for example, of the potential for vocalized misery in the series of 'uhs' – and Mosca's agility in exploiting each petitioner's weakness and desperation.

We meet a different kind of three-person set-up in Act II of *Don Juan* by Molière. Don Juan is speaking to Charlotte, one of two peasant girls he has been pleased to woo: 'I shall be the happiest man alive. I wouldn't give my good fortune for anything in the world. What bliss it will be when you are my wife, and . . .' Whereupon Mathurine, the other one, appears:

MATHURINE [*to* DON JUAN]	Sir, what are you doing there with Charlotte? Are you courting her as well?
DON JUAN [*aside* to MATHURINE]	No, no. It's *she* who wants to marry *me*. But I've told her I am engaged to you.
CHARLOTTE [*to* DON JUAN]	What's Mathurine got to say to you?
DON JUAN [*aside to* CHARLOTTE]	She's jealous of my speaking to you. She insists that I'm engaged to her. But I've told her that you're the one I want.[10]

Bodied logic would seem to place Don Juan between the two young women: he is trying desperately to keep them apart so they cannot compare notes, even as he explains away the other's behaviour by way of assuring each one in turn that she is the one he loves. It's a deceptively active little scene, which goes on much longer than this, and offers ample room for comic performance. Let us note that the near tediousness of lines on the page compared to the bodied dynamic on the stage highlights vital differences between armchair reading and the theatre embodiment it is called upon to generate. The stage of the mind must seek to account for and retain just those vital elements of three-dimensional life that dissipate in the parade of lines on paper (see the box on page 100). As most comedy relies very heavily on gesture, action and tempo (as well as the vocal intonation mentioned above), only the reader's ability to think in theatre will rescue it from the flatness of the page.

There is another way we can improve our imagining of this scene, and, perhaps, comedy in general. In reading a novel, we are asked to concretize the fictional world directly, including, of course, its characters. In concretizing a play, we should look to imagine characters made from competent actors, not the stuff of 'real' people. No matter how fully and effectively an actor immerses himself in a role there is always the bodied presence of a person before us (in the audience), who displays physical and aesthetic characteristics which are non-fictional. This difference in metaphysical quality becomes evident if we think about the appearance of an actual or mythical person in a dramatic text. Recall our discussion of Terry Johnson's *Hysteria* and Aristophanes' *The Frogs* in Chapter 3. The characters of Sigmund Freud in the first and Dionysos in the second can only ever mean to be embodied by actors, outlined as their referents through casting, language, costume, etc. If these were literary texts, we would be meant to imagine the person (or god) 'in the flesh' – in these plays it is better to imagine actors. There is a difference, which is much more than theoretical, and it goes to the heart of our competency in reading comedy.

The defective exchange

The 'defective exchange' is a staple of comic drama. It works by way of a momentary misunderstanding brought on by some violation of philosopher Paul Grice's maxims for 'ordinary' conversation, which basically advise us to use language considerately and efficiently, not to be verbose or obtuse and to stick to the subject in play. Our everyday dialogue serves us quite well enough, even though we routinely break the maxims. Circumstance, gesture and relationship supply sufficient glue to hold most of our conversations together. Under comic circumstances, though, distraction, urgency, social unease, a conversational leap or, indeed, wilful mischief will bring about a collision of humorously juxtaposed frames.

It can be difficult to trace the full value of comic misdirection from the armchair because of the relatively antiseptic succession of lines and attributions on the page, rather than the three-dimensional enactment for which they stand. In Act I of *Absurd Person Singular*, we are in Sidney's kitchen. He is there along with Geoffrey and Ronald, whose observations about the goings-on in the next room inevitably move toward the life of the party, Dick Potter, and his attractive wife Lottie. Sidney tries to impart interesting information about the couple – they're both teachers and work with youth groups, whom they take hiking in the mountains – only belatedly picking up on their sexual innuendo:

> GEOFFREY   . . . Nice pair of legs.
> RONALD   Yes.
> SIDNEY   Dick?
> GEOFFREY His wife.
> SIDNEY   Lottie? Oh, yes. Mind you, I don't think I've really noticed them . . . [11]

In performance, it should be much easier to see Geoffrey and Ronald conversing at some level past the awareness of Sidney, who might optimally be situated between them (see Figure 4.1). He earnestly tries to share his appreciation of Dick's community-minded pursuits, while the two other men are only interested in coveting their neighbour's wife. It is, admittedly, a bit odd to think that Dick's legs should be the subject of their collective admiration, and that's what makes it potentially amusing. Sidney's relative innocence, though, and the fact that he was just talking about Dick, make it more than a gratuitous gag.

Figure 4.1 *Absurd Person Singular* by Alan Ayckbourn. In the context of the scripted scene, in which Ronald and Geoffrey have a conversation at least partly over the head of Sidney, one can see how this particular stage arrangement supports the comic sense. The Garrick Theatre, London, 2007.

As an additional point of interest, we can see in Sidney's final line in the above extract a scripted example of that delayed recognition that comic characters sometimes experience. Whether Sidney really has noticed Lottie's legs or whether he's just being polite, I think it desirable for his appreciation to have some energy behind it so he really does have to slam on the brakes and reverse direction, as he registers his indiscretion.

In the above scene, rather than confess his duplicity at being caught out so obviously, Don Juan invites amusement with mutually exclusive outlines of devotion to each woman. Comic playing will benefit from varied and 'heartfelt' parries of the damsels' growing attacks, as well as the ability to make crisp transitions between them (the side-by-side signifiers which make for effective reversals). The point here, coupled with the example from *Volpone*, is this: there is a conceptual wit behind the scripting of the above sequences, but they rely in the end on the *performers* to fill the lines to a full comic potential, not on actual people. These routines do not proffer formal jokes so much as situational confections awaiting the addition of body, voice, energy and, it might be said, a comic aptitude for outlining, all conjured in the moment of performance. The command of voice and body, invention of the inspired gag and its execution 'without a net', the traces of tireless training and rehearsal and, on the other hand, spontaneity and inspiration, all stand upon the actor's real-life abilities in the here and now in front of an audience.

William Gruber tells us that 'audiences respond to the representing as well as to the representation itself. The actor's body is too obviously present as a resource to be confined wholly within the "dramatic illusion"'.[12] There is, indeed, an aspect of performance in which the actor's or actress's proficiency or charisma bleed through (if not supersede) the onstage fiction. States coins the phrase 'self-expressive mode' to refer to the aspect of performance in which the performer seems to say 'See what I can do',[13] in a display of physical or vocal dexterity, a blast of emotional energy or a riveting command of the stage. No matter how well a gag is conceived or written, the performer's real-life artistry becomes an indisputable element in its success 'on the spot'. Because the comic actor courts the spontaneous expression of approval through audience laughter, we might identify a layer of 'self-expressive mode' in *every* execution of stage humour, which, to oversimplify, has much to do with an instinct and ability to outline.

As I said previously, a comic conceit reaches deep inside our experience of life and living for its potency. But these sequences have also been conceived according to a bodied palette of performance inscribed in the words, which does not quite follow the rules of 'real life'. This speaks to the main project of this chapter (and perhaps the whole book): *it serves our reading to imagine proficient actors and actresses embodying these roles and uttering these lines, rather than fictional or (especially) 'real' people.*

Textually, the above excerpts can be seen as astutely conceived and virtually self-contained set pieces, featuring quintessential comic characters or relationships. As such they direct us toward an inevitable rendezvous with the origins of modern comedy in performance: the *commedia dell'arte*, its masks and *lazzi*.

The *commedia dell'arte*

We have already seen that time and culture suffuse a dramatic text, that the pragmatics of theatre performance leave their fingerprints in, say, the number of speaking roles in a scene from Old Comedy or the stock set involving three entrances in New Comedy. This chapter, however, does not concern itself with the distinctions we could make about the comic practice of any particular period. It has, to the contrary, to do with fundamental consistencies related to comic performance which may help us read comic texts.

It is widely regarded that Western comic performance's life blood flows from the full-bodied artistry of Italy's *commedia dell'arte*. Yet this leads us into tricky territory in the crucial area of historical certainty about the actuality of performance. In discussing prototypical comic drama from Ancient Greece and Rome, although much detail about performance will always remain beyond our reach, we are able to inspect something of the originating comic force resident in those extant texts, as they were scripted prior to performance. We have benefited greatly from the examination of some of these texts, recovered from what was, in some respect, a 'writer's theatre'. We have no such point of direct access to the *commedia dell'arte*, which was a 'performer's theatre', first and foremost. Its vitality sprang from the actors' physical and vocal contributions. With its emphasis on improvization and physicality, there are no scripts to be unearthed and pored over. Its creative engine *was* the current of spontaneous energy and skill. This most valuable feature is all but unrecoverable, hinted at only in written accounts and in artists' and engravers' images of masked, physically extravagant performances, usually portrayed on makeshift outdoor stages.

There remains uncertainty, as well, about the historical details of the *commedia dell'arte* and the breadth of its daily existence. It had taken identifiable shape by the 1540s, emerging in Italy as a marketplace entertainment. It soon introduced the actress to the Italian (and thereafter the European) stage; its professional companies came to play in theatres and halls and sought patronage from the nobility. Eventually it spread beyond Italy into other European countries, particularly France, where Italian companies toured or took up residence. The late sixteenth and early seventeenth centuries are considered the golden years of the *commedia dell'arte*, and it is reckoned to have entered a long period of decline by the 1700s as standards dropped and, perhaps, inspiration waned.

The name *commedia dell'arte* did not come into use until well into its final phase, found in the first written instance in a work by Italian playwright Carlo Goldoni (1707–93). The phrase *commedia dell'arte* refers in its historical context literally to a 'comedy of the professional guild'. We should think of it as a comic theatre – despite the fact that the repertoire came to include non-comedies as well – featuring a mix of masked and unmasked performers, who improvised according to prescribed scenarios, but also incorporated practised set pieces. And we should think of the performers as professional, both in the level of their skill and discipline and in the fact that they did it quite seriously for a living.

An actor cultivated a speciality in a particular character, based upon a combination of that character's generic traits and his or her individualized creative persona. Actors became adept at various *lazzi*, or set pieces, which might be incorporated during performance in flight and adapted to the specific situation. It is possible, then, to consider their performances as simultaneously well-rehearsed *and* open to the inspiration of the moment, a meeting of structured control and spontaneous creativity, which has been compared by Antonio Fava, a contemporary practitioner and authority on *commedia dell'arte*, to the improvisations of contemporary jazz musicians. Fava also sees the twentieth-century animated cartoon series as 'the modern expression closest to Commedia': 'It has fixed types, recurrent behaviours, perfectly recognizable characters; *lazzi* or gags; standard situations; fixed schema.'[14] (The comparison can be argued as more than metaphoric, by connecting acknowledged historical dots from the *commedia dell'arte* to nineteenth-century vaudeville and music hall to silent-film performance and finally to the first wave of animated cartoons.)

Each performance built itself around a scenario, which provided a backbone in terms of characters, relationships and plot points, noting specific information that had to be disclosed during a given scene. It is said that the *commedia erudita*, acted by amateurs, scripted, unmasked and performed on private indoor stages, gave the *commedia dell'arte* its plot structures and stock characters from Plautus and Terence. Some of these scenarios have survived, the earliest of which is a collection published in 1611 by Flaminio Scala, an actor from one of the leading companies of the time.

With this basic context established, we can better focus upon the appointed purpose of this chapter – contributions to the practices of comic enactment – by saying a bit more about masks and *lazzi*.

Masks

Not all characters in a *commedia dell'arte* performance were masked in the sense that the actors wore facial coverings with fixed features. The old men and the comic servants wore masks, but the young lovers and female servants did not. Nonetheless, in discussion of the historical *commedia dell'arte*, all characters are referred to as 'masks', because of their generic plot functions and consistent, recognizable features.

Surviving scenarios suggest that plots were designed to make use of a consistent enough configuration of masks so that a *commedia dell'arte* company could promise a 'new' show every day for quite a long time. The context and precise relationships might change, but the performers were apprised of the specific day's details, with, perhaps a copy of the scenario posted offstage for reference. Rather than full-scale rehearsal and rote memorization of fixed scripts, performances were built from a confidence and comfort in one's character, a warehouse of personal material, an ability to engage instinctively with an audience and cooperation with the rest of the cast in advancing the scenario.

We should acknowledge that, for all the impression of a foregrounded physicality imparted by visual documentation, a certain amount of comic value was drawn from verbal humour, based on, for example, a mask's pomposity or gullibility. The masks of the *commedia dell'arte* were comic prototypes associated with particular regions, and bore their character credentials in the way they spoke. Pantalone was a Venetian skinflint, Dottore a Bolognese blowhard, and the various *zanni*, usually comic servants including the likes of Arlecchino, were essentially peasants from the country seeking to fill their stomachs however they might. Capitano was a braggart foreigner with military pretensions, who might speak in Spanish, for example. The *innamorati*, or lovers, expressed their romantic passions in florid literary language.

There were masks with other names comparable to the above characters, but these represent the main generic types. According to Kenneth and Laura Richards in *The Commedia dell'arte* (1990) a company might have carried two *vecchi* (or old men), like Pantalone and Dottore; two or more *zanni*; a 'free-ranging' figure like Capitano; and two or more pairs of lovers. They might also have used a *servetta* or female *zanni*, called Colombina, Franceschina or Smeraldina, among others, and there may have been other masks particular to a company.

The masks would appear to serve as archetypal social lampoons, capable of laying bare transcendent human weaknesses across hundreds of years of Western culture. Yet we should not forget that the masks also displayed localized features, noted above in their customary dialects, and therefore inaccessible to those of us looking on from a different time and place. It is interesting that something about the behaviours codified in these caricatures remains constant over time, although culture and subculture would tend to delineate their own variations. (Think about dialects and outlined behaviours, for example, through which one might translate Dottore's hollow pomposity into contemporary terms.)

Pantalone and Arlecchino, as archetypal master and servant masks, embody an enduring relationship in our comic-performance tradition, inherent in their clearly determined power dynamic (see the box on page 106). Richard Andrews observes: 'A great deal of *commedia dell'arte* laughter, to judge both by scenarios and by visual material, was based on the infliction of pain and humiliation by one character on another.'[15] The authority figure was always a prime target for trickery and indignity, just as the subservient character could be expected, sooner or later, to garner slapstick punishment.

Alazon and *eiron*

It is a matter of some interest that stock comic archetypes described by Aristotle and employed by Aristophanes over 2,400 years ago can still be seen to inform characterization here in the twenty-first century. The *eiron*, who ironically 'dissembles his real qualities and abilities', and the *alazon*, who 'loudly lays claim to qualities and abilities not rightly his',[16] remain key agents for humour in popular Western drama.

In the Pantalone/Arlecchino (or, more generally, *vecchi/zanni*) relationship we can see the *alazon/eiron* in tandem: the pretentious or unyielding *alazon* opposed by the flexible or self-deprecating *eiron*. Frye observes: 'The multitudes of comic scenes in which one character complacently soliloquizes while another makes sarcastic asides to the audience show the contest of *eiron* and *alazon* in its purest form, and show too that the audience is sympathetic to the *eiron* side.'[17]

The nature and function of the pairing evokes a strategy reminiscent of a traditional European circus's entrée clown act, comprised of a 'whiteface' and 'auguste' partner:

> It is only through their relationships that their comic characters make sense. An entree could not be performed on the merits of just one clown or the other working alone in the ring. For example, the authoritarian whiteface, who simply wants his plan to be accomplished properly, defines the bad manners, incompetence, and lowly status of his auguste partners, who never seem to be able to provide their elegant friend with the necessary help.[18]

We should recognize that the *alazon* and *eiron* do not necessarily come as a pair. It is possible to identify one without the other in a given text. Malvolio, from *Twelfth Night*, is very much an *alazon* on his own. Sganarelle, the central character in *The Reluctant Doctor (Le Médecin malgré lui*, 1666) by Molière can be considered an *eiron*. What *alazons* and *eirons* can you think of in modern-day drama, film and television?

There is another essential component to consider when imagining mask performance and it lies in the contribution of the specific actor, how a particular human supplies life and breath to a fictional construct and thereby distinguishes it through individual appearance and personality, abilities and sensibilities. Performers applied (and could not help but apply) something of themselves to the mask, through expressive and virtuosic individuality, as Fava observes: 'The masked actor combines his unique and repeatable human and artistic peculiarities with the universal and archetypal qualities of the mask.'[19]

In the constellation of *commedia dell'arte* masks, a Dottore, for example, thrived on vocal dexterity, while the *zanni* made particular use of physical and acrobatic abilities, even while they assumed archetypal features of the mask. As a parallel, consider the ways in which Charlie Chaplin, Buster Keaton and Harold Lloyd, all well-known clowns (whom we might even call *zanni*) of the silent-film era, cultivated personas cut from the same cloth, though distinctively shaped by who they were in terms of personality and physicality.

Lazzi

The scenario's story and details are intended primarily to supply situation, relationship and motivation for opportunities in comic performance. Because so many elements of the scenarios are interchangeable, an array of set pieces – verbal and physical – could be devised and rehearsed for inclusion in performance. These comic set pieces grow from a specific character in a given situation, but in effect lay plot development to the side for the benefit of laughter-generating business.

Commedia dell'arte actors built up stockpiles of comic speeches, routines and business for insertion into performance. These *lazzi* (the singular of which is *lazzo*) are characterized by Mel Gordon as 'any discrete, or inde-pendent, comic and repeatable activity that guaranteed laughs for its participants'.[20] A certain *lazzo* might be considered an obvious fit for a particular point in a scenario, and be planned in advance. But a company would also have a set of discreet signals so that, should an opportune moment arise during performance – in response to developing action or audience response – an actor could cue the beginning of a *lazzo*, which might involve a solo turn or an ensemble effort. A *lazzo* including two or more performers might display a well-rehearsed physical or vocal sequence, thereby emphasizing a collective virtuosity in its pacing and precision.

Gordon has assembled a collection of documented *lazzi* from *commedia dell'arte* companies performing in Europe between 1550 and 1750. It is striking to note the extent to which the comic sensibilities behind these joking enactments align with our culturally inscribed sense of dramatic humour. In a classic *lazzo*, 'Arlecchino...pulls the chair away from the Captain just before he is to sit down.'[21] This most timeworn of stage gags nonetheless evokes characterization and relationship, while inviting an amplified physical outlining which underscores the reversal of social pos-ition. The traditionally arrogant Capitano is brought delectably low by the rascally servant (sometimes considered the First *Zanni*); perhaps in another company, he is delivered unceremoniously and unwittingly to the ground by a stupid servant (the Second *Zanni*). Both the timing of the action and the comic fall itself required rehearsal and skill for maximum effect.

We can refer again to Chaplin, Keaton and Lloyd, whose films essentially used simple narrative contexts as road maps for the more immediate purpose of affording exquisitely conceived and executed comic detours or, we might say, *lazzi*. As you may already have gleaned, this is very much along the lines of the *commedia dell'arte* performer's relationship to plot, role and audience. The scenario's fictional circumstances gave rise to a parade of comic turns, and the performer's abilities were of primary interest to everyone involved, in contrast to a contemporary mode of performance in which actors are expected to immerse themselves completely 'inside' a character for the more effective illusion of an unfolding reality.

We remember Charlie Chaplin eating his shoe in *The Gold Rush* (1925), Lucille Ball trying desperately to wrap chocolates in the *I Love Lucy* episode, 'Job switching' (1952; see Figure 4.2), and Jim Carrey beating himself up in the lavatory in *Liar Liar* (1997). These three sequences spring from plot and character, yet easily stand outside them as set pieces through which the performer's distinctive personality and talents shine.

What we call a 'sketch' in vaudeville or music-hall terms is essentially a free-standing *lazzo*, which goes on for as long as the writers/performers foresee it as bearing its comic weight. The 'Dead parrot' sketch from *Monty Python's Flying Circus* (1969–74), for example, has the John Cleese character reaching for a string of euphemisms to describe the dead parrot he has been duped into buying, while Michael Palin's shopkeeper steadfastly refuses to acknowledge the dodgy sale. This strategy of constructing a humorous conceit – or, in effect, a scripted *lazzo* – based on delay, protraction, extension or reinforcement can be seen in a few of the sequences cited thus far (e.g., Anna and Freud, in the previous chapter, speaking at cross-purposes about the light pull), and is a mainstay of writing for comic performance.

Despite, or perhaps because of, the amount of experience and rehearsal that contributed to a *lazzo*'s success, Andrews proposes that *commedia* dialogue was structured, though not set, and that the actors improvised the actual words subject to audience response and inspiration of the moment. Speeches might also be learned if not memorized (in the manner of a stand-up comic). He says that, 'In memorizing and performing the sequence, the stress would lie on conveying the information and/or getting the laugh, rather than on repeating the words identically every time.'[22]

By examining period texts, Andrews has gained insights into the nature of the *commedia dell'arte*'s improvisational technique, identifying what he calls modular structure and the 'elastic gag'. With a comic conceit primed – e.g., a mischievous servant on the verge of imparting a piece of information

Figure 4.2. In the vintage 1950s comedy series, *I Love Lucy*, Lucy and Ethel adopt increasingly desperate measures for dealing with a conveyor belt gone amok with unwrapped chocolates, a markedly physical, detachable comic set piece reminiscent of the *commedia dell'arte's lazzi.*

his master is desperately eager to receive – the actors could continue to manufacture dialogue for as long (or short) as the audience kept laughing, just by improvising variations on the basic model for the exchange. He proposes that we can see in such constructs the direct influence of elastic improvisation upon scripted texts, and that 'such modular components are a sign of improvisation technique, of a mode of performance in which an actor's existing repertoire of jokes, long and short, can be adapted and inserted into any plot with which they do not actually clash'.[23]

Carlo Goldoni has been credited with both the death blow and resuscitation of the *commedia dell'arte* in the mid-eighteenth century. He took back the creative initiative from the actor, doing away with the use of face masks and improvisation. His best-known play, *The Servant of Two Masters*

(*Arlecchino servitore di due padroni*, 1753), features variations on trad-itional mask characters and a number of identifiable *lazzi* set-ups. We can see scripted versions of the elastic-gag strategy in the above sequences from *Volpone* and *Don Juan*: a potent comic set-up, which, though scripted, *could* have gone on longer or shorter (and the reader is directed to the full versions of the scenes for a better idea of what I am talking about). Jonson places Mosca in control of the scenes with the three unscrupulous sup-plicants for Volpone's alleged fortune. Although each scene is shrewdly varied according to the precise nature of the visiting character's venality, once established they offer a series of reversals based on the same set-up – Jonson has simply written them to some instinctive ideal length. The same is true of Molière's writing, above. Attempting simultaneously to appease the two young women *and* keep them apart, the trio of actors could the-oretically improvise along the same lines for as long as the audience keeps laughing.

This overview of the *commedia dell'arte* and brief discussions of its two defining features has been intended to further a way of thinking about character and comic performance for reading comedy. Although rooted in real life, mask performance seeks to outline a selective universality about human behaviours. The *lazzo*, in turn, should instruct us to think in terms of the rehearsal, skill and resulting precision which will serve to highlight the elements of set-up and reversal. An emphasis on physicality draws attention to the performing body and embraces a combination of playfulness and proficiency. Again, this amounts to a mode of performance which acknowledges, plays *for* and plays *with* the spectator.

   We should take from this section an awareness of the extent to which a physical-vocal vitality and control assist in the fluid, three-dimensional joking of much comic performance. Physical comedy teases our bodies *directly*, and we should be on the lookout for these kinds of reversals having been foreseen (and, in fact, enabled) by the playwright. When reading a comic text, we should ask ourselves not only, 'What does it *ask* the performer(s) to do?', but, 'What does it *allow* them to do?'

The clown

In close historic proximity to the *zanni* of the *commedia dell'arte*, we find the clown. The clown is said to have evolved from the Vice character in medieval English drama, who manifested the unapproved side of the moral compass (see the box on page 156). It is hard to ignore the fact that both the English clown and the Italian *zanni* came into the world as targets of ridicule in urbanizing societies because of their country-bred, low social status (and there would seem to remain an inherited naïvety even in our modern conception of the clown). In contemporary Western culture we use the term primarily to refer to a circus (or circus-style) entertainer, the stereotypical appearance and performance persona of which we joked about in the preceding chapter (see the box below).

Clowning

From the historically specific origins recounted in this chapter, clowning now stands as a populist performance mode, always signalling an intention to joke. David Wiles shows in historical terms how 'the clown's primary "language" is physical rather than verbal',[24] and we might observe that a non-speaking status has become a part of its modern connotation. Clown performance places a minimum of interpretive demand upon the spectator, and often supplies a child's introduction to live performance. It is not, however, necessary to display the red nose, baggy pants and oversized shoes to avail oneself of its conventions – we recognize a clowning persona in extravagance of gesture, facial expression and what we might call a humour of innocence. Animated cartoons and children's-show humour rely heavily on clowning personas and patterns.

   Recalling the silent clowns of early cinema, Charlie Chaplin, Buster Keaton and Harold Lloyd, and mid-century clowns like Jacques Tati and Lucille Ball, Rowan Atkinson's creation Mr Bean is probably the best known of modern clown figures. Krusty the Clown of *The Simpsons* is a misanthropic, emphysemic send-up of Bozo the Clown, a 1950s-America children's television host, with a sly nod to Soupy Sales, another such host whose own causticity was famously caught on air, and an entrepreneurial sneer at Ronald McDonald, the hamburger salesclown.

   The so-called New Vaudeville of the 1980s and 1990s produced the likes of Bill Irwin, who applied an acrobatic, physical dexterity to conventional clowning patterns and a postmodern sensibility. One of Irwin's signature routines saw his body sucked by an inexplicable gravitational pull toward the stage-left wings whenever he ventured too near them.

   Clown figures usually invoke a direct relationship with the audience, exacting an interesting flavour of authorization from the spectator. As privileged agents of the unfranchised they allow a universal identification with uphill struggle. At the same time they encourage, through laughter, an assertion of superiority. Despite unswerving determination and fantastic invention, clowns spend much of their time failing. In fact, according to Wolfgang Iser, the clown arrives inscribed for reception with a general metaphysical brief: 'Everything he does goes wrong, but he persists, as if the repetition denoted constant success.'[25] Enid Welsford observes that 'the clown depends, not upon the external conflicts of hostile groups, but upon a certain inner contradiction in the soul of every man'.[26]

Wiles, in his book *Shakespeare's Clown: Actor and Text in the Elizabethan Playhouse* (1987), explores in-depth the English origins of the clown figure in drama. He emphasizes that 'clown' became the professional label for a company's principal comic actor, which is why it sometimes takes the place of a character name in a text. This allowed the clown to occupy a meta-physical level of being detached or detachable from the rest of the stage world and straddling the divide between fiction and real life.

Clearly the scripted activities of a clown figure are of immediate interest to us, as we investigate how the words of a dramatic text ask to be imagined in performance. Wiles supports the proposition that Shakespeare reworked *The Two Gentlemen of Verona* (1593–8) following Will Kemp's attachment to the Chamberlain's company, and regards it as a turning point for the playwright in writing for comic performance.[27] Shakespeare appears to have added the role of Launce specifically for Kemp, cleverly incorporating him into the fabric of the play while allowing him the kind of bravura comic turn upon which he had already built a reputation as a minstrel. Two scenes in the extant play involve *lazzo*-like monologues to the audience delivered by Launce, who, in both cases is accompanied by his dog, Crab (which may well have been played by a real animal).

The scenes are much to be admired for facilitating maximum advantage of a simple comic conceit. Launce enters in the throes of sorrow, having wrenched himself from his family, a scene he describes here:

> I think Crab my dog be the sourest-natured dog that lives: my mother weeping; my father wailing; my sister crying; our maid howling; our cat wringing her hands, and all our house in a great perplexity; yet did not this cruel-hearted cur shed one tear.[28]

Launce seeks the audience's empathy over the heartless companion placed before them, using the (real or stuffed) dog's innate obliviousness to brilliant comic advantage. A committed emotional state outlined by the actor will generate a comic juxtaposition with whatever may be readable from the canine scene partner. The above words shrewdly direct the spectator's attention to the dog. The actor then delineates the list of family reactions through voice, body and feeling, invested perhaps with an emotional build, all of which is undercut by 'the cat wringing her hands', before focus is returned to the dog. The piece may have been based on Kemp's solo entertainments, but hints at the advantage of astute scripting in its clean shaping and calculated direction of attention to Launce's scene partner.

The monologue soon enters another phase in which the actor attempts to act out the scene of woe using items to hand as stand-ins for the various family members:

> Nay, I'll show you the manner of it. This shoe is my father. No, this left shoe is my father; no, no, this left shoe is my mother; nay, that cannot be so neither. Yes, it is so, it is so: it hath the worser sole. This shoe with the hole in it is my mother; and this is my father. A vengeance on't, there 'tis. Now, sir, this staff is my sister; for, look you, she is as white as a lily, and as small as a wand. This hat is Nan our maid. I am the dog. No, the dog is himself, and I am the dog. O, the dog is me, and I am myself.[29]

A tried-and-true premise for a comic monologue is the recounting of a story or description of a scene in which the speaker becomes somehow overly caught up in the telling.[30] Shepherd has several interesting things to say about this speech, pointing up the comic wisdom of Launce casting inanimate objects for family members allegedly wracked with grief, even as he grapples emotionally with his dog's bespoken disinterest. The conditions are foreseen by the playwright for Launce in his distress to be surrounded by embodied indifference in two registers (the dog and the objects).

The clowning drive very often involves an unremitting fixation upon a single goal, defined as comic by its seeming lack of importance or worth in the overall scheme of things. We can see it manifested here in Launce's fretting over which shoe should represent which parent. Shepherd also perceives in the lines a sense of the character being 'taken over by the internal rhythm of his activity'.[31] A language of emotionality, a shortening of sentences and sudden changes in thought indicative of a distraught mind, here and in other dramatic texts do indeed harbour instruction for the performer – it is the ludicrous logic spiralling downward into self-pity which stands to facilitate comic effect.

The physical activity foreseen by this speech remains a defining element of generic clown performance. The clowning impulse often applies itself to problem-solving, and we can find it driving stage business in many a non-clowning text. The clowning spirit will often be dedicated to some quest pursued with too much or too little diligence or for which conditions lead to a disarming resourcefulness.

In Alan Ayckbourn's *Absurd Person Singular* (1972), which shows us three suburban couples on three successive Christmases, one of the women spends the entire second act trying to kill herself. Eva never says a word during this act (save for singing in a semi-sedated daze toward the end), but keeps writing suicide notes while turning to various resources one might find in a kitchen to accomplish her task. Neither does she make any attempt to hide what she is doing: her husband talks for four pages before he realizes what she is up to, after which the partygoers one at a time frustrate her plans by mistaking each effort for some manner of domestic endeavour.[32]

There is something we might call life-affirming in Eva's unflagging pursuit of self-extermination, an artful reversal upon Langer's contention that the clown figure is 'the personified *élan vital*'.[33] The spectator may be caught wanting Eva to succeed because she applies herself with such quiet persistence and unflinching invention. It should, though, become apparent that she will not – I doubt anyone would really want her to – so that her series of failures turns into the saddest of triumphs.

I should like to point out that this sort of identification of clown pattern in a text is no mere analytical exercise. It should cue the reader (or actress) to keep in mind the kind of clear and precise outlining with which a clown might approach the non-verbal communication of thought process, action and reaction. This, of course, exists as a subset of our broader imperative to imagine actors and actresses in a sort of provisional or inchoate performance. The practised reader comes to perceive what and how humorous potential resides in character, situation and textual pattern.

Reading comic character (mask)

The *commedia dell'arte* found comic resonance in its masks because they were based on cultural types and behaviours particular to the world around it. They were marked for immediate recognition through social context, dialect and a defining behavioural excess, all of which were specific to time and place. We can notice concurrently that some part of these masks had been inherited from the Ancient Roman comedy of Plautus and Terence, recognizable in our work in Chapter 3 on characters like the penny-pinching old man and the witty slave. In our times, older men still get a hard time from comedy, and the unpretentious but cheeky young man has become one of Hollywood's favoured central characters.

Shepherd contends that the words of a dramatic text signal instruction for the body. He endorses the view that an awareness of rhythm in dialogue 'can turn reading into feeling,'[34] and I commented on this above in the use of short sentences for Launce's speech. In Oscar Wilde's *An Ideal Husband* (1895), Mabel Chiltern is a lovely young Englishwoman of respectable social standing. Here she is talking to her sister-in-law about the attentions of her brother's clerk:

> Well, Tommy has proposed to me again. Tommy really does nothing but propose to me. He proposed to me last night in the music-room, when I was quite unprotected, as there was an elaborate trio going on. I didn't dare to make the smallest repartee, I need hardly tell you. If I had, it would have stopped the music at once. Musical people are so absurdly unreasonable. They always want one to be perfectly dumb at the very moment when one is longing to be absolutely deaf. Then he proposed to me in broad daylight this morning, in front of that dreadful statue of Achilles. Really, the things that go on in front of that work of art are quite appalling. The police should interfere. At luncheon I saw by the glare in his eye that he was going to propose again, and I just managed to check him in time by assuring him that I was a bimetallist. Fortunately I don't know what bimetallism means.[35]

The upright propriety and physical articulation of good manners strongly suggest a bodied bearing in delivery. The cultured choice of words, the rhetorical play of repetition and variation, the air of unimpeachable authority in the phrasing – this linguistic suggestion of a decorous, self-possessed bodied register serves best to outline that humorous mismatch of a subject and its treatment.

We can, then, find amusement in a young woman's response to a young man's persistence, the quirky sense of inconvenience with occasional conversational footnotes, as well as the carefree self-assurance with which it is pronounced from the great heights of youthful fancy. He proposed when she 'was quite unprotected, as there was an elaborate trio going on', then 'in broad daylight this morning, in front of that dreadful statue of Achilles'. The conditions are wryly detailed and the suitor's hapless determination carries clownish overtones. The experienced reader will come to know that Wilde's characters love to talk and they love to render opinions in aphoristic fashion.

Let's look at a contrasting character in body, culture and nature. This is a speech by Bunny, a character in *The House of Blue Leaves* (1971) by John Guare:

> I'm not good in bed. It's no insult. I took that sex test in the *Reader's Digest* two weeks ago and I scored twelve. Twelve, Artie! I ran out of that dentist office with tears gushing out of my face. But I face up to the truth about myself. So if I cooked for you now and said I won't sleep with you till we're married, you'd look forward to sleeping with me so much that by the time we did get to that motel near Hollywood,

> I'd be such a disappointment, you'd never forgive me. My cooking is
> the only thing I got to lure you on with and hold you with. Artie, we
> got to keep some magic for the honeymoon. It's my first honeymoon
> and I want it to be so good, I'm aiming for two million calories. I want
> to cook for you so bad I walk by the A & P, I get all hot jabs of chili
> powder inside my thighs.[36]

Inadequate sexual performance bores too deeply into issues of identity
and intimacy to brook joking for most of us. Bunny's blunt announcement
bursts through the normal boundaries of candour for such matters; her
pragmatic variation on 'saving oneself' for the wedding night makes perfect
comic sense.

This body projects itself as much less reserved than the previous one
(though you might, as an experiment, try reading these two monologues
with the 'wrong' characters). Bunny's speech is plain-spoken, perhaps
alarmingly so, and hyperbolic. Its feeling is unapologetic, implying a
brashness of twentieth-century urban character. The play is rooted specifically in time and place – an apartment in Sunnyside, Queens on 4 October,
1965, the day the Pope arrived in New York. Though not hundreds of years
old, it was written almost forty years ago. We can read the character of
Bunny, then, as just that combination of specific and universal upon which
all comic characters cannot help but be based. There is surely a strong
element of the late twentieth-century 'Stage New Yorker' readable in this
speech, a stereotype available to the Western world in the movies of Woody
Allen and television series like *Everybody Loves Raymond* (1996–2005) and
The King of Queens (1998–2007).

Bergson observes, 'A comic effect is always obtainable by transposing the
natural expression of an idea into another key.'[37] When reading dramatic
texts, we should remember that this other key is produced by the performing
body and voice, even though our attention centres on the words. Akin to the
commedia dell'arte, the above speeches can be seen as *lazzo*-like routines,
conceived for the masks current to time and culture, and reliant for their
comic resonance upon the actress's delineation. They should, then, be read
with the text's attempt to foresee an actress's expressive capabilities kept in
mind. (It sometimes helps to imagine a specific actress in the role.)

Opportunities for comic enactment arise whenever a character attempts in
some way to accept centre stage, either in the company of other characters or
directly with the audience. This, in effect, produces concentric spotlights and
a double challenge for the actor – as character and as performer. Indeed, a
character/performer holding the stage in a play or role associated with
comedy virtually incurs a joking obligation.

A comic character may read, recite, sing, imitate, tell a story or otherwise adopt a presentational stance within the stage world, allowing us to see their expressive capabilities. Shakespearean characters sometimes work through a problem via soliloquy, which allows for an embodiment of dramatic conflict within a single person. In comic terms Launcelot Gobbo in *The Merchant of Venice* (1596–7), listed as 'the clown, servant to Shylock', engages in an internal wrestling match over whether to desert his despised master or maintain his position with honour (Act II, Scene ii, lines 1–33). He enacts the ethical tug-of-war between the good and bad aspects of his conscience, transparently giving away his preference for the 'most courageous fiend' telling him to get out while he can. The monologue enables potent comic embodiment for the two opposing forces as well as his own thinly disguised cowardice as moderator of the debate.

A scene frequently played out in comedy involves a character rehearsing for an imminent interview or confrontation. It often involves that character attempting to perform some level of competency in a role or situation for which they are not entirely suited, or which appears utterly opposed to their established nature. In William Congreve's *The Way of the World*, Lady Wishfort prepares to entertain Sir Rowland, asking advice and support from her woman in waiting, Foible:

> Well, and how shall I receive him? In what figure shall I give his heart the first impression? There is a great deal in the first impression. Shall I sit? – No, I won't sit – I'll walk – ay, I'll walk from the door upon his entrance; and then turn full upon him. – No, that will be too sudden. I'll lie – ay, I'll lie down – I'll receive him in my little dressing-room, there's a couch – yes, yes, I'll give the first impression on a couch – I won't lie neither, but loll and lean upon one elbow; with one foot a little dangling off, jogging in a thoughtful way – yes – and then as soon as he appears, start, ay start and be surprised, and rise to meet him in a pretty disorder – yes – O, nothing is more alluring than a levee from a couch in some confusion. – It shows the foot to advantage, and furnishes with blushes, and re-composing airs beyond comparison. Hark! There's a coach.[38]

Lady Wishfort is a choice target for gulling, constructed in the play as a spiteful and hypocritical blocking figure. Congreve marks her card clearly via Restoration naming convention by labelling her with a contraction of 'Wish for it'. We are therefore urged to read the preparation enacted here as a rehearsal of modesty perhaps awkwardly and/or incompetently executed. The playwright has supplied *tour de force* conditions for physical embodiment, and J. L. Styan admires in the writing the room for vocal possibility as well, 'a complete development in range of feeling from apprehension to exhilaration'.[39]

Comic custom, inherited from the *commedia dell'arte* models discussed previously, prescribes maximum and prolonged humiliation for this character. In an echo of the Old Man/Servant relationship, Wishfort is attended here by her woman in waiting, Foible. The latter goads her mistress while her new husband, Waitwell, readies himself to assume the role of the fictional suitor, Sir Rowland. A survey of reviews from the past century assures us that casting and tone are capable of swinging performance of this speech between broad comedy and disconcerting cruelty. It is, in any case, easy to see even in a cursory reading how much physical playing is invited by the words. Lady Wishfort continually questions and edits her approach. Does she monitor Foible's responses and change accordingly? Does she become suddenly aware of her own ungainliness in certain ways? Do physical mishaps occur, causing her to decide not to risk inelegance? Does her apprehension get the better of her? There are, of course, many possibilities up to and including comic falls and grotesquely seductive poses, depending on the palette adopted by a given production. Phrases like, 'I'll give the first impression on a couch' and 'but loll and lean upon one elbow; with one foot a little dangling off, jogging in a thoughtful way' and 'rise and meet him in a pretty disorder' invite the performer to find a comic divergence between the words and the effect the character 'thinks' she is achieving.

We might say that the comic monologue encourages us to imagine the potential for exploration of mask in a *commedia dell'arte* sense, by asking what human foible is being held up for ridicule, and in what cultural stereotype does it sit most recognizably. Once again, though, we try to anticipate a gap between intention and effect. Susan Purdie, who provided illumination in the previous chapter, does so again:

> Characters are comic through a carefully structured culmination of incoherences: their behaviour is not commensurate with their (constructed) motivation; other characters' responses are not in measure with their intended effects; all their signification is inappropriate; and this incites the Audience to notice the disjuncture between the 'presentation' and 'representation' of the text.[40]

We can only ever read a text from our position in time and place, and with regard to our dramatic and cultural experience (even though an awareness of historical conditions and conventions may augment our understanding). As suggested above, we can intuit ideal mismatches between material and its delivery, between conscious behaviour and its unconscious appearance, between a character's apprehension of circumstances and what the spectator knows them to be.

To be sure, outlining conventions differ from one pocket of historical performance to another. But it serves the reader to imagine a conscious attention to clear and advantageous framing in a comic text, and this does not always mean it needs to be broad or exaggerated. Even in the television series, *The Office*, whose faux-documentary style pretends there is no performing going on, we can see an impressive use of bodied detail, particularly by Ricky Gervais as David Brent. This show, in fact, frequently focuses on the ways in which the subtleties of body language and facial expression betray honest feeling (see the box below).

Acting comedy v. acting funny

Concentration on the nature of outlining comic worlds prompts an important reminder (especially for readers with more than a passing interest in acting or directing): our first-order experience with real life and its behaviours authorizes all comic performance – it is the shared unspoken knowledge upon which comic acting predicates itself. The foregoing emphasis upon skilled outlining and expressive proficiency should not be taken as advice to privilege the artificiality of performance over genuine situational behaviour. I am not trying to oversimplify the process of comic performance by advising you to imagine actors and actresses 'acting funny'.

It is sometimes easier to see the 'Here's a joke!' outline than the joke-in-itself. A performer's delivery, a playwright's linguistic set-up, a director's pacing – any and all of these factors may point toward an intended reversal. Spectators become schooled in the conventions surrounding a sequence of performed humour, so that elements like vocal, physical and facial nuance and joking rhythms may well provoke a show of amusement, regardless of the actual joking material. (The canned laughter added to many a television comedy is designed to coax a response from the spectator at home by artificially embellishing one of the surrounding indicators of successful humour.)

Overblown characters and responses, sudden changes in energy, silly faces or voices – these strategies may appear as short cuts in courting audience response, as they have come to act as pre-emptive signs for humour. When outlining overshadows situation, we sometimes call it 'mugging' or 'over-the-top' acting. Any accomplished comic practitioner will tell you that without the real, honest or serious dedication to circumstances, a performance threatens to lose an essential comic integrity.

Steve Seidman, writing about some of the best comedians in Hollywood history, notes the element of unabashed performing even within the confines of fourth-wall illusion: 'While the success of the actor or actress in nineteenth-century theatre was predicated on the performer's becoming a "he" or "she", the performer's success in vaudeville and its descendants was contingent on presenting the "I", exhibiting the self in such a way as to induce an immediate response (laughter, applause, singing along) from the audience.'[41] We might take the liberty of extending this shift in emphasis by saying that the two-person comic scene is contingent on presenting the 'we'.

Reading comic dialogue (*lazzi*)

The two-person scene represents a basic unit of comic performance, involving a shift of the spotlight from the single actor to a cooperative ensemble. It asks for something more than a display of individual artistry in the outlining of character, set-up and reversal. We should, however, carry over that sense of keeping a third eye openly trained upon the audience. Comic performance, even at its most self-effacing, endeavours to shape or 'improve upon' the surfaces of real life toward several ends: clear framing of character and emotional state within a situation; management of pace and rhythm so as to pull the audience along without leaving them behind; shuffling of expectation and surprise; and clean springing of the psychic traps of reversal. This process, as I have suggested, differs according to whether a single performer is in full charge, or two or more performers share the onus of orchestration.

We observed in Chapter 1 a 'craftedness' to the dialogue in the opening scene of Molière's *Scapin the Schemer*. One character asks a series of questions to which the other responds in short affirmative or repetitive answers. The pattern appears too purposeful to be taken for natural conversation, and that is one of the reasons we know to check for comic intent. The passage resembles a *lazzo* in its clear provision of a detachable comic routine. As such, we should imagine a well-rehearsed workmanship to the sequence, two performers working in concert for optimum rhythm and precision.

We can perceive comic rhythm in its larger shapes by identifying a build-up of momentum to a climactic punchline. The screen scene from Sheridan's *The School for Scandal*, part of which we looked at in the preceding chapter, shows things getting increasingly uncomfortable for Joseph Surface. His machinations are unravelling rapidly, and with Sir Peter and Charles Surface inconveniently on hand, he has gone downstairs to get rid of yet another unwanted visitor. Sir Peter's wife's presence behind the dressing screen is thus far known only to Joseph, who has told him it is 'a little French milliner' waiting to resume a dalliance with him. Implored by Joseph not to disclose her presence, Sir Peter naturally does, and then realizes Joseph will return imminently:

> CHARLES   Behind the screen! Odds life, let's unveil her!
> SIR PETER   No, no – he's coming – you shan't indeed!
> CHARLES   Oh, egad, we'll have a peep at the little milliner!
> SIR PETER   Not for the world! – Joseph will never forgive me.
> CHARLES   I'll stand by you –
> SIR PETER   Odds, here he is!
> [JOSEPH *enters just as* CHARLES *throws down the screen*]
> CHARLES   Lady Teazle – by all that's wonderful!
> SIR PETER   Lady Teazle, by all that's damnable![42]

This is but the crowning stretch of comic opportunity in a scene during which, as Katharine Worth says, 'every opportunity for hiding, being hidden and overhearing has been exploited to the full'.[43] Over its course Joseph parries each new threat to his respectable image and self-serving aims. A full reading of the scene (Act IV, Scene iii) is necessary to gain full appreciation of the internal orchestration of each subsequence, between the arrival of one character and the next, and the rhythmic pauses taken for Joseph and the spectator to catch their breaths and review the state of play. Sheridan offers up a comic shell game composed of variety, expectation, surprise and discomfort stretched deliciously and then suddenly deferred or reversed.[44] The playwright has implied a rush of emotional and physical activity to ensure a topping comic high point to the scene: Charles and Sir Peter appear to be engaged in an escalating tussle about whether they should look behind the screen, and on the point of Joseph's re-entrance, Charles throws down the screen. Lady Teazle is at last exposed – no doubt in a momentary freeze to put a neat button on the onstage action – the disclosure we have been dreading and hoping for since Sir Peter's entrance. The complementary exclamations by Charles and Sir Peter reflect this ambivalence in the spectator, and the mischievous Charles rides the wave with a further wisecrack: 'Sir Peter, this is one of the smartest French milliners I ever saw. Egad, you seem all to have been diverting yourselves here at hide and seek, and I don't see who is out of the secret.'[45] The insightful reader will recognize the importance this physical flurry and sudden stillness play in organizing the comic enactment, in the way, perhaps, that a literary writer uses paragraphing and subchapters to organize a different kind of reading experience. Let us recognize, in anticipation of our next topic, how Joseph, Lady Teazle and Sir Peter are decidedly omitted from any sense of the comic about their situation, while Charles appears to derive an amusement which serves as a bridge to the spectator's experience.

In the preceding chapter I asserted that a joke made by one person to another anticipates the more complex humorous transaction between stage and audience. This notion is worth looking into a bit further, because of an ambiguity inherent in the several cross-functional levels upon which the fictional stage world and its actual embodiment unfold.

In his essay on 'Humour' (1927), Freud contends that the joking trans-action follows one of two models:

> It may take place in regard to a single person, who himself adopts the humorous attitude, while a second person plays the part of the spec-tator who derives enjoyment from it; or it may take place between two persons, of whom one takes no part at all in the humorous process, but is made the object of humorous contemplation by the other.[46]

In the first model, all the ramifications of the moment are acknowledged between the two people involved in the transaction; not so in the second, in which the initiator and spectator find amusement at the expense of the 'object of humorous contemplation' or butt of the joke. The first model suggests collusion between joke teller and listener; the second implies some sort of exclusion. Although all jokes are made at someone or something's expense (even if it doesn't seem like it), this model can be seen to describe the difference between 'laughing with' and 'laughing at'.

The first model generally induces a feeling of involvement or equal footing between the joking entity – whether a character or the whole stage world – and spectator ('laughing with'); the second ('laughing at'), tends to urge a more observational, judgemental slant, the playwright and production complicit with the reader/spectator at the expense of the stage world or its inhabitant(s).

Traditional comic style most often parallels the second model, in which humorous implication is launched over the heads of the characters. A character may have 'awareness' of making a joke at another's expense or at the expense of society, culture, or human nature. But comic convention usually dictates that the joke's butt – which may be one or more of the characters, or their entire 'world' – exhibits insufficient or indirect awareness that a potentially humorous act has taken place. In preceding examples, we are invited to laugh at Lady Wishfort and David Brent, who, within the confines of their worlds, show no awareness that they may be held up to ridicule (and should not, according to comic wisdom).

Characters do, of course, acknowledge that a joke has been made or that something laughable has occurred, which we saw in Griffiths's *Comedians* in the preceding chapter. In that case we saw the characters acknowledge the joke by withholding laughter, which may or may not turn them into objects of humorous contemplation for the playwright and the spectator. I noted at the time that the play takes serious issue with comedy. It is, in fact, in more serious stage worlds that, when a joke is made or humour perceived, the characters are likely to acknowledge it, approximating the first of Freud's models. One can, in any case, see how a range of subtleties in the relationships between stage world, individual characters and audience can be calibrated by writer and practitioner.

Comic pairing

The comic team or double act bases its humour strategies on the dialogue (verbal or non-verbal), and usually features that blend of cooperation and precision prescribed in this chapter's section on 'Reading comic dialogue (*lazzi*)'. A crucial element offered by the two-performer configuration lies in relationship. Oppositions between personality and status supply vital hues to the joking transaction.

Commedia dell'arte historians and practitioners classify comic servants as either a *First Zanni* or *Second Zanni*. The *First Zanni* occupies a primary place in the plotting, a throwback to the 'witty slave' of Roman times who takes the lead in scheming; the *Second Zanni* is more likely to be the comic foil, the slower or more innocent of the two. The comedy team or double act, as represented on the variety stage and in film and television, has in notable instances carried through this dynamic in double acts like Laurel and Hardy, Abbott and Costello, and Peter Cook and Dudley Moore. Our musings in this chapter should make sense of the inclination for double acts to avail themselves of contrasts in nature and physicality, an inclination which, perhaps carries out an ongoing interrogation of balance in the human condition.

Comic pairs abound in dramatic texts, from Sir Toby Belch and Sir Andrew Aguecheek in Shakespeare's *Twelfth Night* to Felix Ungar and Oscar Madison in Neil Simon's *The Odd Couple* (1965; reborn for a female cast with the characters' names as Florence and Olive in 1985). In light of these considerations, how might we visualize Don Juan and Sganarelle, for example, Zangler and Melchior in *On the Razzle*, and Dionysos and Xanthias in *The Frogs*? It is worth thinking about the hypothetical dynamic of these and other pairings in concrete terms. Again, it is interesting and entirely useful to imagine known actors in the roles, perhaps even auditioning various combinations in the mind, because it contributes a crucial shade of actuality even to an armchair reading.

Conflict supplies a universal fuel for drama, and conflict or competition remains a common premise for comic enactment. I have remarked upon the classic comic tandem of master and servant, which thrived on a perpetual cycle of beating and trickery. In the way that problem-solving provides an active paradigmatic thrust for a single comic performer, comic conflict between two characters often takes the form of a battle of wits or one-upmanship. As a dramatic figure, it parallels a tennis match in the equal parts of aggression and gamesmanship. The serve-and-volley pattern has comparable implications for the spectator watching from the theatre seat.

Ever a popular template for two or more clowns, we can look to early screen comedy for expressly physical manifestations of this pattern (see the box on page 123). Laurel and Hardy enjoin any number of tit-for-tat exchanges throughout their films, though two of the more celebrated sequences provide variations: the duo, as a team, engage James Finlayson in the escalating destruction of a house and automobile in *Big Business* (1929); and the two initiate the greatest pie fight ever filmed in *Battle of the Century* (1927). Of course, in animated cartoons, where physical possibility is not constrained by the laws of biology or physics, Bugs Bunny and Daffy Duck have had classic confrontations, sometimes welcoming Elmer Fudd into the fray. Tom and Jerry serve as the cat-and-mouse original for *The Simpsons*' Itchy and Scratchy, who go well beyond the usual bloodless resiliency of slapstick, thereby lampooning the very comic model we are discussing.

A brilliant adaptation of this comic pattern in physical terms can be found in the beating competition from Aristophanes' *The Frogs*, which follows on from a scene cited in the previous chapter. You may recall that Dionysos and his slave, Xanthias, are following in the footsteps of Herakles, who seems to have left bad feelings on his journey to the underworld. Aiakos the gate-keeper – via a series of loopy logical steps – intends to beat each one in turn until one of them betrays the pain which would mark him as a non-deity. He hits Xanthias first:

> AIAKOS   There.
> XANTHIAS   Ready when you are.
> AIAKOS   I've just hit you.
> XANTHIAS   You're joking.
> AIAKOS   *I* see. His turn, then. [He hits Dionysos.]
> DIONYSOS   Get on with it.
> AIAKOS   I've done it.
> DIONYSOS   I'd have felt the draught.
> AIAKOS   Back to the other one.
> XANTHIAS   Ready when you – hoo!
> AIAKOS   What d'you mean, yoohoo? Felt that, did you?
> XANTHIAS   Felt what? I was waving to the audience.[47]

We don't often find such a clever anticipation of verbal and physical comedy entwined built upon this pattern. In reading the above extract, we should recall that the mythic Dionysos is portrayed as somewhat less than heroic and that Xanthias is the conventionally put-upon yet sharp-witted slave. Aiakos gives the impression of a brawny sergeant-at-arms, who is not quite observant enough to notice the suppressed reactions to his beatings. We can see opportunity for the actors to confer great comic force upon his blows, then resolutely collect themselves for the denials. Here is where the art of reading comedy lies: recognizing something of the possibility for actualization of humour in performance, bred by the particularities of character response in a given situation. Such actualization may involve a gap between exterior enactment and (what we in the audience know to be) interior feeling or thought; a gap opened by character reactions (physical and/or verbal) which appear too quick, too slow or otherwise incommensurate with the situation; quirky or extravagant use of the performing body or spectacular cooperation between bodies; and the potential for rhythmic enhancement of humour's workings.

The tit-for-tat comic template at its most basic taps directly into humour's playful-aggressive impulse, and in dramatic texts its attacks are more likely to take verbal form. It bears a *lazzo*-like facility for ubiquitous incorporation, and remains another one of those staple templates for situation comedy on television. More often than not, it appears as a sequence of alternating insults. Here are the well-known verbal jousters and reluctant lovers, Beatrice and Benedick from Shakespeare's *Much Ado About Nothing* (1598), in their very first exchange:

> BEATRICE   I wonder that you will still be talking, Signior Benedick.
>   Nobody marks you.
> BENEDICK   What, my dear Lady Disdain! are you yet living?[48]

There is, of course, much missing from this exchange, with regard to how much actual venom, sarcasm or flirtation goes into each salvo. The interplay between these characters is rendered in prose, the language of clowning, held to foster a more down-to-earth and impromptu feel than the verse-speaking of most Shakespearean romances. But the pattern is as up to date as the latest romantic comedy from Hollywood. It may reflect something about the psychic anxieties accompanying deep affection that would-be (or will-again) lovers have often been launched into this kind of comic combat. The humorous sparring in plays like Aphra Behn's *The Rover* (1677), Noel Coward's *Private Lives* (1930), and David Mamet's *Boston Marriage* (1999) can turn sharp. But we read through it a common human ambivalence toward objects of affection, as if our egos struggle to retain dominance over deep feelings in spite of ourselves.

Tit-for-tat sequences are not, of course, limited to sublimated or mis-directed amorousness. In a cultural context like Restoration England, the gatherings of high society become public arenas in which standing is won through contests of wit, recalling age-old traditions of competitive verbal abuse like *flyting*. We can see a tongue-in-cheek version of this pattern in some of the dialogue between Cecily and Gwendolen in *The Importance of Being Earnest*, especially when they both believe themselves engaged to Ernest (when, in fact, their respective suitors both happen to call themselves Ernest):

GWENDOLEN   . . . I am so sorry, dear Cecily, if it is any disappoint-ment to you, but I am afraid I have the prior claim.

CECILY   It would distress me more than I can tell you, dear Gwendolen, if it caused you any mental or physical anguish, but I feel bound to point out that since Ernest proposed to you he clearly has changed his mind.

GWENDOLEN   [*meditatively*] If the poor fellow has been entrapped into any foolish promise I shall consider it my duty to rescue him at once, and with a firm hand.

CECILY   [*thoughtfully and sadly*] Whatever unfortunate entangle-ment my dear boy may have got into, I will never reproach him with it after we are married.[49]

This version of the alternating pattern opens its humorous gap by opposing the emotional stakes inherent in such an argument with a more-civilized-than-thou competition. The bodies, owing to propriety and lin-guistic authority, likely incline toward control. In an opposite direction lie Martin McDonagh's warring brothers Valene and Coleman in *The Lonesome West* (1997). The Connor brothers live together in close-quarter dysfunction on the west coast of Ireland. Father Welsh, the parish priest, has been conversing with Coleman, when Valene arrives with a few new religious figurines for his prized collection:

VALENE   Fibreglass.
COLEMAN   [*pause*] Feck fibreglass.
VALENE   No, feck you instead of feck fibreglass.
COLEMAN   No, feck you two times instead of feck fibreglass . . .
WELSH   Hey now!! [*Pause*] Jesus![50]

The tit-for-tat pattern is reduced to the barely articulate bickering of foul-mouthed children, and it is, perhaps, a good part of the joke that the dia-logue is placed in the mouths of grown men. The hostility between the brothers will ultimately turn violent, and their bitter contention over the most mundane of subjects is what stands to give the play its sardonically comic tone. In this case, there can be little question of the open rancour with which the retorts are intended.

This sequence also offers another reminder to look for rhythm on the page. We can see the increase in words, line by line, as well as the playwright's advice for pausing. The risible squabble takes place in front of the hapless clergyman, who nips it in the bud and goes on himself to blaspheme. These bodies are not self-aware like the ones in the scene from *The Importance of Being Earnest*, and may not be able to bridle their antagonism or, indeed, refrain from presenting a pugnacious physical posture.

The idea, ultimately, is not to presume the ability to predict exactly what the bodies will do, but only to remember that they are there, and that they shoulder their own responsibilities and offer their own possibilities to advance comic effect.

Comic metaphysics

Peter L. Berger tells us 'the comic conjures up a *separate world*, different from the world of ordinary reality, operating by different rules'.[51] Comic worlds, as we have seen, render the world playfully, which in bodied terms means a simultaneous loosening and refashioning of life's metaphysical fabric. This propensity in some regard defies generalization – comic worlds shift as needs arise for purposes of surprise and incongruity. There are, however, a handful of comic-leaning principles which bear keeping in mind, ways in which a mental image of performance technique supports better reading.

Metaphysical caprice

Repetition of utterances, gestures, or situations appears to jar with our sense of life's natural fluidity. Bergson in his essay on 'Laughter' (1900) famously claimed that we tend to laugh at '[s]omething mechanical encrusted on the living'.[52] We know through an instinctual sense of being in the world that the endless river of changing circumstances militates against anything happening *exactly* the same way twice (or more), and so the use of repetition in an artistic depiction toys with our bodied knowledge of the world.

The opening of *Scapin the Schemer* (from Chapter 1) pointedly repeats the dialogic pattern of rhetorical query and short response a number of times, leading to the constructed feel which makes us suspect comic intent. In the last act of *A Little Hotel on the Side*, Pinglet has nearly and miraculously escaped being caught out when Mathieu shows up, the one person who would inadvertently incriminate him. Pinglet keeps trying to push Mathieu out of the room, but he bounces right back, recalling the jack-in-the-box, another metaphor invoked by Bergson.[53]

A short step sideways leads to the informally termed Rule of Three, which remains an ingrained rhythm for comic metaphysics: a series of two actions, utterances or units of information sets up a third, which somehow supplies a reversal. Many a joke will describe three people (of differing nationalities, religions or drinking preferences, with the order depending on the stereotypical behaviour being ridiculed) entering a bar, or send a man to the doctor three times. It is easy to see that this 'rule' comes about because a sequence of three is the shortest series in which a pattern can be established and then broken. In the opening of *The Suicide*, which we treated in Chapter 1, the same basic sequence plays through twice, in which Semyon wakes up his wife, she screams, and he has to calm her down. The reader is right to suspect that, when Semyon tries to wake her the third time, he will get to ask what he wants or there will otherwise be some resolution. Sure enough Masha answers, 'No', the next time he asks if she is asleep, and he makes his deflating request about the liver sausage. There is a third scream shortly after the above section, but this time it's from Semyon, who has fallen asleep during a speech in which Masha chastizes him for his self-centredness. In fact, the whole 'What's wrong' pattern is then repeated with the roles reversed, a bonus exploitation of the sequence which should still be in the spectator's mind.

It is also unlikely, in the flow of real events, that identical actions will occur at exactly the same time (and this, perhaps, is related to comedy's propensity for coincidence noted in the previous chapter). Toward the climax of Goldoni's *The Servant of Two Masters*, two desolate lovers attempt to hang themselves at the same time on opposite sides of the stage. Theatrical convention allows such events to happen within close physical proximity, while in this case selective disattention fortuitously prevents them from seeing one another until dramatically (or comically) desirable. The desperate act is undertaken by the two characters with unlikely simultaneity, while genre convention and, no doubt, comic outlining assure us that they will be interrupted just in time.

It is easy to find explicit traces of repetition and simultaneity in dramatic texts, as I have done here. But, as clowning and physical-comedy patterns, they need not be confined to verbal construction. It is possible to infer them in non-verbal sequences and beneath scripted dialogue, as they may be so discovered in the rehearsal room. Repetition or simultaneity in gesture and tone might well find its way into the staging for the above scenes from *The Importance of Being Earnest* and *The Lonesome West.*

The comic body

In the second act of *A Little Hotel on the Side*, the farcical hero, Pinglet, is standing against a hotel-room wall, on the verge of consummating an illicit relationship with the lovely Marcelle, his neighbour's wife. Outside the room, the voyeuristic hotel desk assistant has taken a hand drill to the wall in the hope of gaining a peephole upon their activities. Comic coincidence places the drill's point of entry at the precise location of Pinglet's backside. As the drill makes progress (all according to stage directions), several verbal exchanges elapse before anything like pain registers upon Pinglet – he seems vaguely uncertain as to what is going on down there. Under real-world conditions, one would know soon enough and register quite sharply if this fantastically unfortunate coincidence had occurred.

The comic body gains humorous effect by appearing to be made from stuff other than the expected organic materials. Eric Bentley considers farce 'the theatre of the surrealist body',[54] but this description applies to many a comic world outside those formal confines. The comic body in performance is capable of changing qualities without warning, purely at the whim of comic convenience. It recomposes the laws of nature, skews physical sensation, and, as intimated in the above example, stretches or shrinks reaction times (see the box on page 130). This is an area in which the theatre performer's athleticism, agility and precision create the effect. In the modern age, tricks of film-making and post-production stand to assist the body's natural abilities, and in a literary text like Rabelais' *Gargantua and Pantagruel* (*La Vie de Gargantua et de Pantagruel*, 1532–64), the reader's imagination gives form to the physically impossible sight gag.

A large category of physical comedy follows from the potential for comic violence, whether in tit-for-tat conflicts, master/slave interludes, or the inadvertent kind described above. 'Slapstick' is a term usually applied to comic violence. It refers to the prop paddle once used in music hall and vaudeville, which made a sharp crack upon contact with a victim, and derives from the wooden bat once used by clowns to administer comic blows. For some people the word has come to refer to something more than that, usually any kind of broad or physical comedy. Slapstick violence is a mode of performance humour which, in its conventional guise, denies or distorts the real-life implications of physical aggression and bodily harm, featuring motivation, effervescence and resiliency and, as I've noted, silly substitutions for biological accuracy. (Animated worlds have a particular advantage in this regard, in that bodies are capable of anything a cartoonist can draw as well as immediate recovery; we should note further the part that sound effects play in augmenting cartoon comedy.)

Comic reactions

A 'take' is actor's jargon for a reactive look or gesture intended to register or emphasize some comic point. A 'double take' bases itself on a delayed reaction: one version has the actor look in the direction of some unlikely sight, turn back to business as if there is nothing irregular to note, then suddenly register the vision, jerking his head to look again, finally 'seeing' it. A variation places an intermediary take to the audience, as if to ask, 'Could I really have seen that?', before confirming the unexpected sight. A character may also display a delayed or prolonged response – sometimes called a 'slow burn' – in which a realization dawns later or more gradually than seems warranted by circumstances (e.g., his trousers are on fire or there's a goat in the room). Vintage examples of these types of comic reactions appear in the films of Laurel and Hardy: Stan Laurel (the skinny one) specialized in the double take, Oliver Hardy (the fat one) in the slow burn. Daffy Duck and Wile E. Coyote are also quite good at these.

It should be noted that these comic conventions do not arise from thin air, but anchor themselves in the fact that lags in sensory processing do occur in humans. We might, for example, have to look at something a second time to confirm that we've seen what we think we've seen, especially when concentrating on something else. These reactions represent a prime strategy of the comic body: the projection of a whimsical disjunction between inner and outer tracks of human behaviour as we know it.

The ability to regulate the pace at which a gag is sprung for the purpose of gaining maximum effect is a skill (some would say an instinct) we call 'timing'. Maurice Charney says: 'Comedy works in time (or duration), and timing is the high art of controlling the passage of time, either speeding it up or slowing it down for some calculated purpose.'[55]

The prospects of the comic body may be the least evident of all elements in a play script, and the highly competent reader of comedy comes to recognize promising textual conditions for physicalized humour, even when they are not prescribed by stage directions. This chapter has pointed to the *commedia dell' arte* as an historical source for comic outlining and performance patterns, which surely remain embedded in our cultural notions of body. In the next chapter we shall see how comic patterns, verbal and physical, have affected stage worlds beyond the conventional reaches of comedy.

Chapter 5

Comedy's range

Dramatic texture and the comic

We have in the past two chapters surveyed signatures of the comic across time and text. We have also observed some general principles of humour and comic performance upon which they might be based. This should not be taken to imply a sameness in all worlds with comic lineage. To the contrary, every world incorporating the comic harbours a singular feeling, owing to its precise mix and use of elements. An essential project of this chapter is to direct the reader toward a more discerning apprehension of the stage world as a whole, and the ways in which comic elements interact with their worldly settings.

We discussed in Chapter 1 the complex means by which we read the world of a work into existence from the page of a novel or play, and the super-abundant scope for expression of which genre framing is capable. Each of the dramatic texts to which I have thus far referred in the name of comedy proffers a weave of its own, differentiating itself at a textual level through the specific mingling of historical theatre convention, surrounding culture, theme, tone and the playwright's creative infusion. (There remains, of course, a further indefinable range of meaning and feeling, prior to con-cretization in actual performance, the comic implications of which I will discuss at the end of this chapter.) So, although I have in recent chapters been at pains to demonstrate the ways in which aspects of comic texts resemble one another, I would now like to shift the emphasis from the universal to the specific, thereby considering the ways in which a text as topographical blueprint is always something entirely its own.

This avenue of investigation implies the need for a completed reading of the text. In fact a second full reading is desirable, so that any given comic ingredient can be gauged within an overarching awareness of the stage world's contours. Reflect upon the four manifestations of tit-for-tat comic structure sampled in the preceding chapter (*The Frogs*, *Much Ado About Nothing*, *The Importance of Being Earnest* and *The Lonesome West*) in the broader context of the plays. Think about the dialectic between these comic sequences and the textual 'personalities' of their respective worlds. How does the use of language inform comic performance in each case? How about the nature and tone of relationship? What part does a third character (or lack thereof) play in the sequence? How does sociocultural context commission and shade the comic work?

We should also ask how the various endings of the plays reflect back upon the quality of humour in these extracts. A full reading of *The Lonesome West*, for example, reveals an actual tit-for-tat drive to the stage world in the brothers' perpetual cycle of cruel and petty one-upmanship. Violence and death grin perversely upon the world of this play, with gags about the brutal conduct of the local under-twelves girls' football team placed alongside the offstage suicide of the troubled Father Welsh. This is comedy late-twentieth-century style, cynical and close to the bone, and its particular manifestation in these slyly vicious brothers gives us something palpable to apply to the short early extract cited in Chapter 4. Having identified textbook comic constructions within plays like *The Suicide, Hysteria* and *Absurd Person Singular,* we should now observe that each of these textual fabrics exhibits darker, troubling or uncertain threads. All of them provide something quite removed from the symbolic marriage classically associated with comedy's conclusion. The practised reader comes to look at the complexity of every text's weave, and the practised reader of comedy comes to contemplate the potential effects in and by the comic elements for a multi-layered stage world.

The comic and the tragic

Comedy amid tragedy

Bad things have always happened in comedy, as malicious acts and outrageous misfortunes are visited upon its favoured inhabitants. In conventional comic worlds the light shines at such an angle as to obscure darker implications and cast a sunny sheen over life after the final curtain. Bentley nonetheless recognizes the sobering pull of comedy's elemental subject matter: 'The tone says: life is fun. The undertone suggests that life is a catastrophe.'[1]

Let us now consider the effects of that thematic ballast in more detail, as we move on to those stage worlds that are not so buoyant and forgiving, and in which life's disappointment and brutality cannot be kept at arm's length. We might begin by acknowledging how tragedy sometimes imports the comic for temporary relief, to stretch the tension and to augment its argument.

In Sophocles' *Antigone* (*c.* 442 BC) the inexorable march toward tragedy begins with the title character's burial of her brother – a personal act of public defiance, given the new king Creon's edict against such respect for a fallen enemy. It is relatively early in the play: Antigone has announced her unhesitating intention to honour her brother's remains, knowing full well that the act invites a death sentence. Creon declares in lofty, uncompromising rhetoric that allegiance to the state is a paramount obligation for all subjects, and that Polynices' fall as head of a foreign army merits the formal disgrace of non-burial.

Into this mounting clash of wills comes a Soldier (called Sentry or Guard in some translations), to announce that Polynices' body has indeed been given a respectful covering by the unidentified hand we know to be Antigone's. This Soldier, however, displays every bit the opposite of heroic stature and dutiful resolve we come to expect from the denizens of tragedy, betraying an everyman's instinct for self-preservation:

> My Lord Creon . . . sir! If I can hardly speak
> For lack of breath . . . it's not 'cos I ran . . .
> I kept on stopping, as a matter of fact,
> Half a dozen times, and I hung about
> As much as I dared. I haven't thought about anything
> So much for a long time. 'Listen, don't hurry,'
> I said to myself, 'the chances are,
> Poor sod, you'll cop it when you get there.'
> But then I said to myself, you see,
> 'Hang about,' I said, 'or rather, don't,
> Because if Creon hears this from somebody else,
> You're really in trouble.' So I hurried here
> As slow as I could, going round and round
> In circles, in my head, as well as with my feet![2]

The Soldier's report is usually translated in this type of vernacular register. His exceedingly candid admission of fear cracks open a comic window, jarring with the loftier tragic mood and specifically with Creon's preceding pronouncement upon the contemptibility of a 'ruler who fears the consequences of his actions'.[3] Any given production will decide for itself how much rein should be given (if any) to the outright clowning pattern displayed in the hand-wringing vacillation contained in the words. But the passage slyly regulates the accumulation of tension, while presenting a more modestly human perspective upon Creon's wielding of authority.

In a similar way, the brutal world of Shakespeare's *Macbeth* (1606) pauses after the intensity of the first murder for the drunken Porter's comic commentary. Styan's book, *The Dark Comedy*, deals centrally with the intense pull by the comic upon the serious seen in twentieth-century drama (at least until 1968, when the second edition was published). He paves the way, however, with a tour of earlier Western theatre history, showing that the impulse has always been there, despite the comfort some people seem to find in advancing a sort of purity of generic feeling in comedy and tragedy.

Styan refers to the great Shakespearean tragedies when he emphasizes the projected impact of a carefully wrought dramatic fabric, including 'the many and detailed moments misleadingly called comic "relief", moments carefully thrust into the tragic action to make the pain the more acute'.[4] Making a point that is of utmost importance for our study, he reminds us that the full value of these scenes emerges from the playwright's well-judged anticipation of fluid and immediate production:

> These patterns are especially likely to be missed in reading: in per-formance we become immediately aware that a scene in Shakespearean tragedy is written always as a stage in the cumulative extortion of feeling from an audience, a well-planned turning of the screw.[5]

Although Styan here is discussing Shakespeare in the context of Eliza-bethan staging conditions like the neutral stage and close proximity of the audience, I would hold that it bears relevance for skilled playwrights throughout Western theatre history.

Medieval drama took its religion-based remit seriously. Nonetheless, the morality play, *Everyman* (*c.* 1520), harbours humorous potential in exposing the superficiality in much of what we think anchors our lives. Everyman, for example, tries first to buy his way out of Death's plans: 'Yea, a thousand pound shalt thou have, / And defer this matter till another day.'[6] Despite the archaic speech it is easy to read several kinds of comic character into this utterance (one of which could include a suggestion of the twenty-first-century business executive, who attempts to brush away the intrusion on his or her high-powered schedule). Everyman eventually reconciles himself to his fate. It then becomes clear that, for all the fair-weather avowals of soli-darity from those who surround him, none of these people are prepared to offer meaningful support on the journey to meet his maker:

EVERYMAN   My Cousin, will you not with me go?
COUSIN   No, by our Lady! I have the cramp in my toe.[7]

This laughably unworthy excuse benefits further from the neatness of its simple rhyme. Bergson tells us that 'laughter aims at correcting',[8] and what better way to impress a serious sense of spiritual duty than by humorous chastisement? We find it used similarly in the medieval English mystery plays, day-long cycles of Bible stories enacted throughout towns like Chester and York from the late 1300s for the next two hundred years. In *The Killing of Abel*, the aggressive irreverence of Cain and his servant boy directed straight to the audience ridicules in advance the indolence and blasphemy against which God instructs.

From the Towneley cycle comes the broadly comic *Second Shepherd's Play*, which offers humorous banter between husband and wife, who then try to cover the presence of a stolen sheep in farcical manner by pretending it is their newborn baby bundled in its crib. The play provides a parodic parallel to the birth of Jesus, then puts joking aside to end on notes of grace and reverence appropriate to the sacred event. Styan reckons that in its historical context the comic transposition did nothing to diminish the holy message, nor could it be seen as pandering to a popular audience – on the contrary:

> In a divine order of things the incongruity of man's baseness and stupidity was part of the sacred pattern. The human world of littleness and sin is set on the same stage with the emblems of heaven, and is all part of the same story.[9]

In more recent times, Marina Carr applies comic inflection to selected characters in *By the Bog of Cats . . .* (1998), a play with more than an echo of the horrific tragedy seen in Euripides' *Medea* (431 BC). Here, like *Everyman*, the central character encounters a harbinger of death. Carr's Hester Swane, though, engages the so-called Ghost Fancier with an almost flirtatious scepticism ('So what do you do, Mr Ghost Fancier? Eye up ghosts? Have love affairs with them?').[10] In a short opening scene, the Ghost Fancier realizes he's arrived at sunrise rather than sunset ('Then I'm too previous. I mistook this hour for dusk. A thousand apologies'). We don't think of the Grim Reaper or his agents as vulnerable to such mortal displays of disorientation. Although Hester has entered the scene dragging '[*the corpse of a black swan after her*]', the tongue-in-cheek tone of this introductory dialogue denies the tragic portent a primary colour of feeling, tempering it with a sense of play.

Carr then charts a course in the opening pages of Act II through various registers imbued with the comic. Alone at the table, Catwoman, a village seer, conducts a rather whimsical interview with a waiter. His exit is overlapped by the ghost of Joseph Swane, '[*entering; bloodstained shirt and trousers, a throat wound*]'. Catwoman senses an other-worldly presence and, upon confirmation, says, 'Ah Christ, not another ghost.'[11] Her sense of mundane vexation, undercutting the gruesome visitation, frames an otherwise serious expositional scene with an aura of wryness. The tone stands to throw into relief the next scene's emotional gravity, a prenuptial interlude between Carthage – Hester's former lover and the father of her daughter – and his bride-to-be, hinting at insurmountable unease between them.

The character of Mrs Kilbride, Carthage's mother, is capable of bizarrely comic effect. She is drawn as an unkind and uncharitable woman, and takes out her hostility toward Hester upon her young granddaughter. A widow, she remains openly fixated on her son, arriving at the wedding feast dressed very much like a bride herself. Mrs Kilbride is so pleased with her new shoes that she can't resist photographing them, and then puts the finishing touches on her son's embarrassment – and the rest of the wedding party's discomfort – by delivering a toast which ends: 'And that if Carthage will be as good a son to Caroline as he's been a husband to me then she'll have no complaints'.[12] Mrs Kilbride's brittle pettiness allows for ready assignment to a comic league with the old men of the *commedia dell'arte*. As such she is a figure toward whom we would be inclined to accept an invitation to mockery. With all that has come before, her apparent obliviousness to any confusion in the wording of her toast makes for an unmistakable Freudian confession with an unsavoury backwash. We will note in the next chapter Frye's postulation that comedy is designed 'to ridicule a lack of self-knowledge'; in darker characters, such as Mrs Kilbride, there is a meatier bite to the derision.

The spotlight turns next upon Father Willow, the 80-year-old village clergyman. His loopy mix of absent-mindedness, confusion, and uncensored impulse shifts the humour register a few tones lighter. He has arrived at the dinner having celebrated Mass in his hat, with vestments inside out and pyjamas visible beneath his trousers. He has been invited to say grace:

FATHER WILLOW	In the name of the Father and of the Son and of the Holy Ghost, it may or may not surprise yees all if I tould yees I was almost a groom meself wance. Her name was Elizabeth Kennedy, no that was me mother's name, her name was – it'll come to me, anyway it wasn't to be, in the end we fell out over a duck egg on a walkin' holiday by the Shannon, what was her name at all? Helen? No.
MRS KILBRIDE	Would ya say the grace, Father Willow, and be –
FATHER WILLOW	The grace, yes, how does it go again?
MRS KILBRIDE	Bless us, oh Lord, and these thy gifts which of –
FATHER WILLOW	Rowena. That was it. Rowena Phelan. I should never have ate that duck egg – no – [*Stands there lost in thought.*]
	[*Enter Hester in her wedding dress, veil, shoes, the works*][13]

The meanderings of Father Willow's mind steer the mood toward all-purpose amusement – an elderly, forgetful priest, whose regard of women appears to exceed a clergyman's proper contemplation – serving as set-up for a jarring appearance by Hester. The feeling of an irresistible move toward tragedy may recede substantially during this passage, setting up what may qualify as the inverse of comic reversal with the sudden image of Hester's party-crashing. The set-up involves an overall lightness of mood which is suddenly reversed by *withdrawing* the humorous attitude – a powerful tempering of emotion foreseen by the playwright.

The primary argument of this chapter is that, insofar as every dramatic text proffers its own field of thought and feeling, the inclusion of comic elements informs that field in meaningful ways. A play like *By the Bog of Cats* . . . is not just a tragedy with humorous bits added. Comically tinged characters and moods make it a different world from the one that it would be without them – they augment the affective range of the stage world as well as its thematic impact. Styan reminds us: 'The unity of a play is not to be conceived narrowly as a matter of forms, as unity of "action", but as a final tone and climate, a "fourth" unity in which opposites may flourish together in the audience's mind.'[14] Rather than the less authoritative alternative to serious discourse it is often held to be, the comic remains an effective tool for illumination and impact in its own right, and has a powerful contribution to make to the resonance of tragic worlds.

Tragicomedy: it is easy to find dramatic texts throughout Western theatre history in which the comic intrudes upon or supports the tragic, as in the examples shown above. No one would think of *Antigone*, *Macbeth* or *By the Bog of Cats* . . . as anything other than tragedies, even though we have been able to identify textual traces of humour used to regulate feeling and enrich thematic resonance. In other cases, however, tragic and comic elements mingle to confound easy classification as one or the other.

The term 'tragicomedy' generally refers, as one would expect, to a text that bears a coalition of the component genres. Bentley sanctions use of the label in two veins, the first of which is 'tragedy with a happy ending', the second, not surprisingly, 'comedy with an unhappy ending',[15] though we will discover this description to be more tidy than useful. Styan warns against stodgy adherence to labels that limit the full breadth of what an inspired dramatic concoction can accomplish. For him, 'a play may legitimately refuse to be a failed tragedy or a failed comedy – because the response it wants may be of neither kind, and the forms and conventions it uses may bear no relation to either'.[16] Indeed, we will see later in this chapter that, for many a twentieth-century text, Bentley's neatly symmetrical formulation appears all too naïve.

We should also keep in mind that any effect of tragic and comic elements is provisional, prior to actual choices made in production. It is easy to tip the see-saw one way or the other, and even to change its orientation through outlining – and we will discuss briefly the ability to 'season' a stage world in this chapter's final section.

For now, let's concentrate on the interplay of textual elements that may make a play difficult to categorize. We have discussed comedy in terms of its propensity to deal in the common details of everyday life, in opposition to the greater consequence of tragedy's business. Albert Cook, in laying out his own philosophy of comedy, offers another way to look at these tensions. Cook associates realms of comedy with the 'probable' and tragedy with the 'non-probable' or 'wonderful'.[17] These designations assist us in distinguishing an accumulated weight from specific textual features like humour or 'ending in death'. They therefore help us talk about the interpenetration of elements in worlds which invite the tragicomic label.

Shakespeare's *Measure for Measure* (1604) can be a play about many things, including sex, morality and justice. Angelo, the Viennese deputy temporarily in command, has invoked a disused city law to sentence young Claudio to death for sexual immorality – Claudio has got his intended wife with child prior to marriage. Claudio's sister Isabella, a novice nun, goes to Angelo to plead for her brother's life. Angelo ultimately tells her that her brother's only hope for clemency lies in her agreement to become his lover.

It is possible to imagine such a situation treated comically by, say, Plautus, especially because Isabella manages to sidestep the deal through trickery *and* her brother eventually avoids execution and marries his beloved. A short sample of the text's emotional register, however, shows little room for lightness. Isabella's high poetic dudgeon incurs an indisputable seriousness; nor does her brother, Claudio, speak like a traditional comic coward:

> CLAUDIO   Sweet sister, let me live.
> What sin you do to save a brother's life,
> Nature dispenses with the deed so far
> That it becomes a virtue.
> ISABELLA   O you beast,
> O faithless coward, O dishonest wretch!
> Wilt thou be made a man out of my vice?
> Is't not a kind of incest, to take life
> From thine own sister's shame?[18]

Isabella claims her moral high ground with the iron resolve of an Antigone, a Hester Swayne, or any other character touched by Cook's sense of the 'wonderful', giving the world a feeling of deadly seriousness.

The Duke precipitates the events of the play by purporting to take temporary leave of his domain, returning in disguise to observe the goings-on. We might argue that the world of the play is always under comic protection because of the Duke's surveillance, but the eventual survival of Claudio and endings in marriage are never foregone conclusions (and prove unsatisfying for some readers/spectators). Isabella preserves her virtue by submitting to an assignation, then secretly substituting a former lover of Angelo's under cover of darkness.

Disguise and trickery are common comic devices, but are not here employed for the usual purpose of gulling or humorous confusion. We have clowns and fools (Pompey, Froth and Elbow) transposing the issue of womanly virtue to a lower key, but all in the shadow of a hypocritical and unscrupulous villain who raises the stakes of this world well above the bar conventionally set for comedy. Styan says:

> In this profound and constantly engrossing play, Shakespeare compels us to weigh in one scale the meaning of life, as illuminated by death both tragic and comic, against, in the other, the meaning of 'honour', as illuminated by lechery both tragic and comic; then he coolly asks us whether it is God or man who holds the scales.[19]

To be sure, the probable and wonderful deliver striking visions of life, but there is value to the breadth of feeling bred by their compounding. Styan identifies the 'dark comic attitude' particularly descriptive of much Western drama beginning with Ibsen, Strindberg and Chekhov. It represents a cutting down to size of deep feeling and purpose, once thought proper only for gods and royals. There are, after all, momentous consequences within each and every life, sweeping implications arising from ordinary actions: 'The hero of twentieth-century dark comedy is the character who makes the grand speech, but who has to clear his throat and scratch his nose.'[20] This is Styan's way of branding central characters like Madame Ranevskaya in Chekhov's *The Cherry Orchard* (1904), so as to acknowledge heroine and fool in the same being, visible from different angles of dramatic perception.

The point here, is not to be lulled into simplifying the texture of a world or the significance of a character according to rigid formulations. The fluid mixture of probable and wonderful may breed a more encompassing reflection of life on the ground. There is more often than not a push and pull between comic and tragic poles, a weave made from familiar devices and patterns, but modulated by a totality of influences deriving from those orientations. The psychic tousle between these dramatic modes, however, sinks its tendrils far deeper into our bodied lives when death gains entry upon the scene.

The deadly serious treated playfully

In the past century or so we find stage worlds with light and dark elements interwoven, to the extent that it becomes difficult to disentangle one from the other. It generates an affective action Albert Bermel calls 'comic agony', which 'brings an experience of sacrifice or suffering into harmony – or, more likely, collision – with an experience of triumph and uplift'.[21] Literary texts like Kurt Vonnegut's *Slaughterhouse Five* (1969), television series like *The Sopranos* (1999–2007), and films like *M*A*S*H* (1970) represent a certain species of comic agony, in which death and violence mix freely with and even spawn humour.

Freud assigns humour (as distinct from jokes and wit) the explicit task of protecting the emotions: 'the super-ego tries, by means of humour, to console the ego and protect it from suffering'.[22] By way of example, he cites the story about a 'rogue' being led out to execution on a Monday morning and remarking, 'Well, this week's beginning nicely.' One can broadly suppose that the doomed man's incongruously cheerful pronouncement denies mortality the weight of its imminence – his life force rallies feeling, mind and body to an act of psychic defiance, even in the shadow of the gallows.

As alluded to above with regard to the extract from *The Lonesome West*, the pitch-dark comedy particular to recent stage, film and television reflects a super-thickening of the Western skin toward injustice and dehumanization. We are invited to find amusement not only in the negligence with which life, body and civilized values are treated, but in its joking manner of blithe disregard. The humour boasts its lack of feeling, and its edge may be too jagged for some readers/spectators.

Ben Elton's *Popcorn* (1996) demonstrates vividly the use of a common comic stratagem in which serious or urgent circumstances are undercut by intrusion from the trivial or mundane. Unlike conventional comedy and farce, this stage world deals seriously in pain, blood and death. The play, in fact, addresses just that culture of violence in our streets, our newscasts and our popular entertainment that prompts questions about where the cycle among them finds its impetus. In the play, Bruce Delamitri, a Hollywood film director, fancies himself quite the artistic interrogator of psycho-cultural dysfunction. His film about a latter-day Bonnie and Clyde's sex- and drug-fuelled murder spree has been nominated for an Academy Award. He wins the Oscar and brings home Brooke, a *Playboy* model, to celebrate. The award is already controversial, as his work has drawn accusations that, whatever its pretensions, it exploits and glamorizes the remorseless killers it portrays. The charges literally come home to roost as Bruce and Brooke suddenly find themselves captives of the Mall Murderers, Wayne and Scout, real-life versions of Delamitri's fictional anti-heroes.

In the following extract Bruce and Brooke have begun to realize the hair-trigger danger of their situation. Brooke tries to initiate a personal rapport with Scout, perhaps to insinuate a wedge between her and her boyfriend:

> BROOKE   Sure, you're a pretty girl, you know that? Real pretty.
> SCOUT   [*coyly*] Oh, I don't think so.
> BROOKE   Of course you are Scout, and I think you know it too. Except you don't make as much of yourself as you could. Like for instance you have beautiful hair, but you haven't done anything with it.
> SCOUT   Well, all blood and bits of brain and stuff got in it when Wayne pumped this guy who was serving me a soda so I had to rinse it through and now it's a mess.[23]

Although taken out of context, it should be easy enough to recognize the collision of frames. Brooke no doubt seeks to negotiate a tone of address both sincere and solicitous, at least partly in the name of self-preservation. Scout responds like a self-conscious schoolgirl, a register at grotesque odds with her incidental detailing of human slaughter.

It is, however, important to take the measure of the world that surrounds this and other such extracts, as this amounts to a recurring pattern in the play: Scout's status as one half of a ruthless homicidal team is periodically undercut by her decided lack of worldliness. Scout is no fool, though, and in a later scene she smashes Brooke in the face with the butt of her gun for trying to turn her against her man.

Even before their actual arrival in the house we have met the Mall Murderers on the job in a short scene. To sounds of gun fire and screaming, we see Wayne and Scout begin to catch sexual fire:

> SCOUT   We are in a bank, Wayne! This is a public place! There are people here!
> WAYNE   No problem, baby doll.
>   [WAYNE *fires his machine gun this way and that, out into the darkness. We hear screams and sobs.* WAYNE *stops firing; the screaming subsides to a few sobs.*]
> SCOUT   Oh Wayne, I surely do love you.[24]

The massacre is implied by theatrical means (rather than shown explicitly), and the stage world's acid cynicism toward the aesthetic exploitation of violence has already been framed. Wayne's stupefyingly casual gunning and Scout's melting appreciation of her boyfriend's can-do romanticism provide grossly incompatible utterances in succession – the conditions for mordantly mocking humour.

This kind of humour preys upon the torque between biological self (body), conscious self (mind) and the psychic tides that possess them (emotion). It also facilitates demonstration of the way humour is capable of relieving us, in the way Freud diagnosed, of our troubling vulnerability to life's harsher experiences. Human beings are never purely brute thing nor bare consciousness, and humour affords a momentary loosening of the 'serious', survivalist grip they maintain on one another. Psychologist Nico Frijda rephrases humour's bisociation principle as key to a certain kind of emotional coping: 'Serious events are divested of part of their seriousness by discerning features that include them in a different context . . . They do not deny, avoid, or diminish personal involvement, but give it a double implication, by discerning both implications in the events.'[25] The adjustment implies an alternate bearing for emotion, which allows for laughter at awful incongruities – and not every spectator is able to negotiate this stance.

In the above extracts from *Popcorn*, the playwright foresees something remarkable for the perceiving body by inveigling the spectator to laugh at authenticated human suffering. The effect recalls aspects of Luigi Pirandello's prescription for humour. 'Comedy', claims Pirandello, is taken up by '*perception* of the opposite'. In his famous example, we catch a glimpse of an old woman 'dolling herself up' so as to appear young and alluring, and we laugh at the ridiculous image. It is, however, the '*feeling* of the opposite', an empathy derived from emotional reflection upon what causes the poor woman to behave so, which constitutes the more desirable achievement of 'humour'. Genuine humour, Pirandello says, makes one feel as though suspended between forces: 'I feel like laughing, and I do laugh, but my laughter is troubled and obstructed by something that stems from the representation itself.'[26]

The comic beyond the 'realistic'

Despite the broad potential for content, form and register to supply a unique feeling of life on the stage (or screen or television), we should take account of some of the limits imposed by conventional dramatic practice. After all, comedy and tragedy, as the founding genres of Western drama, set their worlds in similar structural forms even though they approach them with contrasting spirits and preferred techniques. They share a generic narrative motion – roughly reducible to exposition, development, climax and dénouement – which they have passed along to offspring like farce, melodrama and the kinds of tragicomedy discussed so far. These structural factors alone shape the world within a corridor of meaning, necessarily excluding other ways of expressing experience.

They have also bred a sort of default approach to representing the world according to its external appearance, primarily in the way that the stage world is populated by embodiments of real or imagined people (we call 'characters') in situations taken from, inspired by or extended from real (or mythic) life. To be sure, a play like *Everyman* contains characters representing abstract ideas like Good Deeds, and Time makes an appearance in the form of a Chorus in Shakespeare's *The Winter's Tale* (1611). But for the most part, we are used to a 'realistic' one-to-one correspondence between the construction and embodiment of the fictional world and the one in which we live, primarily with regard to the actor/character tandem.[27] The capacities for generating meaning and feeling expand quite a bit, though, if we throw off some of the formal constraints described above, as Western drama has done over the past century or so.

New orientations toward reality

The rise of theatrical Realism in the late nineteenth century, typified by Henrik Ibsen's *Ghosts* (1881), was itself a reaction to the anodyne romances and melodramas of the previous era, and aspired to confront the audience with undistorted representations of socially relevant issues. Its surface reflection of ordinary contemporary experience behind an imaginary fourth wall, however, spawned alternative convictions about the nature and purpose of theatre. There arose from some quarters an artistic will to challenge both the dramatist's preoccupation with the trappings of middle-class life, and the spectator's all-too decorous partition from the theatre event.

In practical terms Realism and its close associate, Naturalism (often invoked interchangeably in lower-case usage), staked the integrity of their portrayals on exterior detail with its corresponding interior thoughts and feelings. They pretended a self-effacement of the theatre event, presenting themselves as objective examinations of contemporary life through which the emotional implications of social issues might be scrutinized. A handful of movements arose in reaction to this general aesthetic philosophy, arguing that more valuable truths could be revealed by rendering experience from other angles, and that the sense of theatrical event should be exploited without dissembling.

The comic, particularly in the form of humour practice, easily gained entrance to the anti-realistic theatrical visions advanced in the late 1800s and early 1900s. The anarchic Dada movement effectively based itself on the puncturing or downright demolition of artistic convention and intellectual thought. Epic Theatre resolved to do away with illusionistic pretence as it targeted the spectator's social conscience. Expressionism proposed the use of theatrical means to articulate subjective experience, thereby opening itself to juxtaposition or distortion of elements easily perceived as incongruous.

These disparate movements can, perhaps, be seen as a tendency to deplore an excess of civilization, not only in theme and practice, but in the theatre event itself. Antonin Artaud (1896–1948) advocated nothing less than a full sensory, spiritual absorption of stage and spectator. He envisaged a performance fabric which no longer privileged carefully wrought (and culturally endorsed) dialogue, but 'giving words approximately the value they have in dreams'.[28] In this formulation he found sympathy with the Surrealist impulse, which endeavoured to give artistic form to the uncensored psychic swirl of subconscious experience.

The conceptual underpinnings, of Surrealism, as a natural breeding ground for the comic, invite a closer look. The term was coined by the writer Guillaume Apollinaire (1880–1918) to suggest a higher register of reality (*sur-reality*) available to those who cast off the strictures of rational expression. His play, *The Mammaries of Tiresias* (*Les Mamelles de Tirésias*, 1917), reads like an unhinged series of farcical sketches couched in a fairground spirit. The characters are instructed to speak lines through a megaphone, they sometimes invade the audience and there are musical intrusions on bagpipe (*musette*), bass drum, accordion, sleigh bells, castanets and child's trumpet, not to mention broken crockery. Any sense of the psychological continuity presumed by naturalistic representation is made nonsensical through sight, sound and behaviour. The play includes a character called The People of Zanzibar, who never speaks, but is responsible for the stage world's sound effects; another portrays a singing and dancing news Kiosk. An early series of lines delivered by the central character, Therese, are punctuated by stage instructions like, '[*She has hysterics*]', '[*Sneezes*]', '[*She cackles*]' and, finally, '[*Sneezes, cackles, then imitates the noise of a train*]'.[29] Therese turns into a man (Tiresias of the title) before the audience's eyes, as her breasts (also of the title) are released from her blouse as blue and red balloons, which she then explodes with a cigarette lighter while growing a beard and moustache. The text prescribes rude wordplay reminiscent of Shakespearean verbal clowning, Punch-and-Judy violence (including duellists shot fatally, who simply get up and rejoin the action because they are 'tired of being dead'), and many other visual and verbal *non sequiturs*, as we learn that the Husband (turned woman) has produced 40,050 children in a day.

It should become evident that the very sense of unrestrained playfulness which commissions this stage world represents an extreme state of the defining condition for the comic attitude. If we are to be picky, we might note that there is more nonsense than actual humour – incongruity without much of a gap to be bridged – but a competently staged production might incline toward the wacky exaggerations of a classic Bugs Bunny cartoon. As we move toward mid-twentieth century and the Theatre of the Absurd, this pointlessness of cosmic purpose becomes an underlying punchline for stage worlds.

Surrealism, as redefined by André Breton in the 1920s, calls for a sort of automatic writing of the psyche – uninhibited, free-flowing, revelatory of our deeper humanity and therefore utterly confounding to rational perception. Breton also identifies the concept of 'black humour' as central to the Surrealist attitude. In his introductory essay to the *Anthology of Black Humor* (1979 [1939]), he characterizes black humour as 'the mortal enemy of sentimentality',[30] and nominates Jonathan Swift (1667–1745) as its 'true initiator'. One need only sample the chilling deadpan delivery of Swift's satirical pamphlet, *A Modest Proposal* (1729) – which authoritatively presents a case for the Irish to ease their economic hardship by selling poverty-stricken children as a culinary delicacy for wealthy gentlefolk – to recognize that ruthless comic step too far, taken more and more frequently by writers in our own time. As the *Anthology's* translator Mark Polizzotti points out, this unflinching comic acidity can be identified in literary works by, for instance, Kurt Vonnegut and John Barth, and the films of David Lynch and the Coen Brothers.

Theatre of the Absurd

Black humour gets its punch from the moral void at the heart of Surrealistic worlds, and leads to a strong family resemblance among texts we associate with the Theatre of the Absurd. Martin Esslin was the first to characterize the movement and give it its name in his book *The Theatre of the Absurd* in 1961. He coined the label with reference to Albert Camus's essay, *The Myth of Sisyphus* (1942), to describe a text's inherent 'sense of metaphysical anguish at the absurdity of the human condition'.[31]

Although Esslin defines the Theatre of the Absurd as a mid-twentieth-century form, he marks its actual birth in the first performance of Alfred Jarry's *Ubu the King* (*Ubu Roi*) on 10 December 1896. Here was a play that decimated theatrical convention and stage decorum from its very first word, an elongated obscenity delivered by an actor in a padded costume and pear-shaped mask, instructed to act like a puppet.

The play begins with Mère and Père Ubu (Mum and Dad Ubu) as travesty incarnations of Shakespeare's Macbeth and Lady Macbeth. After trading a few crass insults, Mère Ubu sets about inveigling her boorish husband to murder the entire royal family for the purpose of gaining power and riches. *Ubu the King* proceeds as a barbarous romp of mockery and coarseness, first conceived during Jarry's school days, and offering up a blanket disrespect toward civilized values and Western theatre convention. There remains in its reading a strong scent of adolescent cheekiness in its scatological humour and casual atrocity. Esslin, however, saw the title character as a damning symbol for our basest nature when he wrote *The Theatre of the Absurd*. Half a century on, the critique has only gained in resonance:

> Ubu is a savage caricature of a stupid, selfish bourgeois seen through the cruel eyes of a schoolboy, but this Rabelaisian character, with his Falstaffian greed and cowardice, is more than mere social satire. He is a terrifying image of the animal nature of man, cruelty and ruthlessness.[32]

In terms of the comic we can perceive a childish glee in the gratuitous tossing off of socially taboo language. The aforementioned opening obscenity in the French was, 'Merdre', the additional (second) 'r' facilitating a more indulgent, prolonged delivery for the actor. It has been translated as 'Pschitt' and 'Crrrap' in two versions, attempting to afford the English speaker a similar opportunity to sensationalize the offence.

There are, though, more genuinely comic constructions. Père Ubu issues a compliment to his wife, 'Mère Ubu, you look really ugly today. Is it because we're expecting visitors?', which obviously reverses the marital ideal, but surely calls attention to their outlandish appearances. Père Ubu rushes to embrace his comrade, Captain Brubbish, as they confirm their assassination pact:

PÈRE UBU	Oh! Oh! I love you dearly, Brubbish.
CAPTAIN BRUBBISH	Pooh! You stink, Père Ubu. Don't you ever wash?
PÈRE UBU	Scarcely ever.
MÈRE UBU	Never![33]

This passage, with its revolting bodily comic premise, is reversed by Père Ubu's admission, in which he declines to make any pretension toward acceptable personal hygiene. It is then topped by Mère Ubu's excessively truthful deflation. The sequence would not seem out of place in some brashly cynical contemporary comic worlds, like television's *Curb Your Enthusiasm* or the animated *Family Guy* (1999–).

It is instructive to note a few of the choices made in Jarry's original production, as a means of underlining the potential for comic effect through the manner of representation. The King of Poland's family are outlined linguistically as inhabitants of a high romantic, if not Shakespearean, world:

> THE QUEEN   O Buggerlas! When I recall how happy we were before the coming of that Père Ubu! But now, alas! Everything is changed!
>
> BUGGERLAS   What can I say! Let us wait in hope and never give up our rights.
>
> THE QUEEN   'Tis my hope for you, dear son, but for my part, I shall not live to see that happy day.[34]

The high-flown register claimed by the lines was debased in Jarry's original production. Buggerlas 'was dressed as an outsize baby, in skirts and a bonnet',[35] while the actress playing the Queen spoke in the French equivalent of a stereotypical countrified drawl. If one follows Jarry's production notes, a single soldier should be used to represent an entire army, allowing for the opening of a comic gap when Père Ubu cries, 'What a gang, what a stampede, what a crowd, how can I get myself out of this mess?'[36]

These examples should suggest the extent to which the humour principle of playful disjunction can be applied to any dramatic text – gratuitously so if one seeks merely to ridicule a serious play or its characters, but cleverly in worlds primed for ironic or satiric comment (see the sections on 'Irony' and 'Satire' in the next chapter). Texts like *Ubu the King*, which depart wilfully from realistic detail, are quite open to (perhaps even demanding of) imaginative representation and therefore welcoming to pointed mischief.

The grotesque

We come now to a distinguishing feature of *Ubu the King*'s constitution, which literally sets the tone for the Theatre of the Absurd and many a jaundiced fictional world conceived since. In remarking upon the stage world's comic elements, it is important to note the co-present serious attitude toward killing and brutality contained in the lines and implied by the stage directions. The text includes instructions like, '[*He splits his skull*]', '[*He tears him to pieces*]', and '[*He massacres the Poles*]'. Buggerlas attacks Père Ubu and, according to the stage directions, '[*With a terrible blow of his sword, he splits his belly*]' (a serious-sounding injury about which we hear nothing further).

We find undisguised slapstick in the way Père Ubu stomps on the King's foot to launch the murderous assault on the Polish royal family. Theatre practitioners are quite resourceful. It may or may not be possible to discover some stage equivalent of the animated 'Itchy and Scratchy' cartoons in *The Simpsons*, in which the violent effects are so exaggerated as to pass through the nauseating to the laughable (though not, perhaps, for every viewer). Productions of Martin McDonagh's play, *The Lieutenant of Inishmore* (2001), have spattered buckets of stage blood with comic intent in the service of deflating the pretence of paramilitary violence. In a scene from Quentin Tarantino's *Pulp Fiction* (1994), we see an informant riding in the back seat of a car with the featured hit men up front (played by Samuel L. Jackson and John Travolta). One of them is talking and waving his gun absently as the camera view switches outside the car, whereupon we hear a gun shot and see a concentrated spray of blood hit the rear window. The moment is staged like a joke: bridging the gap, we conclude that the gun has gone off accidentally, and blown away the back-seat passenger's head. It is both laughable in its sudden, excessive misfortune and horrific (if not stomach-churning) in its gratuitous, blood-soaked taking of a human life.

We can refer to the effect of these co-present opposing motions as 'grotesque'. It is a concept wholly applicable to *Ubu*, absurdism and after. Although the grotesque is yet another concept whose definition tends to change shape according to the theorist, Philip Thomson's approach in his little book on *The Grotesque* is a useful place to start. He describes it basically as 'the unresolved clash of incompatibles in work and response',[37] a desirable formulation for our purposes because it considers both the practitioner's and spectator's part in the transaction. He also contends that the grotesque engages body and emotion (again, good for our purposes), that it exhibits an element of excessiveness and that it involves a conscious effort on the part of the producer to unsettle the reader or spectator.

Importantly, Thomson considers the comic a virtually indispensable component of the grotesque; it is, as it were, the secret ingredient that raises the impact above the mere 'appalling' or 'disgusting'. He acknowledges that

> laughter at the grotesque is not 'free', that the horrifying or disgusting aspect cuts across our amusement: the guffaw becomes a grimace. But one can also describe this the other way round and say that our

response to the horrifying is undercut by our appreciation of the comic side of the grotesque.[38]

In the next sentence, and in a somewhat Freudian spirit, he proposes that the grotesque brings 'the horrifying and disgusting aspects of existence to the surface, there to be rendered less harmful by the introduction of a comic perspective'. We might observe that a gallows amusement at the forcible unmasking of an unfeeling and unreasonable universe supplies a psychological bass note for the absurdist project, which has sounded through areas of drama, film and literature ever since.

To be sure, by the middle of the twentieth century some playwrights and novelists were admitting to the distinct impression that there was no one at the wheel of the universe in the way religion had always assured. Fundamental doubt extended to the motives and workings of political systems and their rulers. The Industrial Revolution, in the name of propelling us forward as a civilization, merely provided a distressing metaphor for a society in which people came to resemble interchangeable machine parts.

This new model for drama led to a decline in the expected clarity and resolution of existing Western theatre genres. It punctured the pretence of an all-seeing, all-controlling spirit which has some investment in us, values good over bad, and measures out fortune and catastrophe according to just deserts. Some dramatists could no longer bring themselves to tell entertaining and/or instructive stories, and instead sought to manifest a response to contemporary human existence in theatrical terms.

Circular plots

These new kinds of worlds were made from some of the same old ingredients, but stretched the boundaries of meaning and feeling by enlisting unlikely elements. According to Esslin, the Theatre of the Absurd recombines a number of historical comic practices, including *commedia dell'arte* and clowning, drawing particularly upon the comedy of the silent screen:

> It has the dreamlike strangeness of a world seen from outside with the uncomprehending eyes of one cut off from reality. It has the quality of nightmare and displays a world in constant, and wholly purposeless, movement. And it repeatedly demonstrates the deep poetic power of wordless and purposeless action. The great performers of this cinema, Chaplin and Buster Keaton, are the perfect embodiments of the

stoicism of man when faced with a world of mechanical devices that have got out of hand.[39]

We should acknowledge that the exploits of these silent comic protagonists took place in worlds that treated them merely mischievously and that they usually resolved happily. When reassigned to the context of an uncaring or hostile universe, this resourceful, resilient comic spirit resounds with pathetic overtones. The grotesque, according to Polish critic Jan Kott, is comparable to tragic defeat, but with a crucial added element of double-edged mockery. In tragedy, it is the gods or God or Fate or history that presides over one's downfall. Kott's grotesque epitomizes the absurd by simultaneously scorning these notions of the 'absolute' *and* our belief in them:

> The grotesque is a criticism of the absolute in the name of frail human experience. That is why tragedy brings catharsis, while grotesque offers no consolation whatsoever.[40]

We may laugh at the pathos inherent in the human condition, but in the absence of any larger entity to supply our earthly travails with meaning, the joke turns its ridicule back upon us. And if we see life as ultimately pointless, what hope is there for death? This notion aligns with the Existentialist philosophical movement, which gained ascendancy in the early twentieth century, and is epitomized by Camus's aforementioned essay. The absurdist impulse brings a whole new meaning (or purposeful lack thereof) to the dramatic concept of The End by declining to offer the sense of closure generically guaranteed by classic forms. *Waiting for Godot*, for example, draws to a close with the following:

> VLADIMIR   Well? Shall we go?
> ESTRAGON   Yes, let's go.
> [*They do not move.*]
> [*Curtain*][41]

The characters' pointed inaction following their agreement to 'go' can even be seen as set-up and reversal, lending a bitterly comic inflection to the stage world's parting impact. Regardless of the accumulated feeling of any given production, this final moment would appear pitched to embody some quality of persistent metaphysical stalemate – coupled with the fact that the first act ended with the same exchange and inertia, but with the speakers reversed. The curtain falls in a different tone on Eugène Ionesco's *The Bald Soprano* (*La Cantatrice chauve*, 1950) as the play reruns its opening sequence – a daft send-up of dramatic convention, banal domesticity and language itself. With the dialogue replayed through the mouths of two different characters than the ones who enacted it the first time through, the text advances an impression of existence as a tiresome loop with interchangeable players. The final tableau for Harold Pinter's *The Homecoming* (1965) projects a discomforting ambiguity, suggesting the three hard men of the household (a father and two grownup sons) will jockey for the maternal and/or sexual favours of their absent brother's wife, Ruth. Although Ruth is new to the mix, the final configuration echoes the seamy domestic order prior to the mother's death years earlier. These variations on the circularity of experience deny even the artificial respite of a conventional narrative ending. They point to life without succour beyond the final image.

This circular structural pattern proposes that people are unable to change, progress or escape their circumstances. It represents a surrender to the unfortunate nature of things, which appears by now well integrated into our Western dramatic circuitry. *The Lonesome West*, discussed previously, may suggest a deepening of the brothers' mutual loathing, but no real change in their living situation. Mark Ravenhill's *Shopping and Fucking* (1996) concludes with the central trio of lovers feeding each other once again, echoing the play's opening activity and intimating a return to foetal comfort following some cruel and brutal episodes. These kinds of endings to these kinds of worlds constitute sad, cynical jokes at the expense of our cultural injunction to believe in a better tomorrow. The life spirit triumphs – or does it?

Familiar comic patterns in the absurd: absurdity is the basis for all humour, so we should not be surprised to find rampant incongruity in worlds manifesting a loss of faith in serious discourses. Eugène Ionesco and Samuel Beckett are prone to furnishing outlandish images to be undercut by everyday language: rhinoceroses stampeding through the square of a provincial town in the first instance ('Well of all things!'); a woman buried waist deep in a mound of earth and holding a parasol in the second ('Another heavenly day', see Figure 5.1).

The Bald Soprano, even without such conceptual oddities, sports a wealth of comic strategies, familiar in construction, but unhinged absurdly in context. At the very start of the play the clock strikes seventeen times, prompting the first line, 'There, it's nine o'clock',[42] inviting laughter at the normality with which the impossible is greeted (rather than, say, 'We really must get that clock fixed'). There is in this text an implication of words without thought or feeling beneath them, as if people speak according to rote patterns or cultural programming, or are otherwise disengaged from

Figure 5.1 Samuel Beckett's *Happy Days* predicates itself on the incongruous image of a woman going about her daily routine while buried up to her waist in an earthen mound. Billie Whitelaw as Winnie at the Royal Court Theatre, 1979.

genuine interaction with each other and their environment. One passage begins like this:

MR MARTIN   Excuse me, madam, but it seems to me, unless I'm mistaken, that I've met you somewhere before.
MRS MARTIN   I, too, sir. It seems to me that I've met you somewhere before.[43]

In talking, these two people, speaking politely and formally, determine through an extended series of 'bizarre coincidences' that they are Elizabeth and Donald, husband and wife. The long, extended reversal of discovery plays upon the template of an interaction in which two people meet, match a series of remembrances and discover they once went to the same school or something of the kind. It is overlaid comically upon the relationship of a married couple, so that the tone of bizarre coincidence at the end becomes laughable: 'Then, madam, we live in the same room and we sleep in the same bed, dear lady. It is perhaps there that we have met!' The stage directions prescribe a mode of performance which would read as mechanical, superficial or disengaged (e.g., '[*They embrace without expression*]'). Mary the maid then steals in '[*on tiptoe, a finger to her lips*]', to inform us: 'Elizabeth and Donald are now too happy to be able to hear me. I can therefore let you in on a secret. Elizabeth is not Elizabeth, Donald is not Donald.'[44] Mary discloses a misapprehended detail upon which the logic of their discovery falls apart, before declaring, 'My real name is Sherlock Holmes.' Mary's disclosure reverses upon the preceding sequence, but in the absurd fabric of this world it proposes an utter lack of metaphysical integrity in our own.

The sequence's comic conceit could stand well enough on its own as a sketch. But the text's accumulation of trite chatter, supported by stage directions encouraging the performers away from realistic outlining, anticipates a comic light more garish than that trained upon social manners by, say, a Noel Coward or an A. R. Gurney. Non-naturalistic playing (e.g., mechanical, uninflected or overinflected) could emphasize to a grotesque extent the abandonment or superficiality of human feeling between people (and you should try reading passages of this play with a friend, experimenting with mechanical, melodramatic, uncaring and other styles). Such a theatrical context suffuses the gaps to be bridged with blatant cynicism toward the existence of sincere or distinctive relationships among humans.

Comic tropes, some of which we have surveyed in previous chapters, are easy to locate in absurdist texts from this mid-century era. Jean Genet is particularly fond of role-playing, as seen in *The Maids* (*Les Bonnes*, 1947) and *The Balcony* (*Le Balcon*, 1956). These two plays begin with extended jokes on the audience, as false 'realities' are played out by characters who suddenly drop out of their fictional scenarios. Ionesco's *Rhinoceros* (*Rhinocéros*, 1959), in the scene to which I alluded above, contains runaway repetition ('Oh, a rhinoceros!') and crossed conversations. Beckett's *Waiting for Godot* stars a standard double act in Vladimir and Estragon, one the straight man, the other his comic foil, representing polarities of human nature. There is, as well, a mutation of the classic master–slave relationship in Pozzo and Lucky. Styan lists a host of actions prescribed by Beckett's stage directions, like the swapping-hat routine in the second act, which evoke the slapstick *lazzi* of the *commedia dell'arte*.

Language and the absurd

Patterns for comic dialogue placed in absurdist environments express a fatal distrust of language. The slippage or compromise of understanding upon which wordplay is based takes on censorious overtones. Absurdist contexts refute language's claims of neutrality, let alone goodwill. Language arouses further suspicion in its role as conduit for logical discourse, the epitome of stiff-necked serious mode. Language – long held up as the sturdiest of bridges connecting human hearts and minds – is exposed with a cynical glee by the likes of Ionesco, Beckett and Pinter as useless among strangers, untrustworthy between friends and lovers and downright duplicitous in the mouths of authority and the academy.

The kind of nimble wordplay and crosstalk we found in Shakespearean worlds becomes the distinguishing feature for routines in American vaudeville and the British music hall. It is, however, interesting to note how these rapid-fire exchanges resonate at different frequencies when used by playwrights associated with the absurd. Ionesco foresees an intricately crossed series of verbal breakdowns in *Rhinoceros*, whereby two separate conversations weave in and out of one another, reversing and echoing all the while. In double-act fashion, the supercilious Jean conducts a critique of the beleaguered Berenger's personal habits. Entwined with this dialogue is a faux-philosophical discussion between characters named the Logician and the Old Gentleman, giving rise to passages like the following:

BERENGER	I sometimes wonder if I exist myself.
JEAN	You don't exist, my dear Berenger, because you don't think. Start thinking, then you will.
LOGICIAN	[*to the Old Gentleman*] Another syllogism. All cats die. Socrates is dead. Therefore Socrates is a cat.
OLD GENTLEMAN	And he's got four paws. That's true. I've got a cat named Socrates.
LOGICIAN	There you are, you see[45]

In the context of the play we would presume that Berenger, a character who also appears in other Ionesco plays as an Everyman figure, gives voice to a twentieth-century crisis of metaphysical faith. Jean offers no genuine insight whatsoever, playing loosely enough with meanings of the word 'think' as to open a gap for the ridicule of Cartesian principle ('I think, therefore I am'). The Logician, whose lesson in reasoning has thus far led to some utterly inane statements, proposes another mindless leap of logic. Via the kind of coincidence that occurs only in comedy, the Old Gentleman's revelation about the name of his cat reverses upon the Logician's incredible conclusion about felines and a certain Greek philosopher – allowing the Logician to button the sequence with a self-satisfied claim of validation. The Logician's fatuous lecturing and the Old Gentleman's complaisance frame the Jean–Berenger scene with a baggy-pants devaluation of language and logic as controlling instruments of authority.

This can be the most difficult kind of comic pattern to read from the page, because of the necessity of maintaining the through-lines of separate dia-logues. Both conversations are being carried out seriously and without awareness of the other. A degree of technical modulation is required in the playing, so spectators can maintain a grasp of both conversational tracks, as well as the gestalt utterance they comprise. The effect though, stands to augment the value of humour strategies we identified in earlier texts – we now stand to perceive such crosstalk not just as playing with language and logic, but as the post-industrial babble which suffocates Berenger's earnest efforts to make sense of his life.

In *The Birthday Party*, Pinter ratchets up the pressure on language and logic. The once freewheeling nonsense of music-hall patter now finds itself the instrument of interrogational bullying. The speed of response foreseen by performance no longer serves just an efficient set-up and reversal; it embodies the gathering force of a police grilling that would trip up the most innocent of subjects.

This world, in common Pinteresque fashion, withholds specificity by either declining to confirm key details or at various times supplying con-flicting accounts – and therein lies the menace that hangs in the air between the lines. We are presented with the '[*living room of a house in a seaside town*]', an alleged boarding house tended by a couple in their sixties, Meg and Petey. The only resident is a man named Stanley, who claims to have been a concert pianist, hounded out of his profession under shadowy cir-cumstances. Goldberg and McCann arrive, agents from some unnamed yet powerful organization, to bring Stanley to book over a similarly unclear yet grievous offence.

Here is a case in point regarding the importance of weighing a comic pattern in the context of the fabric within which it is woven. Beholden to a different cosmic context from Vladimir and Estragon – their patter aimed at fending off the creeping desolation of an existence without movement –

Goldberg and McCann operate in tighter metaphysical quarters. They, too, present themselves as an old-fashioned double act, this time the comic yoking of stage Jew and stage Irishman suggested by their names. Goldberg is garrulous and self-possessed, McCann edgy and introverted; speech is power for them, as they submit Stanley to high-pressure cross-examination:

> GOLDBERG   What have you done with your wife?
> MCCANN   He's killed his wife!
> GOLDBERG   Why did you kill your wife?
> STANLEY   [*sitting, his back to the audience*] What wife?[46]

The sequence, based on an escalating series of skewed conversational steps, exhibits the cracked logic of a Marx Brothers routine. In this case, however, the 'straight man' is not a Margaret Dumont character, ever the gull for verbal shell games and meriting humiliation because of her haughty demeanour. It is the increasingly desperate Stanley, fighting to maintain a position of credibility under pressure of unspecified life-and-death stakes. The textual pattern cites a performance model of unrelieved comic intent; the dramatic context supplies a level of threat which cannot be laughed away.

The character of Goldberg, at once avuncular and sinister, unsettles the mood with his ability to shift unpredictably from quaint reminiscence to avenging inquisition, as well as many other situational guises. Elin Diamond sees in him an incarnation of the medieval Vice figure (see the box below), describing him as 'the funniest as well as the most frightening character on stage'.[47]

The Vice

The Vice figure, referred to in the preceding chapter as a forerunner of the clown, represented the forces of Satan on the medieval stage, emerging as an entertaining embodiment of all the instincts opposing good Christian living. The Vice developed as quite a stage-worthy character, perhaps due to an understandable ambivalence in the spectator between the secret allure of unapproved behaviour and its comic condemnation. He also came fitted with the Devil's penchant for disguise and trickery, by nature quite theatrical, not to mention comic, performance traits.

Importantly, the Vice practices evil for the fun of it, not out of psychological motivation. He has been associated with Iago from Shakespeare's *Othello* (1604), who may be one of the early descendants of today's action-film villains, many of whom go about their heinous business with pure delight. On the lighter side, Mosca, the comic servant in Ben Jonson's *Volpone*, orchestrates the play's trickery on his master's behalf, pausing at one point to soliloquize rhapsodically about his 'most excellent nature'.

> Diamond considers Goldberg, from Pinter's *The Birthday Party*, a Vice figure
> poised interestingly between – or, perhaps straddling – the sinister and the comic.
> Like those before him, Goldberg exhibits 'the Vice's clever scheming, his
> dissembling, his gulling of simple characters, his boastful monologuing, his
> merriment, his energy, and, most of all, his motiveless malice'.[48] For all of these
> reasons, the role of Goldberg calls for a bravura performance, effectively driving
> the play, entertaining and intimidating.
> What other Vice inheritors can you think of in drama and cinema?

Pinter's *The Homecoming* is terser than *The Birthday Party*, even though, as Diamond points out, there are some visible comic patterns from a textual standpoint. Speeches by Max and Lenny reveal an X-ray impression of music-hall construction, but their content can be startlingly vicious. In some sequences, one can read the potential for stock comic responses in purely comic worlds. Son and brother Teddy returns to the house after an extended absence, with his wife Ruth in tow. The room is empty and it is night:

> RUTH   Shouldn't you wake someone up? Tell them you're here?
> TEDDY   Not at this time of night. It's too late.
> [*Pause*]
> Shall I go up?
> [*He goes into the hall, looks up the stairs, comes back.*]
> Why don't you sit down?
> [*Pause*]
> I'll just go up . . . have a look.[49]

This passage simulates what we might presume to dub the 'Lazzo of the False Exit', in which one character keeps trying to bluff the other into saying or doing something despite clear indications that no response will be forthcoming ('OK, this time I'm *really* going'). Later in the play, Ruth has delivered a potentially provocative speech, inviting focus upon her leg and lips. Max stands, breaking the silence:

> MAX   Well, it's time to go to the gym. Time for your workout, Joey.
> LENNY   [*standing*] I'll come with you.
> [JOEY *sits looking at* RUTH.]
> MAX   Joe.
> [JOEY *stands. The three go out.*][50]

We can call this one the 'Lazzo of Transfixion'. Joey has been thoroughly mesmerized by Ruth's preceding performance, and fails to take successive hints that it's time to go. We can imagine the comic outlining this basic routine would receive in other worlds. Ruth is a powerful and enigmatic character, and these two ostensibly joking sequences crystallize Ruth's singular ability to unsettle the family of men. In the first instance, she has no intention of taking her husband's instruction, explicit or otherwise; in the second, she has rendered the most physically formidable male on the stage a mere love-struck clown.

Comic constructions in a dramatic text like this could evaporate entirely in a given production. But to whatever extent they insist upon their humour potential in performance, they carry out some interesting work on behalf of a strangely weighted stage world. Devoid of obligations toward realistic interpretation, a text can be read in a more poetic vein, with comic devices expanding the range of feeling beyond the effects of simple joking.

It is worth emphasizing that the Theatre of the Absurd refers properly to a wide band of dramatic texts and their authors, observed in retrospect around the middle of the twentieth century. Notably, from our perspective, the comic plays an elemental part in these worlds in uneasy alliance with the deadly serious; arguably, this mixture produces a double-sided slant upon experience that we know to be more revelatory of human existence than can be painted in primary colours.

Absurdist texts grew from dramatic practice before them, and in turn exerted influence upon many a playwright to follow. John Orr, for one, prefers to discuss these texts, before, during and after the absurd, with regard to a 'modern turn' in tragicomedy, thereby allowing for a more overarching grasp of their project. It should be noted that *Waiting for Godot*, a text definitively associated with the absurd impulse, is subtitled 'A tragicomedy in two acts'. Richard Dutton draws a direct line between Beckett and the upsurge of Renaissance tragicomedy which included works like *The Winter's Tale*. This line continues on through plays by Pinter, Edward Albee and Tom Stoppard, in which, as we have seen, the comic undertakes some heavy lifting with regard to theme and mood. Subsequent uses of the comic in the worlds of David Mamet, Caryl Churchill and Sam Shepard, and later in Sarah Kane, Mark Ravenhill and Neil Labute, inherit obviously from this aesthetic current.

In his take on modern tragicomedy, Orr locates a defining play ('*ludic*') spirit amid twentieth-century theatre's efforts to cope dramatically with the fullness of modern being:

> Play is tragicomedy's elusive response to the moral void it perceives in modern culture. It can be dramatised as boredom and invention, simulation and performance, extemporising and make-believe, as anything to ward off, however briefly, the loss of human control.[51]

And where there is play, there is always an opening for the comic. Playwrights now presume joking permission with regard to our endlessly precarious human condition and, as Orr says, 'the laughter here is not really a laughing away of human folly, because it is shadowed by the darkness of human downfall which cannot be exhausted by rational explanation'.[52] Western culture once seemed so sure of itself, or at least clung to its faith in God and progress. In the twentieth century we began to wonder what, if anything, we *could* proclaim with certainty – even the nature of who we are and how we feel.

Orr directs us to the works of Luigi Pirandello, mentioned briefly above, as a sort of breakaway influence for the spirit of modernist play. The Italian playwright does indeed present a remarkable theatrical voice, emerging from that gamut of turn-of-the-century impulses surveyed above. Pirandello's *Six Characters in Search of an Author* (*Sei personaggi in cerca d'autore*, 1921) takes a sideways leap from the old-fashioned play-within-a-play concept, by situating an exploration of identity and authenticity in the ambiguous phenomenological overlap among human actor and dramatic character.

The gap between actor (person) and character (fictional construct) has been exploited for comic effect in, for example, Shakespeare's *A Midsummer Night's Dream* (1595–6). *Six Characters* foresees a stage world in which a family of 'characters', launched into being and then deserted by some unknown author, lay claim to an inchoate life and emotional intensity of their own. They constitute among them the relationships that drive a tale fraught with resentment and despair, which includes a sordid encounter between a father and his stepdaughter and the accidental deaths of the family's two young children.

The 'characters' interrupt a rehearsal for a theatre company's new production and beseech the gathered director, actors and actresses to assist in the fulfilment of their dramatic destinies. These surrounding denizens of the theatre are easily read as lampoons of a professional theatre troupe, with its petty politics, egos, seducers and, perhaps most importantly, its self-important, artificial acting. The six 'characters' are made from the stuff of tragedy, full-blooded in their feeling and unswerving in their quest for completion; the theatre people are cut from the two-dimensional cloth of comedy, and are summarily unequipped to respond to the web of raw emotions played out before them.[53]

As we might expect, there is many a reversal in this kind of all-purpose set-up: a tragedy entwined with a comedy in a play about the theatre. A serious exchange or revelation among the 'characters' is followed by a mood-breaking interjection from the performers or director ('What a show this is!'). There are plenty of pokes at the pretensions one might find in a rehearsal studio. There is also room for the humour of enactment, as the

Leading Actor and Leading Actress attempt to breathe life into one of the scenes described by the 'characters' (in response to which the Stepdaughter 'character' cannot control her own laughter).

Pirandello uses the actual materials of theatre – words, bodies, voices and feelings – to create a sort of metaphysical Möbius strip of human authenticity. He probes issues like art, truth, identity and the authenticity of experience, and even dips into questions about the nature of human existence. The Father explains:

> A character, sir, can always ask a man who he is. Because a character truly has a life of his own, marked by his own characteristics, because of which he is always 'someone'. On the other hand, a man – I'm not saying you at this moment – a man in general, can be 'nobody'.[54]

This ostensibly inverted logic echoes wordplay by Shakespearean clowns while looking ahead to the interrogation of language by the absurd. It is true that Pirandello used this play to make aesthetic and philosophical points, as laid out in his Preface to a later edition. But by weaving his themes so astutely into the fibre of performance, he deepened the hold of the comic upon serious material, thereby looking ahead to the striking conceptual conceits of mid-century texts.

The tragicomic label does indeed allow us access to an aesthetic sweep that still commissions the comic to entertain a spirit of play amid the brutal and despairing. It has also, it must be said, led in another part of the dramatic kingdom to the expansive expression of the twentieth-century musical, in which comedy's patterns and structures have also played an integral part (see the box below).

Comedy and musical theatre

Musical expression offers quite another dimension to a stage world, steering it sharply toward the non-naturalistic. Music hall and vaudeville, to which we have referred as popular entertainment forms with formidable influence on absurdist worlds, included 'comedy' or 'speciality' numbers based on standalone comic conceits. Operetta had long since been seen to adopt comic character and structure.

The mid-twentieth-century musical, drawing upon both of these influences, is held to be a particularly American development, with its weaving of musical expression for dramatic purposes as well as entertainment value. We find some of the classic comic devices and patterns in musical comedy that we have observed thus far, with the opportunity for character to manifest itself in another register as the mode of expression shifts into song or dance.

From a textual perspective comic lyrics, like comic verse, put increased demands on the writer to set up and spring a reversal, as he or she has to negotiate poetic form and rhythm as well as supply a clever rhyme. Musical setting also plays a part, sometimes supporting the mood or subject, but also available to supply playful contrast. In 'Adelaide's lament', from *Guys and Dolls* (1950), composer/lyricist Frank Loesser enhances through the music the toll that the character's long-suffering courtship has taken on her state of health ('A person can develop a cold'). Leonard Bernstein's music for 'Gee, officer Krupke', in *West Side Story* (1957), provides a lively vaudevillian tempo for Stephen Sondheim's lyrics, addressing with streetwise candour the ways that family, the courts and social support systems have failed to address basic concerns of the inner-city youth who make up the warring gangs in the play:

> BABY JOHN   [*As Female Social Worker*]
> Eek!
> Officer Krupke, you've done it again.
> This boy don't need a job, he needs a year in the pen.
> It ain't just a question of misunderstood;
> Deep down inside him, he's no good![55]

The premise of teenagers lampooning the grown-ups around them allows for broad role-playing by the performers. In the play, the number follows the fatal knifing of one of the characters during a gang fight, and so the mood and quality of humour becomes a complex mixture, which includes (presumably) a high entertainment quotient in the performing. In more recent times, music and comedy have been joined for satirical purpose as in, for example, *Urinetown* (2001), which sends up many of the conventions of musical theatre itself.

Comic latitude in production

This is a book about reading comedy, and as such I have privileged the plumbing of written text for comic intent. I have tried to stress that comedy's written form remains tied directly to performance practices, and have also stressed the extent to which it helps to keep this in mind for provisional visualizations on the mind's stage. I have introduced the notion of outlining to refer to the performer's contribution in concretizing dramatic text through the use of voice, gesture and feeling. It is incumbent upon us, though, to retain awareness of the radical individuality of all performers, of all productions and of the snarl of cultural-historical influences to which they are owed.

In the light of this chapter's intention to address the provisional performance fabric as a whole for any given dramatic text, we must accommodate the fact that the process of text-into-performance by its very nature leaves room for quite a bit of play. The outlining by one, a few, or all the performers, the influences of design and the attempts at concept and orchestration by the director make it desirable for a reader to ponder some of those parameters for latitude in actual production. There are, of course, other factors in and beyond the control of those involved, as well as the unpredictable and fluid blend of all the elements.

For our purposes, though, the comic and its humour strategies represent a significant fulcrum for the balance of meaning and feeling from text to performance. We oversimplify the issue by suggesting some straightforward pendulum effect between lightness and darkness – there are different qualities of humorous effect, as well as their placement, for example – but it is a place to start. Importantly, the fact that there are so many possibilities for any given production is not the point, but that the accumulation of choices made affects meaning and feeling in the performance fabric.

I have thus far projected upon many a text certain convictions about the prospective embodiment of individual moments and the piece as a whole. But the reading of dramatic texts and the comic in particular will always present a challenge to interpret competently, while remaining aware of a range of possibilities to generate meaning and feeling for a particular audience in a particular sociocultural context at a particular time. Jonathan Miller, in the process of defining the 'afterlife' of a dramatic text as its continuing history of concretizations subsequent to the conditions under which it was written, contends, 'In a sense, one of the measures of a great play is that it has the capacity to generate an almost infinite series of unforeseeable inflexions.'[56] (He then warns against gratuitous manipulation of a text in violation of generic limits, but the interpretation, boundaries and wisdom of this caution remain very much a matter of wide-ranging opinion.) It is, in any case, possible to read across the grain of a dramatic text's inherent comic/tragic profile, and to compelling effect for those of us interested in the workings of comedy.

I once saw a production of *The Comedy of Errors* which appeared to downplay the comic outlining in favour of a more serious investigation of the circumstances. Events and actions seemed to affect the characters at a deeper level than farcical custom would authorize – emotional response was registered within a realistic palette. This tuning probably reduced the fun quotient resident in the dramatic text, but it actualized a striking identification with the characters' plights: what does it mean to be plunged into situations in which strangers treat me as fully familiar, even intimate, or actions have been attributed to me for which I have no recollection? Am I nothing more than the sum total of what other people know about me? What *is* it that constitutes 'who I am'?

On the other hand I have seen a production of *Medea* in which the title character was rendered as a giddy housewife in the early scenes – a quirky, self-deprecating outline with humorous intent, which drew more laughter by far than any conventional production of this play would have seen. She then ceremoniously transformed into the ritual executioner of her sons, with the murders staged in horrific fashion. Clownish behaviour can be used to draw us in, to charm us; in this production Medea established herself as the most appealing character in the stage world. This, whatever one concluded, was one way of approaching the challenge to establish sympathy for a tragic heroine who would have trouble gaining empathy in this day and age as dramatic literature's best-known murdering mother. The counter-comic reversal into tragedy then became sharp and devastating.

To end this chapter, I will make some selective references to the production histories of three dramatic texts as a means of urging the armchair reader to remain mindful of comic choices and their implications for the larger performance fabric. As I noted in an aside to our discussion of Sganarelle's opening speech in *Don Juan* (Chapter 1), Molière wrote the servant part for himself, an experienced comic performer in his own right. Molière's treatment of Don Juan comes to us as an absorbingly open dramatic text. The title character seeks new seductions, even as he dodges pursuit from Dona Elvira, a woman he lured from the convent with a promise of marriage. He conducts himself according to a personal code of honour, and philosophizes about society's manners. He is a 'tormented unbeliever' in God, as David Whitton describes him, and meets his comeuppance in a final, potentially sensational scene, in which the Statue of the Commander comes to life and guides him to the brink, whereupon, '[*Flashes of lightning play upon* DON JUAN. *The earth opens and engulfs him. Flames issue from the place into which he has fallen*].'[57] We should note, of course, that Sganarelle then has the last words, enumerating all who will be satisfied by his master's death, then pleading his own hardship for suddenly having no one to pay his wages.

Whitton, in his historical analysis of the play in production, assures us, 'It can be safely assumed that the many *lazzi* and farce routines that he wrote into the part were played to the hilt' in the original.[58] Whitton then cites criticism from Molière's contemporaries, taking him to task for the character's buffoonery (as writer and actor) and its sabotage of the dialectic defence that should have been pitted against Don Juan's atheistic, amoral conduct.

This poses a vital question in considering the grander effect of the comic on a stage world: where do the arrows of ridicule, always implicit in comic playing, locate their targets? Louis Jouvet, the French director and actor, mounted a landmark production in 1947, which essentially rediscovered the play for the twentieth century. Jouvet played Don Juan, not as the Great Seducer, but as a tragic figure undone by his ambivalence toward the existence of God (perhaps in parallel to the gathering absurdist movement, which expressed the same deeply troubling doubts). Sganarelle was played by Fernand-René, a former music-hall clown, as Whitton describes: 'Departing from the tradition of the buffoonish valet, he interpreted him as a cowardly but tender man who is genuinely fearful for his reckless master's soul and who shed real tears over his grave.'[59] Imagine, then, the difference in meaning and feeling for the parting tone if the final speech, rather than delivered as a clownish, self-centred subversion of his master's spectacular damnation, is spoken with heartfelt grieving.

Whitton suggests that Sganarelle may have been nudged too far outside the spotlight by Jouvet's Don Juan, and that he became 'the backbone of the production' in the 1952 production directed by Jean Meyer at the Comédie-Française in Paris. He describes 'a compelling human reality' to the performance of Fernand Ledoux, accommodating the usual naïvety and cowardice: 'But he also allowed himself a finely judged measure of cheeky irony in the face of his master, and moments of pathos which lifted the performance above conventionality'.[60] Antoine Bourseiller's 1967 production (also at the Comédie-Française) was an avant-garde, abstract staging, recalling the spectres of concentration camps and atomic bombs. Among other interpretive choices (which outraged many a critic), Sganarelle was directed away from the usual comic routines: 'Bourseiller integrated the role fully into the tragic perspective, making him a partner in Don Juan's experience of the absurd.'[61]

Whitton points out that this shifted the whole dynamic of the relationship by including the servant in the master's experience, rather than placing him as a figure of antithesis. This positioning had been highlighted by Vsevolod Meyerhold in a 1910 St Petersburg production, in which an established comic actor played Sganarelle 'as a figure from farce who embodied folk-wisdom and the judgement of popular opinion'.[62] Whitton characterizes the actor, Konstantin Varlamov, as bringing a cheerful and naïve radiance to the performance, but also an element of coarseness which would have found ready comic resonance against Don Juan's refined milieu.

Three productions by stage and film director Ingmar Bergman are discussed by Whitton, the first of which in 1955 revealed Don Juan as a balding, unromantic lecher, dressed and groomed with Sganarelle's help to become the womanizing legend during his opening speech. The servant seasoned his comic playing with an attitude of disgust toward his master's true nature; Don Juan treated him with antagonism and more than a hint of violence. Ten years later, Bergman revived the play with a crowd-pleasing *commedia dell'arte* motif and an emphasis on *lazzi* in and between the lines. In Bergman's 1983 revival, 'all the energy and virility traditionally associated with Don Juan were transferred in this production to his servant'.[63] Sganarelle was the lusty one, while Don Juan had become a tired old shell. For the scene discussed in Chapter 4 between Don Juan and the two women, Sganarelle changed clothes with his master to carry out the double seduction with gusto. As Whitton points out, this meant the two women had made further fools of themselves by falling prey to the charms of a mere servant rather than the nobleman they thought they had snared, who, as it turned out, was watching impotently from a safe remove.

I have urged contemplation primarily of Sganarelle in these productions, to the admitted exclusion of other formidable elements. It is arguable that, with the rise and persistence of the directorial concept, a performance fabric is designed 'from the top down'. A director conceives a political and/or aesthetic take on the text, and proceeds to make choices accordingly, beginning with the casting. But overall meaning and feeling still derive from choices made step by step through the dramatic text, and it is still worth retaining awareness of the larger implications for shadings to any given outlining. In this case, Sganarelle serves as the stage world's host. He is assigned a matrix of comic credentials by text and historical genre, but, as I have tried to suggest, a world of artistic possibility remains in the manner of outlining. The precise rendering of character and relationship to Don Juan comprise essential building blocks for meaning and feeling in a provisional stage world. So it is, to varying degrees, for any character at any textual moment.

By way of a broader illustration, Anton Chekhov's *The Cherry Orchard* (1904) presents a different kind of fabric from a different era. It is considered the pinnacle and last gasp of the naturalistic movement, which sought to stage an objective, detailed image of life as it is lived (and spurred the strong reactive impulses toward overt theatricality and subjective or poetic expression noted above in the build-up to absurdism). The dramatic text centres on a landowning family, their servants and those around them, as a combination of historical forces and personal circumstances conspire to displace them from their ancestral home, with its symbolic cherry orchard. It presents a complex weave of unfulfilled promise, unrequited love and the psychic teetering between longing and hope at the end of an era.

Figure 5.2 The extravagant use of body by Oliver Kieran-Jones as Yasha, in a scene with Natalie Cassidy as Dunyasha, should suggest at least one way in which *The Cherry Orchard* can be shaded. The Chichester Festival Theatre, 2008.

Famously, the play was considered by Chekhov to be a comedy, and by actor and director Konstantin Stanislavsky to be a heart-breaking tragedy. There is no doubt that the profound emotional issues described above would seem to incline toward Stanislavsky's side. There is, however, much in the delineation of character and rhythms that points unreservedly toward comic patterns we have discussed (see Figure 5.2). The clerk, Yepikhodov, for example, appears readily qualified as a comic character, entering upon the opening scene with squeaky boots and bumbling behaviour, which sees him drop his bouquet of flowers and accidentally knock over a piece of furniture. The family's adopted daughter, Varya, has pinned her hopes on a marriage proposal she somehow knows will never come from the family friend and new-breed businessman, Lopakhin. She speaks to her sister, Anya:

> I'll tell you what I think – I think nothing's going to come of it. He's very busy, he hasn't got time for me – he doesn't even notice. Well, good luck to him, but I can't bear the sight of him. Everyone talks about our wedding, everyone keeps congratulating me, but in fact there's nothing there – it's all a kind of dream. [*In a different tone.*] You've got a bumble-bee brooch.[64]

There is potential for humour of character in this stream-of-consciousness flight, even though it springs from disappointment. She (perhaps) suddenly switches tone for what appears to be a random observation, and throughout the play cries far too easily, as Chekhov explained. Prior to this, Lopakhin '[*looks in at the door, and moos*]', then goes out. The play is filled with incongruous little occurrences, which can go unnoticed, outlined for comic effect, or given an assortment of shadings. There is, of course, Firs, the ancient family servant, and Gayev, the girls' uncle, who spouts references to billiards without warning, and speaks with deep-felt affection to a bookcase. Charlotta the governess and Pishchik, a neighbouring landowner, are two more characters outfitted with undeniable comic potential.

James N. Loehlin conducts an act-by-act tour of the text, highlighting interpretive crossroads along the way, and in several cases suggesting the implications for comic accentuation. Loehlin suggests on a more subtle level that the scene between Anya and the perennial student, Trofimov, in which he claims they are 'above such things as love',[65] has ample possibility for a comic ironizing of the dialogue and, by induction, his revolutionary rhetoric. In the next act, Trofimov engages in a highly emotional, deeply personal exchange with the matriarchal Madame Ranevskaya. He goes out, then immediately comes back to deliver his parting shot: 'Everything is finished between us!'[66] He then charges offstage and we hear the crash as he falls downstairs, one of the oldest farcical punchlines in the book.

Loehlin directs our attention to the family's departure at the end of the play, and the handful of bits that precede the final exit: Yepikhodov chokes on a glass of water, Varya inadvertently threatens Lopakhin with her umbrella (again), Trofimov's galoshes are finally found and Gayev's inner circuitry reliably returns him to the subject of billiards. Joking amid sadness shows the life spirit trying gamely to assert itself by consciously denying the downward spiral of feeling. This sequence in microcosm demonstrates why words like 'poignant' and 'bittersweet' always appear in descriptions of *The Cherry Orchard*.

The production history of the past century detailed by Loehlin refers to several productions dedicated to teasing out or emphasizing the comic, including the Italian director Giorgio Strehler's 1974 production, which drew upon *commedia dell'arte* comic touches and conscious forays into absurdist territory. Peter Brook's stripped-down production, which opened in Paris in 1981, tried to avoid the mood of emotional indulgence for which Chekhov has become known. Brook took the following approach, cited by Loehlin from a *New York Times* article: 'From the start, I wanted to avoid sentimentality, a false Chekhovian manner that is not in the text. This is not gloomy, romantic, long and slow. It's a comic play about real life'.[67]

The Romanian-born Andrei Serban directed *The Cherry Orchard* in a renowned 1977 New York production, which adopted a striking all-white, dream-like design concept. It was, however, the comic outlining that concerns us:

> Serban's production went farther than any previous major production in the West in subjecting the characters to slapstick indignities and exuberant pratfalls. In this regard, the standout performance was a star-making turn by the young Meryl Streep as Dunyasha. She mugged, wailed, giggled, and took every gesture to exaggerated extremes; when complaining of her nerves, she fell on the floor in a dead faint. Her attempted seduction of Yasha was a vaudeville *tour de force* that incurred the ire of many traditionalist critics.[68]

The reactionary prejudices of some critics aside, though, Loehlin makes an important observation for our purposes: 'While Serban's use of abrasive comedy provided occasional insights, it also created emotional alienation. Even critics who liked the production acknowledged that this was one of the least moving *Cherry Orchards* they could remember.'[69]

We should not take from this a simplistic lesson about the distancing effects of humour. Rather we should take it as a reminder that there are spectrums of tone and technique *within* the uncertain boundaries of the comic, each of which stands to perform some operation upon the spectator.

Before we move on, I want to make another observation for the perceptive reader to keep in mind, for which I will draw upon David Bradby's production history of *Waiting for Godot*. Throughout this book I have treated the dramatic text's potential for performance as something based on things we know generally about stage practice for bodies, voices and emotions, but still generalized or hypothetical. We should take care, however, never to lose sight of the actual performers for whom plays are intended, who possess these attributes *and more* in their own radically individual ways. Every performer possesses a distinctive chemical make-up, based as much on who they 'are' as who they 'can be'. Directors approach casting almost as a laboratory experiment, looking for particular qualities with regard to the role, and the performer's potential mixture with other 'ingredients'. (Other factors inform the arrival at a particular mixture, sometimes relating to a chosen performer's personality, availability or a particular desire to use a 'name' actor or actress for marketing purposes.)

The first production of *Godot*, which opened in Paris in 1953, featured an actor named Lucien Raimbourg in the role of Vladimir. Bradby advises us that Raimbourg was an experienced music-hall comic with an undeniable knack for causing laughter, sometimes beyond his conscious effort. Pierre Latour, who played Estragon, feared that he was relegated to a secondary position in the relationship, though Bradby says that reports suggest it wasn't the case. In the 1955 London premiere Peter Bull, who played Pozzo, brought the most comic experience to the production: 'Peter Bull was capable of putting on a fierce exterior, and he developed a special booming voice for Pozzo, but there was something childishly exaggerated about his manner of performing, which made him very difficult to take entirely seriously.'[70] For the first American productions in 1956, Bert Lahr, known to most film fans as the Cowardly Lion in *The Wizard of Oz* (1939), played Estragon. Lahr was a vaudeville veteran, with a broad comic style and a sure instinct for the music-hall repartee. After an ill-judged opening in Florida, Lahr resumed the role in a Broadway production opposite E. G. Marshall's Vladimir, in which he was allowed 'free rein to treat Marshall as the straight man and himself as the one who got all the laughs'.[71]

A circumspect reading of the play would acknowledge that, although Vladimir and Estragon can be seen as a music-hall double act, their roles in that relationship are decidedly fluid, suggested by the fact that a verbal exchange may be repeated with the roles reversed (e.g., the lines at the end of each act, as observed previously). As one might expect, this embodiment appeared to privilege Lahr's position in the stage world, to the extent that one reviewer saw him as a sort of 'liaison' to the audience. A spectator would generally be more drawn to the 'comic' member of a double act than to the straight man, and Lahr, it seems, projected an additional, extra-fictional 'warmth and humanity'. Bradby observes: 'It is clear that the effect of Lahr's performance was to reduce the bleak anguish of the situation depicted in the play and to emphasise the moments of warmth and comic insight'.[72]

While not trying to make any pronouncements on how the text 'should' be rendered, the point is that these actual circumstances of embodiment exerted an emphatic effect on the production's meaning and feeling. It should be emphasized that the three production histories to which I have referred contain a far wider scope of material relevant to the process by which we imagine text into performance than I have drawn upon here. I have been extremely selective in fixing upon production moments and comments that relate directly to the argument of comic latitude in performance.

What I have tried to evince via this hurried attention to historic performance is that a comic trace in a dramatic text predetermines no single manner of concretization nor its effect. Quite the opposite: it presents an array of opportunities to make and affect meaning both in the moment and in the greater landscape of performance. In the next and final chapter I will look further into issues surrounding these comic practices and their angles of influence within social and cultural contexts.

Chapter 6

Comedy and society

Comedy's associates

Having trained our sights primarily upon the process of reading comedy in dramatic texts, we shall now alter our focus to take in the act of comic production within its social and cultural contexts. All artistic works try to do things to their audiences, e.g., teach, entertain, convince, affect, provoke, soothe, criticize, etc. Yet, no matter how self-aware the artist, the work also remains embedded in a snarl of agencies, vectors of influence operating under the skin of a society at any historical moment. A work's intentions, stated or presumed, cannot reasonably be held to account for the whole of its potential influence. There is also the matter of subsequent performances for a dramatic text, and we observed in the preceding chapter the extent to which meanings bend and vary in the actuality of theatre production for a specific audience in time and place.

As I have emphasized all along, it is one of comedy's defining impulses to capitalize upon the daily experiences and dispositions of the target reader. I have also noted that comedy draws upon structures and conventions that carry built-in directives about how we should and should not conduct our lives. In going about its business, comedy has become associated with some general textual designs worth contemplating, among other reasons, for the ways they engage a reader/spectator within society. The limited discussions in this chapter are intended primarily to plant in the mind of the con- scientious reader an awareness (though, hopefully, too, a curiosity) of concepts relevant to the study of comedy, the comic and dramatic text, and should not be taken for comprehensive or definitive treatments.

Irony

Irony, like humour, operates in the gap between the said and the unsaid. It is a mode of discourse that challenges the notion of absolute truth or authority by showing us that an utterance can also mean something other than it seems (sometimes the opposite), either in the larger scheme of worldly affairs or due to some discursive intention. Also, like humour, irony lends its services to all manner and sphere of utterance, from private conversation to public speechmaking, from political cartooning to literary writing – and, of course, to drama.

Dramatic representation by nature tends to supply the spectator with a privileged perspective upon the stage world, a view which, if not omniscient, awards awareness beyond the grasp of some, most, or all of the stage world's inhabitants. The arrangement can be manipulated to reveal to the spectator a disparity between a character's reading of a situation and its actual significance. Western drama is rife with examples of this sort of situational or dramatic irony. In many a tragedy a false reading of events is purveyed by villainous forces. In others a character misapprehends actions, events or utterances to tragic effect. Romeo, having failed to receive the letter disclosing Juliet's plan to feign death by taking a sleeping potion, believes her to be dead. The spectator is aware of this misconception as the distraught young lover takes his own life, leading inevitably to Juliet's suicide.

Irony is an ever-present structural component for conventional comedy, building gaps into the stage world which lie ready and willing to be sprung for humorous purpose. This affinity is manifested in the comic plotting features we have observed, like mistaken identity, trickery, avoidance, concealed characters and role playing, all of which lead the spectator to know or expect something the character cannot. D. C. Muecke claims that 'there is a special pleasure in seeing someone serenely unaware of being in a predicament, especially when this predicament is the contrary of the situation he assumes himself to be in'.[1]

We observed how shrewdly awareness can be configured and exploited humorously in our Chapter 3 treatment of the screen scene from *The School for Scandal*. The spectator knows that Lady Teazle is behind the screen and that her husband, Sir Peter, is hiding in a closet, unaware of his wife's presence. The duplicitous Joseph Surface knows of both their locations, and his brother Charles thinks there is no one else in the room. Potent angles of situational irony abound, and it is masterfully orchestrated for comic potential by the playwright.

In *The Importance of Being Earnest*, Cecily and Gwendolyn each believe themselves in love with a man named Ernest, the alter egos adopted both by Jack and Algernon to facilitate their wooing. Much of the comedy in their 'tea-party' scene derives from a mutual lack of awareness about this actual state of affairs, the underlying accurate reading of events that commissions the humour. Ultimately we learn that – ironically – Jack has lived his life thus far unaware that his given name *is* Ernest, allowing him to declare, 'Gwendolyn, it is a terrible thing for a man to find out suddenly that all his life he has been speaking nothing but the truth. Can you forgive me?'[2]

Time and space remain intrinsic generators of irony by exposing our sheer inability to account for the impact of previous, subsequent or simultaneous occurrences in our readings of the present. Tables turn on the arrogant and favour finds the humble; parallel events turn perceived significance inside out. Claire Colebrook proposes an explanation for our fascination with dramatic irony:

> It is as though there is the course of human events and intentions, involving our awarding of rankings and expectations, that exists alongside another order of fate beyond our predictions. This is an irony of situation, or an irony of existence; it is as though human life and its understanding of the world is undercut by some other meaning or design beyond our powers.[3]

Some stage worlds arrange themselves for ironic inference by playing with time and space. The 1934 play, *Merrily We Roll Along*, by George S. Kaufman and Moss Hart (turned into a musical in 1981), tells its story backwards in nine scenes spanning nearly twenty years. Its central character begins the play as an embittered 40-year-old playwright and ends as a bright and promising young man exhorting his classmates to be true to themselves. His upbeat idealism in the final scene is therefore ironized in light of the future succession of compromises he has made to achieve a hollow sort of success. Moira Buffini's *Loveplay* (2001) is composed of ten scenes, all taking place on the same geographical site, and moving from a half-built Roman structure in 79 AD through time to a dating agency in the present. The premise bundles the individual scenes for ironic contemplation, all manifesting tensions between love and sex amid the varied social conditions of general historical eras.

Harold Pinter is well known for reversing the direction of ironic awareness – his characters tend to possess more of the 'whole picture' than those of us looking on from outside the stage world. The spectator may glean or surmise connections along the way, but the stage world floats beyond full grasp by the outsider in the theatre seat, contributing to the mood of nameless threat noted in the previous chapter. Pinter's television and stage play, *The Lover*

(1963), begins with a scene locating itself along two lines connecting to the heart of conventional comic territory – an everyday domestic conversation and the subject of marital inconstancy:

> RICHARD   [*amiably*] Is your lover coming today?
> SARAH   Mmnn.
> RICHARD   What time?
> SARAH   Three.[4]

The naïve spectator assumes (rightly) that Richard and Sarah are married to one another, but is unlikely to realize until much later that Richard is also the lover to whom Sarah refers. The reader/spectator deprived of ironic awareness at the start of the play may read this as a generic comic framing: the exchange overlays a blunt query about an acknowledged extramarital sexual relationship with the more routine framing of, say, a chat over breakfast about some household obligation. The frank acknowledgement of lovers other than one's husband generally leads to far more heated exchanges. A broader awareness of the couple's double relationship explains away the humorous gap, a reversal on the audience rather than the characters. This sense of comedy dangled along the ironic divide between stage world and audience is the mechanism by which Pinter's plays acquire their ambiguous moods.

As we saw in the last chapter, absurdist and other non-naturalistic worlds are capable of extending the metaphysical play of ironic configurations. In Samuel Beckett's *Happy Days* (1961) Winnie, the central character, is a middle-aged woman embedded in an earthen mound. Her first line, 'Another heavenly day',[5] surely invites ironic consideration with regard to her unusual yet significant physical context, and a humorous response at that. Beckett was prone to mark the irony of theatre reception itself, especially the conventional desperation to find clear, straightforward meaning. Winnie later recalls two passers-by, one of whom commented on her predicament: 'What does it mean? he says – What's it meant to mean?'[6] There is every chance that a given spectator already will have formulated this question. Other lines along the way point to the gap between Winnie's everyday world and ours, even to the extent that she confers ironic pity upon us, despite being buried up to her neck: 'What a curse, mobility!'[7]

It is worth distinguishing situational irony from irony directly related to verbal utterance. In everyday life we would be aware of the wink, throat clearance or vocal emphasis which, in effect, places inverted commas around the words someone is about to say. These conversational markers instruct us not to take what follows at face value, although sometimes the signal comes from first-hand knowledge that the speaker feels otherwise about the subject. As a potent rhetorical device, however, Linda Hutcheon attributes to ironic meaning a 'rubbing together' of the implicit *and* explicit. This is why mere sarcasm – saying something with the singular intention of meaning its opposite – falls something short of the genuine article for Hutcheon.

In *The Country Wife*, Wycherley opens an ironic gap beneath the concept of 'honour'. Sir Jasper has confided to Lady Fidget that Horner has returned from France a eunuch – a few moments after Horner has secretly assured her that he has not. Lady Fidget then takes great pleasure in heaping approval upon Horner's 'honour' for the benefit of her husband, confident in the knowledge that the rest of the attendant characters as well as the audience detect her salacious intent:

> But, poor gentleman, could you be so generous, so truly a man of honour, as for the sakes of us women of honour, to cause yourself to be reported no man? No man! And to suffer yourself the greatest shame that could fall upon a man, that none might fall upon us women by your conversation?[8]

On the surface, Lady Jasper appears to be defining Horner's laudable 'honour' as a willingness to admit publicly to his recently contracted impotency so that he can serve as a trusted escort without staining their reputations. For everyone except her husband, the notion of honour diverges cynically from the socially approved, and the intended 'conversation' grows a lewd alternative meaning: the 'honour' she applauds lies in his shrewd advertisement of emasculation, the better to offer a socially approved façade *while* sating her sexual appetite. Lady Fidget's speech insinuates an alternative reading to the surface meaning of the words she utters, and the ironic resonance between the 'poles', as Hutcheon calls them, implies a critique of seemly social conduct (see the box below).

Brechtian defamiliarization

Bertolt Brecht's concept of *Verfremdungseffekt* is best understood as 'defamiliarization' – which some refer to as 'making strange' or showing something in such a way that it becomes revealed in a new light. Peter Brooker cites Brecht's writing that *Verfremdungseffekt* 'means first of all stripping the event of its self-evident, familiar, obvious quality and creating a sense of astonishment and curiosity.[9] In Brecht's avowedly political terms, defamiliarization refers to the theatrical ironizing of an utterance, concept or social role so that we are drawn to question the way society encourages us to take it for granted.

(cont.)

In Brecht's *Mother Courage and her Children* (1941), the very idea of 'courage' is defamiliarized several times, starting with the character's explanation of how she got the name: 'Courage is the name they gave me because I was scared of going broke, so I drove my cart right through the bombardment of Riga with fifty loaves of bread aboard. They were going moldy.'[10] Mother Courage explains the derivation of her name by telling a story that contradicts the accepted definition of a concept quite dear to political rhetoric – it was fear of losing business rather than brave commitment to a cause or principle which earned her the name. The inversion of meaning punctures the valorous ideal of the word, perhaps exposing a more down-to-earth view about its use in rallying populations to causes of war or sacrifice. The ironic swipe spares some of its edge for the reality behind a taken-for-granted economic model that forces ordinary citizens into such untenable positions.

Brecht's approach allies naturally with movements of practice and criticism seeking to resist the overwhelming force field thrown up by dominant Western discourses. Brecht wrote that, 'for art to be "un-political" means only to ally itself with the "ruling" group',[11] which may extend from a specific regime to civilization's ideological presumptions.

In Caryl Churchill's *Cloud Nine* (1979) some cast members play characters of the opposite sex. This aligns with Brecht's urging that a distinction be maintained between actor and character, and Churchill mines this opportunity to expose some of the ideological underpinnings of gender construction (see Figure 6.1).

Figure 6.1 The prescribed casting for Caryl Churchill's *Cloud Nine* calls for a man to play a female character, a woman to play a young boy, a white man to play a black family servant, and a doll to represent a little girl – emphasizing the Brechtian gap between character and performer which in every case is mined for ironic comment. The Almeida Theatre, London, 2007.

Edward, the young son, is played by a woman; Betty, his mother, is played by a man. During one scene a few of the characters throw a ball back and forth, and the following exchange ensues:

> EDWARD   Mama, don't play. You know you can't catch a ball.
> BETTY   He's perfectly right. I can't throw either.[12]

The cross-casting defamiliarizes the parroting of sexist cliché to construct a 'natural order of things', sometimes being so effective as to cause women to participate in their own oppression. The gap between actor and character in the above exchange causes a disjunction between the cultural inscription of male capabilities and the female self-deprecation contained in the line. As we have seen several times in this book, defamiliarization is one of the things that humour does. In cases like this it obtains political potency by ridiculing what we have been led to believe was beyond question.

Theorists like Muecke also believe that an utterance qualifies as irony only if it is possible that some person or group would take it at face value. For dramatic – or more specifically, comic – purposes, this aspect is manifested by a character like Sir Jasper, who remains clueless as to her statement's secondary significance. He gloats gleefully about Horner's presumed sexual disadvantage, confidently sending them off together: 'Well, well, that your ladyship is as virtuous as any she, I know, and him all the town knows, he, he, he! Therefore, now you like him, get you gone to your business together; go, go, to your business, I say, pleasure, whilst I go to my pleasure, business.'[13] This is a character begging for comic comeuppance. Northrop Frye's durable assessment applies to a broad strain of such uppity characters, with the inference that the warning is intended across the footlights: 'Comedy is designed not to condemn evil, but to ridicule a lack of self-knowledge.'[14]

We should also remember, pursuant to the examples at the end of the previous chapter, that the ability of bodied utterance to inform dramatic text leaves plenty of room for ironic inflection. Two line readings from Luc Bondy's 1999 production of *Waiting for Godot*, described by David Bradby, suggest the extent to which words can in good conscience play against the apparent tone:

> Estragon's memory of the maps of the Holy Land, 'I used to say, that's where we'll go for our honeymoon. We'll swim. We'll be happy', was the cue for him to break down into tears, but his line a couple of pages later about the tree, 'No more weeping', was delivered on a rising laugh, almost as if he were congratulating himself for having found a poetic phrase.[15]

Real-life components in and around production are always capable of projecting ironic meaning upon a dramatic text, especially when removed in time and/or place from its originating conditions. Two brief examples show how irony can wedge itself between text and casting to amusing effect. Rudolf Nureyev took on the lead role in the 1989 North American revival of Rodgers and Hammerstein's *The King and I* (1951), creating for audiences an amusing ironic gap between his fame as a world-renowned ballet dancer and the text's strong-headed monarch with two left feet who is taught the polka in the musical number, 'Shall We Dance?'. *The Kings of the Kilburn High Road*, written by Irish playwright Jimmy Murphy in 2000, centred on a gathering of five Irish immigrants in a London pub. The play addresses the vortex of alcohol and alienation into which a wave of Irish immigrants were drawn during the 1970s, pursuing a promise of economic betterment. The text's humour derives primarily from the banter, which drains away as the play moves toward confrontational climax in the second act. The casting of five black men in a 2006 Dublin production supplied a striking layer of irony beneath the entire stage world in light of the waves of African immigrants who have transformed the face of Irish society in the past decade. Overtly racist comments gained a reverse spin, suddenly acquiring a satiric bite; ruminations about home and cultural identity struck surprising parallel chords between Irish text and African actors.

Any literary or artistic text, any film or photograph, even a casual e-mail falls prey to ironic spin in the inescapable wake of unfolding events and changing circumstances. Theatre, always made from materials in the active present tense, has the ability (some would say obligation) to engage proactively with the ironic gap between historic text and current performance.

Parody

Parody, too, seeks to pry open a gap between the expressed and the implied. It evokes a recognizable utterance, text or general cultural practice while pointing to some distance between it and the target text, thereby making it more than mere imitation. Its intent need not be humorous, though it tends to throw off at least some comic value, if only for calling to mind the recognizable in style or subject. Finally, like humour and irony, parody expresses an opinion, even if it is quite generally advising us against an excess of seriousness, confidence or predictability.

Simon Dentith gathers under a broadest possible label of parody 'any cultural practice which makes a relatively polemical allusive imitation of another cultural production or practice'.[16] Parody counts for its effect on the reader's familiarity with an original, thereby effectively opening a 'gap to be bridged' similar to the one we've identified in humour construction.

Aristophanes' plays, our oldest recorded examples for all things comic, are rife with parodic passages. As discussed in Chapter 2, his humour remains notable for its direct engagement with the lives and concerns of the Athenian audience. In *Lysistrata*, the gathered women swear solidarity, parodying an invocation from Aeschylus' *Seven Against Thebes* (467 BC), by referring to the sacrifice of a lamb rather than the more virile bull of the original, and substituting wine for blood. Having occupied the Acropolis with her sisters-in-arms, Lysistrata later pronounces poetically upon their sexual deprivation in the form of tragic song. The practice of deflating a highly serious form like tragedy or opera by filling its recognizable shell with low or mundane content remains a potent configuration for comedy.

Although parody often targets in general, say, the genres of melodrama or disaster films, it sometimes narrows its focus to a specific text or source. David Ives's one-act, *Speed-the-Play* (1989), written for a benefit honouring American playwright David Mamet, will resonate for anyone familiar with the Mamet *oeuvre* in general, and four of his best-known plays in particular. The following extract is taken from its parody of *Speed-the-Plow* (1988), Mamet's look at the trampling of idealistic values by hardball powermongers in a Hollywood production studio. The two producers retain their names from the original in a microcosmic parody of their dialogue:

> FOX   You lift your leg to pee.
> GOULD   You genuflect to pick your nose.
> FOX   You stand on your head to jerk off.
> GOULD   You bounce on a trampoline to defecate.[17]

The series of blunt, aggressive, gratuitously crude accusations may well succeed in signalling comic intent, even for someone unfamiliar with Mamet's original. The first line could pass seriously as a macho put-down of some lower-status male, incorporating a subhuman image of physicality. The ensuing lines, however, take the theme to ridiculous physical lengths, having very little to do with the attending vulgarities. Cued by the short piece's title (if nothing else) the sequence calls the target text(s) to mind for anyone familiar with Mamet's canon and this play in particular. These readers will also recognize the allusion to one of Mamet's calling cards, a swaggering scatological wit composed of articulate formulation and bathroom language. Ives's parody keys directly to a line at the climax of Mamet's play – 'you squat to pee' [18] – intending with chauvinistic bluntness to denigrate Gould's masculinity. By crafty inflation, Ives pushes the verbal pugilism toward physical absurdity, thereby allowing a pinch of ridicule into the gap between target and imitation. The above passage carries a critique of male posturing as well as Mamet's self-styled treatment of it, but it is the pointed attention to a textual 'original' that leads us to think in terms of parody.

Literary texts lend themselves well to parody, because the words on the page are the target text itself. As usual, we must not forget to consider the transition to the actuality of performance in dramatic parody. The above well-conceived send-up of David Mamet's work misses the mark if not performed in something of the precise, penetrating style for which his stage worlds call.

Bodied style itself is a most theatrical target for parody. As I have suggested, it is common in Western drama to find an element of parody in comic situations that call for role playing or impersonation. In George Bernard Shaw's *Pygmalion* (1913), the incorrigible Professor Henry Higgins undertakes to transform the cockney flower girl, Eliza Doolittle, into a 'lady', replete with upper-class accent and manners of high society. Western comedy has frequently used such a comic 'teaching' structure, for which the target behaviour is meant to provide a humorous stereotype, at which the would-be imitator is laughably unsuccessful or else bodily unsuited.

We should be wary of underestimating the sociopolitical implications of dramatic texts that seek comic value from instruction, imitation and disguise. As always, a defining question from a socio-political standpoint, is: at what or whom are we being invited to laugh? Upon what stereotypical bodied behaviour does the text and performance rely? To what extent does the person (and group he or she represents) being held up for ridicule bear the brunt of critique, and to what extent does the imitator (and group he or she represents)? To what extent does comic effect rely on the imitator's competency or failure to master the target body? We are likely to be coaxed inside the magic circle of readers/spectators, which places a certain bodied style as Other, and which seeks to paint ways of being as laughable. In such constructions, there always exists the possibility for a humorous clash of frames between the character's 'natural' body, behaviour and social styling and those of its target. Shepherd, upon whose analysis of the body in performance we drew in Chapter 4, advises close attention to the socio-cultural implications of 'teaching' and role-playing scenes: 'In encouraging audiences to laugh at or admire particular bodies, the theatre plays its part in the mechanisms by which a society scripts and allocates bodily value.'[19]

In Shakespeare's *As You Like It* (1599), Rosalind adopts the guise of a young man named Ganymede, having been banished to the Forest of Arden. She finds that Orlando, with whom she fell in love at court, has pinned to a tree a love poem proclaiming the romantic feelings he was too shy to express when they first met. She meets Orlando in her guise as Ganymede, and agrees to cure his lovesickness by pretending to be the object of his affections (which happens to be herself), as (s)he had done for another smitten suitor in the past:

> He was to imagine me his love, his mistress; and I set him every day to woo me. At which time would I, being but a moonish youth, grieve, be effeminate, changeable, longing and liking, proud, fantastical, apish, shallow, inconstant, full of tears, full of smiles; for every passion something, and for no passion truly anything, as boys and women are for the most part cattle of this colour; would now like him, now loathe him; then entertain him, then forswear him; now weep for him, then spit at him; that I drave my suitor from his mad humour of love to a living humour of madness – which was, to forswear the full stream of the world and to live in a nook merely monastic.[20]

Shakespeare placed this parody in the mouth (and body) of a boy actor playing a young woman disguised as a young man play-acting the part of the young woman she actually is. It is, to be sure, a comedy-friendly layering, offering several ricochets of ironic nuance even without the original casting convention. 'What presumptions and biases are being accessed?' is a question that can only be asked fairly with regard to a given actualization in time and place, but we should always inspect beneath the crust of the obvious for the political implications of meaning and bias. Taking advice from several theoretical approaches, we should query the primacy of Western culture's male/white/heterosexual orientation when seeking explanations as to how and at whose expense the utterance works. We should look for ways in which comedy and the comic collude with dominant ideologies to reinforce notions of the culturally conditioned as 'natural', just as we seek out evidence of its alternative and subversive capabilities.

The speech's flood of contradictory descriptors generates a pile-up of frame clashes that we recognize as a basic pattern for humour construction, but which is also being advanced as an image of 'what women are like'. Along these lines, it would offer obvious opportunities to outline the rush of behavioural changes, if not a full-bodied caricature of 'female' fickleness or unreason. A feminist critic would have cause to point out

that the ridicule of female behaviour as incongruous or illogical has constituted a long-standing tool for the patriarchal dominance of society. It is,
however, the ever-provisional status of a dramatic text that requires us to
withhold pronouncements upon its political action prior to performance
and context. The words, after all, are delivered by a female character, one of
the most witty and observant we are likely to meet in this and many a
stage world. How 'competent' is Rosalind's mastery of masculinity when
disguised as Ganymede, or does she try to inhabit the role at all? What
attitude does she bring to her role playing? The beauty of Shakespeare's
confection is that the character can be embodied with such qualities – for
example, the 'gentle mockery' observed by one critic in Vanessa Redgrave's
celebrated 1961 performance[21] – as to have made her one of the plum
roles in the Shakespeare canon *and* an articulate heroine for feminist and
gay causes.

It is possible to see Rosalind anticipating the field of gender studies,
with its contention that concepts like 'masculine' and 'feminine' lodge in our
minds and bodies as part of cultural inscription. (They are, in fact, secured in

Figure 6.2 The 1990s Cheek by Jowl production of Shakespeare's
As You Like It used an all-male cast to emphasize issues of gender
construction in the text. Patrick Toomey played Orlando and
Adrian Lester played Rosalind. Lyric Hammersmith, London, 1991.

no small part by comic stereotyping in popular entertainment milieus like the sitcom and the panto.) Rosalind could be seen, in speeches like the one above, to be giving a lecture demonstration on gender construction. A production that highlights our performance of gender – through, for example, the all-male casting of Declan Donnellan's 1991 Cheek by Jowl mounting, in which the actors *became* their female characters at the start – could re-route the critique of the above parody to the cultural catalogue of gestures, styles and scripts we come to take as essential evidence of maleness and femaleness (see Figure 6.2).

There is, ultimately, no telling where this speech might lead a Rosalind, nor the stage world over which she presides. The parodic impulse initiated over 400 years ago can only ever be filtered through the performer and production in a sociocultural present, and its political polarities cannot reasonably be gauged outside an actual context. We can, however, observe that critical thought has claimed parody's allegiance both for and against society's dominant discourses – what Hutcheon calls 'the transideological nature of its politics' with regard to irony[22] – as summed up by Dentith:

> On the one hand, it has been seen as conservative in the way that it is used to mock literary and social innovation, policing the boundaries of the sayable in the interests of those who wish to continue to say what has always been said. On the other hand, there is another tradition which celebrates the subversive possibilities of parody as its essential characteristic; parody in this view typically attacks the official word, mocks the pretensions of authoritative discourse, and undermines the seriousness with which subordinates should approach the justification of their betters.[23]

These positions also encapsulate opposing social dynamics for humour and the comic, and characterize the basic positions in debates about their political allegiances.

Satire

Parody, irony and humour always carry evaluative edges, however veiled or unobtrusive. When that critical charge becomes the main force behind the utterance, we tend to call it satire. Matthew Hodgart points out that the satirist's impulse does not manifest itself in direct attack, but by shrewder means: 'his aim is to make the victim lose "face", and the most effective way of humiliating him is by contemptuous laughter'.[24] With ancient ancestry in Roman verse satire – Horace, known for his restrained, reasoning approach, and Juvenal, for his sneering invective – satire is now seen broadly as a free-ranging mode of artistic attack, usually against some real or perceived orthodoxy in thought, attitude or practice.

Satire cannot be reduced to an empiric formula in the ways that we have distinguished for irony and parody, although it often employs these modes to express its disdain. In literary satires like *Candide* and *A Modest Proposal*, to which I have referred in previous chapters, a narrator adopts an identifiable discursive register in detached contrast to the events being described, thereby emphasizing the blithe, blind, or unthinking acceptance of insupportable thought or deed (war and violence in the first instance, eating children in the second).

Dramatic satire, usually deprived of a single narratorial perspective, often looks for generic worlds from which to open critical gaps upon its targets. John Gay's *The Beggar's Opera* (1728), for example, invokes the form of Italian opera popular at the time, replete with heroic characters, high-blown emotions and gratuitous plot turns, for an attack on the hypocrisies of the ruling classes. By filling his stage world with denizens of the criminal underworld, who were at the time of its writing also thinly veiled stand-ins for well-known politicians and popular figures, Gay avails himself of a double deflation. Highwaymen and prostitutes are seen to comport themselves with impeccably 'civilized' manners as they justify the most cynically self-serving behaviour (and, alas, its satire still scores effectively, even without audience knowledge of the original targets). With the criminal protagonist being led to execution, the mass theatregoers' own predilections for escapist fluff are ridiculed – 'for an Opera must end happily' – and the ending is simply changed 'to comply with the taste of the town'.[25]

Satire usually eschews the happy endings of conventional comedy, unless it twists their resonances as above, or subverts the sense of closure, as noted in Chapter 1 with regard to *What the Butler Saw*. Aphra Behn's *The Rover* (1677) ends with conventional comic pairings, but on terms specified by the female playwright amid a staunchly patriarchal society. In the play, Hellena, disinclined to follow the family's wishes by entering the convent, takes the opportunity of carnival time to seek her own romantic fortunes. She sets her sights on Willmore, whom Behn depicts as the hard-drinking rogue and sexual adventurer one might have encountered in her audience. Hellena disarms him with honesty and wit:

> I am as inconstant as you, for I have considered, captain, that a handsome woman has a great deal to do whilst her face is good, for then is our harvest-time to gather friends; and should I in these days of my youth, catch a fit of foolish constancy, I were undone; 'tis loitering by daylight in our great journey.[26]

Their betrothal at the end advances Behn's case for a more honest meeting of men and women and a redressing of the standards against which their respective behaviours are held.

Satiric writers have more than once vented their spleens over the endlessly corruptible nature of those who preside over society and would exemplify its principles, by revealing how readily their venality serves them up as prey for the scamps and conmen they would denounce. The Russian writer Nikolai Gogol was one who dramatized this seemingly permanent human defect in *The Government Inspector* (1836). A down-at-heel clerk, unable to pay his bill at the local inn, is mistaken for the title character expected by the mayor and town officials. Before long he is playing the part to the hilt, accepting bribes from everyone desperate to cover up their indiscretions. He escapes before they come upon his real identity, whereupon the guilty townspeople, reeling from the discovery, are confronted with the *real* government inspector. The notable aspect of this type of world is the absence of any truly admirable character, a most cynical – though not uncommon – satiric view of human nature.

Despite his famous warning, 'Satire is what closes Saturday night' (meaning, presumably, by the end of its first week),[27] the American playwright Kaufman was one of the deftest satirists of the early twentieth century. Plays like *Once in a Lifetime*, which Kaufman wrote with Hart in 1930, can't seem to believe the depths of foolishness, hypocrisy and downright dishonesty of which society and its inhabitants prove themselves capable. The play still has some startling currency, embodying a culture's mindless commercial pursuit for the next big 'trend' in the gold-rush mentality of Hollywood movie-making in the 1920s. The voice of reason is found in a playwright who has been whisked to Hollywood and now prowls a studio reception room, emotionally unravelling at having been given nothing to do in the six months since he arrived from New York, and being unable to talk to anyone in authority:

> I think Hollywood and this darling industry of yours is the most God-awful thing I've ever run into. Everybody behaving in the most fantastic fashion – nobody acting like a human being. I'm brought out here, like a hundred others, paid a fat salary – nobody notices me. Not that I might be any good – it's just an indication. Thousands of dollars thrown away every day. Why do they do that, do you know?[28]

The character's distraught speeches embody a seething exasperation with the current state of reason or civilization, a tone one can detect in many a satiric world.

The stage satirist has particular recourse to non-realistic and multi-textual techniques. Eugène Ionesco's *Rhinoceros* (*Rhinocéros*, 1959) shows the population of a village turned one by one into the stampeding horned creatures of the title. Although it was written in response to Ionesco's particular experiences of Fascism, its satiric power attaches to the troubling human inclination toward herd mentality, whether in thrall to some new cultural fashion or – more dangerously, as history has shown – to religious and political movements. Suzan-Lori Parks's *Venus* (1996) depicts the real-life episode of a Hottentot woman lured from South Africa in the early 1800s to be displayed and exploited in England as a freak. Parks creates a rabid swirl of a stage world, mingling scientific discovery with hucksterism. Her text generates different dramatic and choral styles, interpolated with music, as well as spoken footnotes, testimonies and historical extracts. The piece as a whole makes trenchant points about the root system of racist attitudes toward African-Americans in the United States, while more generally mocking a tendency toward bigotry's all too familiar cocktail of ignorance and arrogance.

Carnival

A few other concepts demand attention in a discussion of comic worlds, particularly with regard to their social workings. Russian theorist Mikhail Bakhtin introduced the influential concept of carnival through his book, *Rabelais and His World*, written in the 1930s and unpublished until 1965. He characterizes the phenomenon of medieval carnival as an officially sanctioned holiday from the usual order of things. The carnival spirit was populist and all-inclusive, Bakhtin observes, and 'one might say that carnival celebrated temporary liberation from the prevailing truth and from the established order; it marked the suspension of all hierarchical rank, privileges, norms, and prohibitions'.[29] He refers, for instance, to the Feast of Fools, a celebration led by lesser clergy, given temporary licence to ridicule church life as well as their superiors.

Anything went during carnival time, when all citizens enjoyed a freedom unavailable in everyday life. Aphra Behn sets *The Rover* during a later version of carnival time in Naples; there is music, dancing, and widespread masquerade, affording almost unlimited opportunity to dare new identities and behaviours. Hellena uses her disguise to wriggle from under the thumb of an oppressively patriarchal society. Despite being reared in a nunnery, she proclaims from the outset not only her interest in male companionship, but her intention to go on the offensive – an initiative unthinkable under everyday social codes of the time: 'Nay, I'm resolved to provide myself this Carnival, if there be e'er a handsome proper fellow of my humour above ground, though I ask first.'[30]

The carnival spirit, according to Bakhtin, is also characterized by a populist outpouring of laughter. It is not surprising, then, that comedy should like to think of itself as the embodiment of carnival spirit, a rising up on behalf of popular desire and the disenfranchised. As we have seen, mocking figures and structures of authority remain evergreen spurs to audience laughter, relating generally to Freudian release at the blatant breaking of taboos. It might be noted, however, that these opportunities for challenges to the ruling order are fixed and limited, and can be seen as a way of containing or diffusing those threatening impulses.

Bakhtin's formulation of the carnivalesque includes the concept of 'grotesque realism', which centres on exaggerations of the body, its orifices and functions, a 'lowering of all that is high, spiritual, ideal, abstract; it is a transfer to the material level, to the sphere of earth and body in their indissoluble unity'.[31] Julia Kristeva, a literary critic and psychoanalyst, excavates similar ground with her notion of 'abjection'. Cultural inscription constructs within us indelible responses toward the trappings of our bodied existences – genitalia, blood, faeces, urine and death, for example. As inescapable parts of bodied living, these sources of revulsion can never be placed 'outside' ourselves, so they also become strange objects of fascination that cannot be ignored. Kristeva's concept addresses the troubling effect of these things too close to our daily being to keep at arm's length: 'It is thus not lack of cleanliness or health that causes abjection but what disturbs identity, system, order.'[32] Andrew Stott, in looking at the body in comedy, proposes: 'Abjection may explain why 'sick', morbid, or scatological humour, or comedy that involves violence and pain, is so popular. Such examples go straight to the worry, addressing the inescapable bodily facts of existence that are elided by manners.'[33] Both these ideas recall our discussion of the grotesque in the preceding chapter, and the body's ambivalent relationship toward its own corporeality.

In Mamet's *Glengarry Glen Ross* (1983), the third scene begins with Roma, the consummate salesman, seated next to a potential customer and in mid-sales pitch: 'all train compartments smell vaguely of shit. It gets so you don't mind it. That's the worst thing that I can confess.'[34] He goes on to toss off several discomfiting thoughts before circling back around to, 'You ever take a dump made you feel you'd just slept for twelve hours?'[35]

The speech involves more than bathroom humour, touching almost randomly upon death, homoeroticism, adultery, pederasty and hell, book-ended by these references to excrement. In a psychological approach to the character, we might surmise that Roma has crafted these philosophical meanderings as the slickest of openings for setting up his next mark. The last line, with its unceremonious wording and metaphoric exaggeration is built like a joke, offering the listening character and the spectator an exit door to relief. Mamet's calculated transgressions of 'taste' in the above passage enter upon a borderline, uneasy humour found in some of Sarah Kane's work and in contemporary plays by Mark Ravenhill and Neil Labute.

Fools and madmen

Mental defect and clinical insanity may be no laughing matters in real life. It cannot be surprising, though, that literature and drama have found comic touchstones in foolishness and madness. They remain human states defined by Western culture in opposition to the rational thought and behaviour upon which civilization is laid. What better candidates, then, for the discursive stratagem we call humour, which thrives on breaking frames and making sense from non-sense?

Welsford's classic study, *The Fool: His Social and Literary History*, follows her subject back into the mists of early civilization, where he served as mascot and scapegoat, poet and clairvoyant, and was found in cultures from east to west. Welsford identifies four orders of fools, from hapless bumpkin to master manipulator:

> [T]here are those who get slapped, there are those who are none the worse for their slapping, there are those who adroitly change places with the slappers, and occasionally there are those who enquire, 'What do slaps matter to the man whose body is of indiarubber, and whose mind is of quicksilver, and who can even – greatest triumph of all – persuade you for the moment that such indeed is your case?'[36]

We touched upon foolery in Chapter 4, with regard to the clown figure. In Elizabethan times the fool and the clown were distinguishable by their costumes, but otherwise became conflated, as the performer who took the clown roles might be called a fool in the stage world – Robert Armin as, for example, the Fool in *King Lear* or Feste in *Twelfth Night*.

A dim character may display cracked logic or judgement – say, the sequence from Shakespeare's *The Two Gentlemen of Verona* involving Launce and his dog discussed in Chapter 4 – but there is still an entertaining sense to the actions, especially when it was performed by a comic virtuoso like Will Kemp. In the above look at *Once in a Lifetime*, part of the satiric value lies in the fact that the fool figure of George should achieve such renown for mental acuity in the mindlessly trend-happy land of Hollywood.

The 'wise fool' on the Elizabethan stage exercises a licence – obligation, in fact – to dispense cheeky advice, especially by confounding the laws of reason. This is the person who may dissemble foolishness toward some end, as does the dog dealer and 'good soldier' transposed from Jaroslav Hasek's novel to *Schweyk in the Second World War* (*Schweyk im zweiten Weltkrieg*, 1957) by Bertolt Brecht. It is never certain that Schweyk is quite the dunderhead he seems, as he survives the deadliest of circumstances by seeming to serve the Third Reich.

Welsford treats the madman as a character akin to the fool in some manifestations, observing that 'there is a widespread notion which is not yet quite extinct that the lunatic is an awe-inspiring figure whose reason has ceased to function normally because he has become the mouthpiece of a spirit, or power external to himself, and so has access to hidden knowledge – especially knowledge of the future'.[37]

Madmen are deployed differently by Shakespeare and his contemporaries from the way they are used by subsequent dramatists. References to madness in Shakespearean comedy arise in *The Comedy of Errors* and *Twelfth Night*, when young men lose faith in their own identities due to confusions with their twins. *Twelfth Night* shows the comic gulling of Malvolio, branded as mad after being lured into displays of ridiculous dress and conduct.[38]

For Michel Foucault, the notion of madness became a post-Enlightenment sorting machine for maintaining strict control over the shape and substance of approved discourses. Characters labelled as mad because of their eccentric behaviours or marginalized status in, say, Kaufman and Hart's *You Can't Take It With You* (1936) and Jean Giraudoux's *The Madwoman of Chaillot* (*La Folle de Chaillot*, 1947) reverse the accusation by holding a mirror up to society and proposing themselves as clearly the saner and certainly the more human.

The first act of Peter Barnes's *The Ruling Class* (1968) uses madness as a comic battering ram against the stalwart English aristocracy and the calcified principles it has too often come to represent. The 14th Earl of Gurney is a young man who earnestly and exuberantly believes himself to be God. The family doctor explains:

> Remember, he's suffering from delusions of *grandeur*. In reality he's an Earl, an English aristocrat, a peer of the realm, a member of the ruling class. Naturally, he's come to believe there's only one person grander than that – the Lord God Almighty Himself.[39]

Barnes borrows the objective authority awarded to medical pronouncements to land many such tongue-in-cheek punches. The Earl hangs upon a crucifix over the gallery when resting, and on his wedding night enters the bedchamber riding a unicycle. His action and thought are unpredictable and uninhibited, both of which serve his construction as mad and serve the purposes of comedy, as Purdie has observed: 'Behaviour which is "mad" and behaviour which is funny are definitionally alike.'[40] The Earl's psychic disjunction at times allows for bolts of the irresistible coherence that we have come to expect from a stage madman: 'You think I'd go around saying I was God if I could help it? Mental hospitals are full of chaps saying they're God.'[41]

The Earl is 'cured' at the end of the first act, whereupon he becomes the overbearing archconservative his family craved in the first place, and is barely able to contain his new delusion as a seething incarnation of Jack the Ripper. Barnes pulls off the neat trick of reversing the comic tide in mid-play: the liberating humour of the first act goes chillingly sardonic in the second. The Earl assumes his rightful place in the Gurney line, more dangerously unbalanced than before, and announces: 'Behaviour which would be considered insanity in a tradesman is looked on as mild eccentricity in a lord'.[42]

This stage world goes further than most by using the instruments of comedy for more than satiric wisecracking. It wields the comic with affective force: with cultural discourses so strongly imprinted upon our psyches, what happens to suppressed or disallowed impulses and desires, especially for those outside a society's 'ruling class'? This concern represents an issue championed by several critical approaches, and is particularly tricky for comedy, which trades on the validation of experience, thought and feeling between individual and group.

Comedy's politics

Comedy and society

Peter Buse, in constructing an argument about the ideological politics of joking, looks at the transaction between teller and listener: 'A successful joke cements a bond between these two in which the butt acts as the glue; in other words, jokes are a way of establishing the borders of a social unit or community.'[43] In theatrical terms, the teller is the playwright as mediated by production; the listener is the reader/spectator; the butt, of course, is the joke's target of ridicule. Comedy can, of course, originate from a minority position – taking aim at official, popular or accepted prey – but it threatens to gain its desired effect solely upon those already inclined to validate its stance. To earn its serious credentials, comedy would seem to have to prove itself capable of something more.

Christopher Innes touches upon this question by distinguishing Alan Ayckbourn and Michael Frayn as playwrights who insistently tried to reclaim the primacy of entertainment value for comic form in the 1980s. He cites Ayckbourn's resentment: 'I'm on a crusade to try and persuade people that theatre can be fun; but every time I start doing that, some hairy bugger from the left comes in and tells them it's instructive, and drives them all out again. If I want to be instructed, I go to night-school'.[44] Innes contends that Ayckbourn's and Frayn's widespread success in making people laugh led to a shortfall in appreciation for their achievements:

> These are easy to pin down in print, unlike the electricity of purely theatrical moments that characterizes farce; and analysing, or even imposing, serious ideas confirms the value of the critic. Conversely, prolific output and wide popularity – achieved so notably by Ayck-bourn – tend to be looked on as superficial, while commercial success is suspect.[45]

Innes makes a fair and welcome point about the devalued status accorded comic discourse due to intellectual and political biases. It remains, however, a separate issue, as neither of these playwrights could be considered uncritical of society's status quo. The ending of Ayckbourn's *Absurd Person Singular*, to which I alluded at the end of Chapter 1, may be seen simultaneously to emulate and bristle against comedy's closing celebration of social harmony. The dancing version of the children's game, musical chairs, turns into a bizarre celebration of Sidney's unlikely ascendancy to the top of the social heap. He discharges his newfound power hysterically, by handing out humiliating 'forfeits' while exhorting the players to continue dancing. It stands, in fact, as quite an impressive achievement that Ayckbourn has pleased such a wide audience by showing them semblances of their own behavioural excesses amid the rocks and hard places of modern social pressures.

The above refocusing upon the actuality of comedy in the public act of performance should remind us about the endlessly provisional nature of the dramatic text in a discussion like this. We observed in the preceding chapter something of the range for embodiment to which any given text, no matter how familiar, is subject. In comedic terms, not only is the degree of humorous intent negotiable, but so are its tones and targets. My short discussion above of Aphra Behn's *The Rover* speaks too confidently about its woman-oriented resonance, which in contemporary performance may be all but smothered by production choices. Shakespeare's *The Taming of the Shrew* (1594) appears on the page to stamp unequivocally the originating culture's patriarchal dominance upon the final scene. I have been aware of several productions of the play here in the early twenty-first century in which all roles were taken by performers of the opposite sex, thereby seeking an ironic inversion for jokes about gender stereotyping and presumptions of sexual dominance.

The fact remains that comedy is a hard character to pin to a consistent political stripe. It can't quite shake its reputation for guarding the status quo by ridiculing difference and confirming allegiance to the social order. While often appearing to champion the spirit of individual expression, comedy nonetheless attempts to throw a normalizing arm around all and sundry, through resolutions that feel pleasing precisely because they reinforce what we've been taught about the natural order of things. In many cases, comedy's humour wears a mask of simple, pleasure-seeking innocence, which can only ever amount to a concealment of the socially conservative face behind the hooting down of accepted targets.

It is, therefore, fairly easy, once you start looking, to compile a list of society's accepted joking butts. The next time you watch a film or television comedy, take note of the stereotypes and biases that the humour attempts to exploit. What social labels have the greatest number of jokes made at their expense, how is the group identified by accent, skin colour, nationality, dress, physique, occupation, social class, part of the country, etc., and what are the traits being held up for ridicule?

However, comedy and the comic have shown the ability to open spaces for the unique and effective challenge of received ideas and encrusted sociocultural conceits. They can jump-start discussion on subjects thought beyond question, thereby stirring controversy (if not downright offence) from quarters unwilling or unable to countenance debate in a playful key.

The rest of this chapter will address a handful of critical orientations in a highly selective fashion. While trying to introduce a sense of what a concept refers to, in all cases these issues are infinitely more complex than their mention here suggests, and would contain competing approaches or strains of thought within them. I have in every instance tried merely to offer a few examples of how the comic has been wielded with regard to these critical areas, trusting that the diligent reader will go on to seek out more (for which Mark Fortier's *Theory/Theatre: An Introduction* provides extremely accessible entries to all these theoretical areas).[46]

Feminist and gay currents

As intimated above, Western civilization is built upon a foundation laid by white, heterosexual men, who continue to claim sociopolitical pre-eminence. Its canon of literature and drama are embedded in this web of presumptions and power relations, not to mention its aesthetic structures. A text's convictions about 'nature', 'common sense' and, well, comedy, always merit interrogation by the likes of Marxist, feminist, gay and lesbian, intercultural and postcolonial critical approaches. There is no need (nor room) to go into all these critical literatures here – suffice to say that there will always be things worth unpacking from mainstream comedic texts in terms of the tenets, passions, characters and groups being held up for validation and ridicule.

A first good question is: do comedy and the comic have the genuine capacities to challenge and change the dominant discourses of our societies? In a celebrated essay titled 'The laugh of the Medusa' ('Le rire de la méduse', 1975), French feminist critic Hélène Cixous announced, 'Woman must write herself',[47] to give original voice to the veracity and fullness of her bodied existence. In *Goodnight Desdemona (Good Morning Juliet)* (1988), Canadian writer Ann-Marie MacDonald tilts the male-oriented worlds of Shakespearian tragedy and modern academia on their axes. Her central character, Constance, is assistant to a professor in a university drama department. She is working on her PhD dissertation, in which she argues that the flimsiness of the tragic crises in *Romeo and Juliet* and *Othello* may be traced to earlier, 'lost' texts from which Shakespeare borrowed. She argues in her thesis that the inability of a Romeo or Othello to save himself (or his beloved) points to missing gravitational pulls in their respective dramatic systems – generated in other plays by a saving influence upon which I have already touched:

> Indeed, in *Othello* and *Romeo and Juliet* the Fool is conspicuous by his very absence, for these two tragedies turn on flimsy mistakes – a lost hanky, a delayed wedding announcement – mistakes too easily concocted and corrected by a Wise Fool.[48]

Constance, hard-working and brilliant in her own right, has been shunted into the shadows of her department, exploited personally and professionally by the cheesy male professor she assists. In a dreamlike plot turn, Constance is sucked into her office wastebasket and into the worlds of *Othello* and *Romeo and Juliet*, where she effectively fulfils the fool function, changing the courses and meanings of the plays. MacDonald weaves a new and festive world from pieces of these exceedingly familiar fabrics. The stage world

incorporates slapstick, comic juxtaposition of the Shakespearean and contemporary, cross-dressing confusion, music-hall gags, and satiric swipes at
the confluence of academia, Shakespeare studies and patriarchal presump-
tion. MacDonald must be writing herself, as Cixous urges, intervening
cleverly in the original plays so as to rediscover their worlds from her own
subject position. A comic infectiousness subverts from within the fusty old
world of tragic predestination, proposing a fresh, female alternative to the
'tunnel vision' and 'certainty' that leads so reliably to piles of bodies at the
end of a play. Coming upon a liberating sense of identity, Constance celebrates her birthday in an alternative to comedy's 'sacred marriage', affirming
her solidarity with newfound friends, Desdemona and Juliet.

I might well have cited from Joe Orton's *What the Butler Saw* in the
above section on madness. The play takes place in a mental clinic, where the
confusion, disguises and misapprehensions of a farcical stage world appear
well suited to a milieu for representing madness – not to mention the
genre's classic set, as one character wonders: 'Why are there so many doors?
Was the house designed by a lunatic?'[49] As discussed earlier with regard to
A Little Hotel on the Side, farce is often driven by sexual desire, which Orton
exploits to throw the doors wide open upon a dizzying exploration of
gender construction and carnal appetite. Dr Rance is a government
inspector, whose power is absolute and whose reasoning inclines toward
the startling. The play's farcical evasion began when the clinic's consultant,
Dr Prentice, attempted to seduce his new secretary, Geraldine; she is now
dressed as a boy:

> RANCE   Do you think of yourself as a girl?
> GERALDINE   No.
> RANCE   Why not?
> GERALDINE   I'm a boy.
> RANCE   [*kindly*] Do you have the evidence about you?
> GERALDINE   [*her eyes flashing an appeal to* DR PRENTICE] I must be
>   a boy. I like girls.
> [DR RANCE *stops and wrinkles his brow, puzzled.*]
> RANCE   [*aside, to* DR PRENTICE] I can't quite follow the rea-
>   soning there.
> PRENTICE   Many men imagine that a preference for women, is *ipso*
>   *facto*, a proof of virility.
> RANCE   [*nodding, sagely*] Someone should really write a book
>   on these folk-myths.[50]

The scene takes the form of an interrogation, with Rance as more police
figure than psychiatric authority. His mystification at Geraldine's response
underplays with comic excess the nod to a strict heterosexual gender typing

which allows no other possibilities. The aside exchange between the two doctors draws upon the considered tones of professional dialogue about mental illness to ridicule further society's party line on sex and gender.

Buse discusses how *What the Butler Saw*, written by a gay playwright during the 1960s, produced split critical opinion about its social posture:

> Some regard Orton's plays as overt challenges to the sexual con-
> formities of his day and therefore figure Orton as an advance guard of
> the revolution, a sort of fifth columnist among the sexual conserva-
> tives. There is, however, an equally convincing case that plays like
> *What the Butler Saw* are so firmly wedged in the closet that they have
> nothing positive to offer a progressive sexual politics, and indeed, that
> Orton, far from being a radical in formation, was quite happy to
> remain in the closet without directly confronting the sexual powers
> that be.[51]

There can be little question that the play exploits medical discourse to equate sanity with heterosexual desire and madness with anything else. One wonders to what extent the disagreement amounts to a debate on the effectiveness of Orton's satiric vehicle, farcical form, in lending sufficient weight to a political statement.

Tony Kushner's *Angels in America, Part One: Millenium Approaches* (1991) uses no such conventional comic template. Subtitled *A Gay Fantasia on National Themes*, the play does its best to forge a genre of its own, and so it presents an interesting counterpoint to the comic dynamic of *What the Butler Saw*. Comic possibility arises from a metaphysical sense of play, through, for example, hallucinations on the part of Harper, an agoraphobic woman, unhappily married to a Mormon in desperate denial of his homosexuality. She is one of two characters who share a 'mutual dream scene' even though they don't know each other, and who proceed to tear up the playwright's own dramatic licence by wondering how such mental activity can be possible. Alongside fictional people, the cast includes a character based on the legendary right-wing lawyer Roy M. Cohn, who died of AIDS in 1986, an imaginary travel agent, an angel and a couple of ghosts.

C. W. E. Bigsby declares *Angels* 'surely the most successful play of the 1990s',[52] implying that it enjoyed the broadest of commercial reaches. Much of its humour manifests itself in jokes made consciously by the characters. A world-weary rabbi is talking to a young man at the cemetery, having just conducted the service for his recently deceased grandmother. Louis, the young man, points to the coffin and asks, 'Why are there just two little wooden pegs holding the lid down?' The rabbi answers, 'So she can get out easier if she wants to.'[53] The young man later sidles toward a confession that he is about to leave his male lover dying of AIDS:

> LOUIS   Rabbi, I'm afraid of the crimes I may commit.
> RABBI ISIDOR   Please, mister. I'm a sick old rabbi facing a long drive
> CHEMELWITZ   home to the Bronx. You want to confess, better
>   you should find a priest.[54]

These are good jokes – rabbis are also known for their sage senses of humour – the second one crafting a mainstream laugh about neighbouring religious practices to normalize the distinctive AIDS-related anguish of gay relationships at the time. Mark Fortier sees in the text a 'minoritizing interest' in gay culture, meaning references to a lifestyle, its vernacular styles and coded referents, which would not include most spectators. Prior, Louis's dying lover, supplies many such minoritizing references to gay culture of the period, identifying with the Shirley Booth character in *Come Back, Little Sheba*, and commenting on Harper's sudden disappearance from his dream ('People come and go so quickly here'), an obvious reference to *The Wizard of Oz*.

If we accept Bigsby's analysis that, in the play's historical context of 1985, 'Prior represents the human need being ignored by those who command the political system, a challenge to the humanity of everyone involved',[55] the character's irrepressible will to quip becomes much more than comic relief. Finally working up the nerve to show Louis his first lesion, an early physical sign of AIDS, Prior jokes, 'I'm a lesionnaire. The Foreign Lesion. The American Lesion. Lesionnaire's disease'.[56] In the symbolic context Bigsby proposes, it is to be sure a man whose sense of humour goes into overdrive as he deals with death's first unmistakable grip upon his arm. It is also an unprecedented enshrinement of the life spirit in its everyday heroism, stepping up when it really counts and painful to witness in light of an establishment making believe it's none of their business. This text in time and culture shows the comic swimming upstream against the tide of official thought – and making legitimate headway with a mainstream audience.

Postmodernism and the comic

Postmodernism is a philosophical and critical concept that means many things to many theorists. It broadly describes an erosion (since around the 1960s) of our faith in the systems and explanations that once inspired confidence in a meaningful, cohesive existence. It expresses distrust toward notions of truth, cohesion and authenticity. This means that there is not usually a seat at the postmodern table for comedy, a time-honoured Western genre with a classical penchant for unity and meaning. It is, however, good news for the comic, which has been known to enter eagerly where cynical treatments of language, religion, authority and the authenticity of experience are required.[57]

Postmodernism oversees our evolution toward a media-hyped, plugged-in global society, constantly bombarding its inhabitants with information and images, jumbling together the profound and mundane without rhyme or reason. In *The Ruling Class*, discussed above, the Earl delivers the occasional unhinged burst of psychic activity:

> Like a river flowing over everything. I pick up a newspaper and I'm everywhere, conducting a Summit Conference, dying of hunger in a Peruvian gutter, accepting the Nobel Prize for Literature, raping a nun in Sumatra.[58]

We can see in his stream of consciousness a string of incongruous activities, perhaps amusing from the perspective of the character's claim to divine ubiquity, but not at all so in light of the final atrocity. Perhaps the utterance serves as a pointed anti-joke about theism, from the mouth of a man who claims to be God.

Postmodernism is drawn naturally to incongruity and scepticism, and generally held to have an affinity for the multiple framings of parody, irony, pastiche and intertextuality. It repudiates the privileging of high culture over low – or even their segregation – making texts like *Monty Python's Flying Circus* (1969–74) and *The Simpsons* natural comic ambassadors.

Postmodernism also sponsors questions about history and its valid representation. The first act of Churchill's *Top Girls* (1982) depicts a dinner party thrown by Marlene, on the occasion of her big promotion. She has invited five women: Lady Nijo, a thirteenth-century Emperor's concubine and Buddhist nun; Griselda, the exceedingly obedient wife in 'The clerk's tale' of Chaucer's *The Canterbury Tales*; Isabella Bird, a Victorian adventurer; Joan, who, disguised as a man, was alleged to have been Pope for three years in the ninth century; and Dull Gret, the warrior subject of a painting by Pieter Brueghel the Elder. They are served throughout the scene by a silent waitress. This impossible cross section of cultural inscription and meta-physical being sets the stage for a particularly postmodern humour, as the scene generates multiple disjunctions of historical, cultural and metaphysical status. Griselda tells her story of being plucked from among the peasants for marriage to the Marquis:

> GRISELDA   I'd rather obey the Marquis than a boy from the village.
> MARLENE   Yes, that's a point.
> JOAN   I never obeyed anyone. They all obeyed me.
> NIJO   And what did you wear? He didn't make you get married in your own clothes? That would be perverse.[59]

Here are three potential comic reversals in a row, following Griselda's assertion. They emanate from the incompatibility of these cultural-historical positions, ripped from real, fictional and undetermined fabrics of existence. As a whole, they bespeak a relativity among all these voices of experience, denying any single claim upon a 'right' or 'valid' position – and this is where the postmodern and the comic have much to offer one another.

Interculturalism and comedy

In an essay on humour and society, sociologist Chris Powell says 'that an anomalous, strange or untoward event, idea or cultural expression is often initially defined as "funny". The converse of this is that a "humour response" is likely when a social role of some kind is perceived as having been in-fracted.'[60] Think how often Western or English-speaking films and plays solicit laughter at the expense of a character visiting from another culture, an immigrant or a non-native speaker.

It can therefore be instructive for Western audiences to read non-Western texts. A play like *The Dilemma of a Ghost* (1964) by the Ghanaian playwright, Ama Ata Aidoo, is particularly revealing because one of the characters is an African-American woman who has accompanied her husband to his home in Ghana. As such she simulates the position of a Western reader as Other in a highly traditional community with strong codes and beliefs. The young man's uncles facetiously refer to him as 'our master, the white man himself',[61] because he has been studying in the United States. Family members mispronounce the young woman's name and cannot fathom the fact that she does not have a tribe. This play was built for a target Ghanaian audience to trade for its comic effect on her ignorance of codes endemic to African culture, with particular reference to the conduct of women, marriage and childbearing.[62]

The mingling of diverse cultures due to shifting populations around the world makes for some interesting developments in intercultural theatre. In

Ireland, Nigerian-born Bisi Adigun and Irish-born Roddy Doyle collaborated on a contemporary version of Synge's *The Playboy of the Western World*. This celebrated text of the Irish canon, described briefly in Chapter 1, shows how young Christy Mahon reinvents himself in the new context of a rural community, growing in stature as he rewrites his identity for the locals. The new version of *The Playboy of the Western World* (2007) makes Christy a Nigerian immigrant entering upon a Dublin pub, providing an opportunity for up-to-date observations on Irish culture as well as an intriguing cross-cultural resonance against the original theme.

Postcolonialism and the comic

Looking at comic drama through a postcolonial lens also calls attention to the relationship between cultural in-groups and out-groups. Post-colonialism, says Mark Fortier, 'aims to give voice to an oppressed group by understanding and critiquing the structures of oppression and articulating and encouraging liberation and revolution. In this case the group is those who have lived under the imperialist domination of Western colonial powers'.[63] Postcolonialism looks to reclaim authority for an occupied or displaced group and to cast a critical eye over the effects of cultural bullying.

Native Canadian playwright Tomson Highway's *The Rez Sisters* (1986) looks at lives on a reservation in Northern Ontario. The play shows the surface tensions and underlying bonds among a group of seven women with a common interest in making the journey to Toronto for The Biggest Bingo in the World. There is a life-on-the-ground humour in their interplay and in the private dreams they impart through a series of monologues. What makes the play particularly interesting for the study of comedy is Highway's stage enshrinement of the trickster figure (see the box on page 200). In *The Rez Sisters*, Highway employs the Ojibway trickster Nanabush, who appears variously as a white seagull, a black nighthawk and the Bingo Master, all played by a male dancer. Highway has written about the trickster's importance to Native Canadian culture as a comic figure with spiritual significance, and Helen Gilbert distils its function in this particular play: 'With Nanabush's intervention, the Rez sisters' quest becomes regenerative, not because it might provide the means to alleviate their poverty but rather because they learn from their experiences to value what they have and to use their own energy and ingenuity to solve problems.'[64]

The trickster figure

The trickster is a type of character or persona found in the mythologies and folk tales of cultures all over the world, an obvious candidate for the spirit (if not soul) of comedy. Although differing variously from one manifestation to another, the trickster is a personification of mischief, wholly adult in body and appetite, yet possessed of a childlike indulgence in whim and desire.

George A. Test contends, 'The trickster figure of mythology, the closest thing to a mythic source that satire can claim, is a figure of deception, roguishness, and illusion. He is a prankster, a jokester; he is unreliable, enormously libidinous, a hell-raiser.'[65] Test's roster of tricksters includes Hermes from Greek mythology, Coyote from the oral tradition of North American Plains Indians, Br'er Rabbit in the tales once told by African slaves in the American South, the Norse god Loki the Mischief-Maker, and the Yoruban god, Eshu.

Trickster appears to express the tension between bodied spirit and social constraint, which we have seen to lie at the constant heart of humour and comedy. Anthropologist Apte describes tricksters as driven entirely by the body's self-gratification to the abject disregard of Other and social unit at large. They appear to possess qualities applicable to *both* hero and buffoon:

> Most tricksters are pranksters and are primarily egotistical. They are powerful, clever, selfish, cruel, deceitful, cunning, and sly. They are also boastful, foolish, lazy, and ineffective. They have no control over their basal desires and seek instant gratification. They are infantile, inordinate, lack restraint, and ignore social responsibilities. Tricksters are prone to blunder and have no ability to distinguish between good and evil, between themselves and others, and between objects and organisms.[66]

Psychiatrist Carl Jung identified the trickster as one of the 'archetypes' found in our species' 'collective unconscious', embodying an aspect of the human psyche's progress toward civilization. He sees the trickster as 'subhuman and superhuman, a bestial and divine being'.[67] The trickster figure would seem to act as goad to the argument within each human between uncurbed animal instinct and normalizing cultural inscription – with a strong input from the spirit of play. Puck from Shakespeare's *A Midsummer Night's Dream* is one of the purest manifestations of the trickster figure in dramatic form.

Although tricksters have been known to adopt female forms, there does appear to be a male bias to this concept, reflecting the patriarchal dominance of most cultures. Edith Kern perceives the mark of the trickster upon Rosalind in *As You Like It* and Dorine in Molière's *Tartuffe* (1664). In *The Female Trickster: The Mask That Reveals*, Ricki Stefanie Tannen celebrates a 'postmodern female Trickster energy', identifiable in the overtly disruptive screen persona of Mae West and what she calls the 'Trickster tales' of *Sex and the City* (1998–2004, 2008).[68]

Clearly, the use of an indigenous (or any other) language likely to exclude certain members of an audience speaks very much to the heart of humorous discourse, emphasizing both the solidarity of the in-group and the otherness of the out-group. Gilbert and co-author Joanne Tompkins cite Highway's use of the Cree language at selected points in the play, to observe that the exclusionary effect on some audience members 'not only disperses any particular discourse's claim to singular authority, but it also opens up new topics which are unsuitable to, or which cannot be translated into, the imperial language'.[69] We might even follow on to say that different cultures joke differently in ways no doubt embodied in their languages, and therefore open singular ways of expressing their identities and experiences.

A postcolonial impulse drives rereading of canonical texts for analysis of their participation in instilling and reifying the mindsets of colonial oppression. For the writer, it sometimes means taking on these texts by reinvention and recontextualization. Daniel Defoe's novel, *Robinson Crusoe* (1719) is seen from a postcolonial perspective as a classic text of Eurocentric colonization. Its story of a shipwrecked white man teaching English and Christianity to the black native he finds on a tropical island replicates in microcosm the action and effect of cultural imperialism. The West Indies playwright, Derek Walcott, transports the text's cultural stereotypes and power relations onto the stage for theatrical dissection in *Pantomime* (1978). Harry Trewe is a retired pantomime actor who owns a guest house on the island of Tobago; Jackson Phillip, a Trinidadian and former calypso musician, works for him. Harry convinces Jackson to take part in a pantomime performance of the Crusoe tale he used to perform with his wife, a premise that allows for continual reframing and inverting of the original, often to comic effect.

Jackson's first utterances in the play sample English and Creole accents, laying the issue on the table from the outset:

> Mr Trewe? [*English accent*] Mr Trewe, your scramble eggs is here! are here! [*Creole accent*] You hear, Mr Trewe? I here wid your eggs! [*English accent*] Are you in there? [*To himself*] And when his eggs get cold, is I to catch.[70]

Here is a potentially humorous contrast between vocal styles of colonizer and colonized, calling attention to the performances of culture we learn without realizing. Jackson continually interrogates the original text in comic fashion, choosing at one point to call himself Thursday instead of Friday.

Cultural performance styles come to the fore in the play's dialogue, especially when Jackson is charged with miming Crusoe's arrival in the island, which he cannot help but undertake in a bodied style that offends Harry's artistic sensibilities. Gilbert and Tompkins observe that 'the pantomime relies on slapstick humour, gender- and race-swapping, and verbal and visual puns to convey its interest in performance as a site of struggle between cultures'.[71]

It is impossible to ignore this play's basic master/slave relationship with regard to Western comic heritage. This is no ordinary double-act treatment, however – the continual replication, inversion and subversion of racial and power roles as the two men negotiate their performance text sometimes becomes laughably convoluted, so that the object of humorous attack is not so much one or the other, but the entire signifying system of cultural performance. Interestingly, especially from the perspective of comic genre, Walcott bypasses an ending which simply reverses the power roles for a glimpse of a more humane and genuine progress.

Doing things with the comic

We have seen that the comic is capable of working for or against the comfortable, accepted, even championed order of things. We laugh at something because we have (or discover we have) a feeling about it *already inside us.* Another good question would have to be: does comedy or the comic possess the capacity to address subjects for which we might not otherwise sit still, without watering down the issues?

Paula Vogel approaches the deeply troubling topic of sexual abuse in her play, *How I Learned to Drive* (1997). The story recounted by the character Li'l Bit, and in which she takes a part in re-enacting, is disturbing. The scenes are shown out of chronological order, representing the difficulty with which she 'remembers' Uncle Peck's first approach when she was 11. The cast includes three 'Chorus' members, who supply comic caricatures of the family and recollections of adolescent social discomfort. The humour operates as a relief valve, but also contributes satiric comment on the social and domestic attitudes that enable such abuse to flourish.

In *The Colored Museum* (1986), George C. Wolfe makes free and inventive use of comic attack modes to take a hard look at his own African-American culture, its literary/dramatic past and present and its relationship to a white-dominated sociocultural context. The piece demonstrates how a revue structure suits broad-based satiric criticism, allowing a comic conceit or clever parody to do its work quickly and efficiently without the onus of sustaining a full-length stage world.

The play's eleven 'exhibits' begin with an opening sketch for which Miss Pat, a '*black, pert, and cute*' mini-skirted airline hostess gives pre-flight instructions for the Celebrity Slaveship:

> Once we reach the desired altitude, the Captain will turn off the 'Fasten Your Shackle' sign . . . [*She efficiently points out the 'Fasten Your Shackle' signs on either side of her, which light up.*] . . . allowing you a chance to stretch and dance in the aisles a bit. But otherwise, shackles must be worn at all times.[72]

We can anticipate how parody of the text and manner of a real-life flight attendant, with her practised, ever-smiling dedication to safety and comfort, sharpens the bite by its casual contrast with the racial injustice and stereotyping to which the speech alludes. Another sequence invokes the cultured context of 'important' television drama to frame an allusion to the first real wave of drama to emerge from African-American writers in the mid-twentieth century (like Lorraine Hansberry's *A Raisin in the Sun*, 1959). The sketch evokes the indomitable Mama figure, ever looking skyward for strength and direction, as well as the Son, an angry young black man, who erupts at every opportunity at the white bosses who oppress him:

> MAMA   [*looking up from her Bible, speaking in a slow manner*] Son, did you wipe your feet?
>
> SON   [*an ever-erupting volcano*] No, Mama, I didn't wipe my feet! Out there, every day, Mama is the Man. The Man Mama. Mr. Charlie! Mr. Bossman! And he's wipin' his feet on me. On me, Mama, every damn day of my life. Ain't that enough for me to deal with? Ain't that enough?[73]

Parodic exaggeration may not be overtly detectable in the writing, but we have surely been cued to look for it in the framing of the sketch (if not the play at large), as an over-the-top response to a quintessentially motherly question. This striking use of a comic gap foresees the negative and positive in one utterance. By citing the gritty, unleashed performance style of the original plays (and the films made from them), it invites reading as a dated expression of outrage even as it acknowledges the animating force behind the original. This sketch, like the piece as a whole, launches comic strikes against the excesses and compromises in African-American culture since the height of the civil-rights movement, as well as the white mainstream's persistent clinging to repressive African-American stereotypes.

The Goat (2002) by Edward Albee is also notable from a comedy-studies perspective. It exploits a humour relationship between the stage world and reader/spectator, who is invited to confirm through laughter a bias against the central character's actions. By the end of the play, the reader/spectator is likely to have been relocated closer to the emotional position of the character, perhaps to unsettle encrusted convictions on the subject of sexual deviance.

The play begins very much like a conventional domestic comedy in which adultery incites the conflict. Amid banter between Martin, a prize-winning architect on his fiftieth birthday, and his wife, Stevie, the question of his having an affair pokes its head into the conversation. The couple playfully transpose the discussion to a parody of a scene from a Noël Coward play, adopting '[*English accents, flamboyant gestures*]':

> STEVIE   I suppose you'd better tell me!
> MARTIN   I can't! I can't!
> STEVIE   Tell me! Tell me!
> MARTIN   Her name is Sylvia!
> STEVIE   Sylvia? Who is Sylvia?
> MARTIN   She's a goat, Sylvia is a goat! [*acting manner dropped; normal tone now; serious, flat*] She's a goat.
> STEVIE   [*long pause; she stares, finally smiles. Giggles, chortles, moves towards the hall; normal tone*] You're too much! [*Exits*[74]

The confession will turn out to be serious: Martin has fallen in love with a goat. Meanwhile, Martin talks to his lifelong friend, Ross, about the fact that his seventeen-year-old son, Billy, is gay. Ross tries to dismiss the revelation as a mere passing stumble on the way to grown heterosexual normality. Martin, who betrays his own anti-gay disposition, recounts telling his son just to be sure about his feelings: 'Says he's sure; loves it, he says.' Ross dismisses the notion with a locker-room wisecrack: 'Well, of course he loves it; he's getting laid, for God's sake!'[75]

The inevitable admission of Martin's affair with a goat introduces an element of absurdism to the play, which relativizes Billy's homosexual orientation: 'At least what I do is with . . . persons!'[76] Martin goes on to speak seriously about his beloved, while Stevie continually undercuts him with sitcom exasperation. There's a passage in which Martin recounts his experiences of going to group therapy for people who engage in bestiality, which is punctuated by Stevie destroying vases, plates and anything else she can get her hands on:

> STEVIE   Did you all take your . . . friends with you – your pigs, your dogs, your goats, your . . .

MARTIN   No. We weren't there to talk about *them*; we were there about ourselves, our . . . our problems, as they called them.
STEVIE   The livestock was all happy, you mean.
MARTIN   Well, no; there was this one . . . goose, I think it was . . . [*Stevie sweeps a bowl off a table.*] Shall we go outside?[77]

These are conventional comic patterns, and the featured ridicule of Martin's 'skewed' behaviour counts upon the reader/spectator assuming a position against its acceptability. The play, however, proceeds to shift the emotional fulcrum by degrees toward sympathy for Martin and his lover. Somewhere along the way, Martin talks in the most heartfelt terms about, for example, looking into Sylvia's eyes for the first time. The ability for this sea change to work relies undeniably on the actor's capacity to embody a transcending honesty of feeling. By then the reader/spectator does stand to find that the textual ground has shifted away from laughable alienation.

In a climactic scene between father and son, Billy gives vent to ambivalent feelings toward the parent whose conduct has suddenly destroyed the family and the father he still loves. Father and son embrace, and Billy '[*starts kissing* MARTIN *on the hands, then on the neck, crying all the while. Then it turns – or does it? – and he kisses* MARTIN *full on the mouth – a deep, sobbing, sexual kiss*]'.[78]

This moment breaks the remaining cultural taboo with regard to sex, through an apparent act of incest. It is, in any case, uncharted territory, an occurrence that neither of the participants will be able to explain to each other or to Ross, who has happened upon the scene and reacts with abject disgust. From the perspective of queer theory, this can be seen as a quint-essentially queer moment – not because it involves a potentially gay kiss, but because it lies beyond accommodation in 'heterocentrist' discourse. John Storey cites an article by Alexander Doty, who uses the term 'queer'

> to mark a flexible space for the expression of all aspects of non (anti-, contra-) straight cultural production and reception. As such, this 'queer space' recognizes the possibility that various and fluctuating queer positions might be occupied whenever *anyone* produces or responds to culture.[79]

This moment may possibly elicit laughter from some audience members, out of discomfort or because we simply don't know what to do with it. It pushes the experience of this stage world another step further from the comic mood at the start, based on the common practice of ridiculing the Other. Ultimately, Stevie returns, dragging the dead and bloodied body of the goat in question. The play, which began so firmly in comic territory ends with a tragic sacrifice. With the help of the comic in form and device, the stage world beckons the reader/spectator toward the safe centre of social inscription, if not then to turn the tables completely, at least to unsettle our certainty about where precisely we sit at them. I would submit that, in many a case, a spectator finds it difficult to deny entirely the symbolic power of the romance between man and goat. It may not justify an acceptance of sexual relationships outside the human species, but it should inspire reflection upon our culture's lingering antagonism toward alternative loves and life-styles. The comic has opened the door for serious discussion of human sexuality with an effectiveness that could not have been guaranteed by a strictly serious stage world.

I have tried to give an impression in this last section of the extent to which comedy and the comic draw power from deep within our social and cultural relations. I have also tried to suggest how comic discourse, despite some critical opinions through the centuries, has the ability to affect the reader/spectator in ways unavailable to non-playful forms and techniques. Throughout the book I have emphasized that comedy draws a circle of inclusion around itself, a polarized field which can serve to exclude or bully. I have returned continually to the fact that the comic taps into the psychic unity of body, mind and feeling, through laughter and ingrained patterns of feeling invoked by generic structure. I have furthermore tried to underline, although it can be difficult to drive home in written argument, the extent to which choices actualized in the here-and-now of production concretize the utterance in a way less ideal but more potent than can ever fully be captured either in words or upon the stage of the mind.

Comedy's endemic associations with pleasure and celebration can be exploited as ends in themselves, without necessarily risking accusations of taking the easy way out. The temptation can be great, on the other hand, to enlist such popular allies and decline to give too much thought to the social consequences. Playwrights and practitioners have discovered, though, that a truth told or a point made by comic means draws the reader/spectator closer, the better to strike bodily or to ambush the overly confident rationality of serious discourse.

Notes

Introduction: thinking about comedy

1 Andy Kempe, 'Reading plays for performance' in D. Hornbrook (ed.), *On the Subject of Drama* (London: Routledge, 1998), pp. 92–111 (pp. 93–4).

2 Erving Goffman, *Frame Analysis: An Essay on the Organization of Experience*, new edn (Boston: Northeastern University Press, 1986), p. 138.

3 D. W. Winnicott, *Playing and Reality* (London: Routledge, 1991), p. 13.

4 Bruce Wilshire, *Role Playing and Identity: The Limits of Theatre as Metaphor* (Bloomington: Indiana University Press, 1982), p. 24.

5 Margaret Lowenfeld, *Play in Childhood*, new edn (London: Mac Keith, 1991), p. 230. The four main purposes quoted after this are from p. 232.

6 Johan Huizinga, *Homo Ludens: A Study of the Play-Element in Culture* (Boston: Beacon, 1955), p. 8.

7 *Ibid.*, p. 9.

8 *Ibid.*, p. 13.

9 Jean-Paul Sartre, 'Play', in R. Denoon Cumming (ed.), *The Philosophy of Jean-Paul Sartre* (New York: Vintage, 1965). pp. 310–16 (p. 310).

10 M. J. Ellis, *Why People Play* (Englewood Cliffs: Prentice Hall, 1973).

11 Richard Schechner, *The Future of Ritual* (London: Routledge, 1993), p. 41.

12 *Ibid.*, p. 43.

13 *Ibid.*, p. 43.

14 Alexander Leggatt, *English Stage Comedy 1490–1990* (London: Routledge, 1998), p. 1.

15 For a further discussion of the derivation and meaning of comedy, and some of these historical conceits, see W. D. Howarth's 'Introduction' to *Comic Drama*. M. S. Silk surveys historical comments on comedy/humour/laughter in the second chapter of *Aristophanes and the Definition of Comedy*.

16 L. J. Potts, *Comedy* (London: Hutchinson & Co, 1957), p. 18.

17 Susanne K. Langer, *Feeling and Form* (New York: Charles Scribner's Sons, 1953), p. 346.

18 *Ibid.*, p. 333.

19 Andrew Bennett and Nicholas Royle, *Introduction to Literature, Criticism and Theory*, new edn (Harlow: Prentice Hall, 1999), p. 251.

20 Northrop Frye, *Anatomy of Criticism* (London: Penguin, 1990), p. 170.

21 Aristotle, *Poetics*, trans. by Malcolm Heath (London: Penguin, 1996), p. 22.

22 Christopher Booker, *The Seven Basic Plots: Why We Tell Stories* (London: Continuum, 2004), p. 123.

23 Walter Kerr, *Tragedy and Comedy* (New York: Da Capo, 1985), p. 78.

24 T. G. A. Nelson, *Comedy: An Introduction to Comedy in Literature, Drama, and Cinema* (Oxford University Press, 1990), p. 2.

25 Alexander Leggatt, *English Stage Comedy*, p. 4.

26 Kerr, *Tragedy and Comedy*, p. 79.

27 Eric Bentley, *The Life of the Drama* (New York: Applause, 1991), p. 306.

28 Robert W. Corrigan, 'Introduction: Comedy and the Comic Spirit' in *Comedy: Meaning and Form* (Scranton: Chandler, 1965), pp. 1–11 (p. 5).

29 Potts, *Comedy*, p. 13.

30 Lane Cooper, *An Aristotelian Theory of Comedy*, pp. 69–70.

31 Elder Olson, *The Theory of Comedy* (Bloomington; Indiana University Press, 1968), pp. 46–7.

32 Richard Janko, *Aristotle on Comedy: Towards a Reconstruction of Poetics II* (London: Dackworth, 2002), p. 93.

33 Umberto Eco, 'Frames of comic freedom' in T. Sebeok (ed.), in *Carnival!*, (Berlin: Mouton, 1984), pp. 1–9 (p. 4).

34 *Ibid.*

35 Aristophanes, *Lysistrata*, trans. by Kenneth McLeish in *Aristophanes plays: One* (London: Methuen, 1993), pp. 183–256 (p. 201).

36 Douglas MacDowell, *Aristophanes and Athens* (Oxford University Press, 1995), p. 247.

37 Lauren K. Taaffe, *Aristophanes and Women* (London: Routledge, 1993), p. 73.

38 Michael Cordner, Peter Holland and John Kerrigan, 'Introduction' in *English Comedy* (Cambridge University Press, 1994), pp. 1–11 (p. 2).

39 Christopher Fry, *An Experience of Critics and the Approach to Dramatic Criticism* (London: Perpetua, 1952), p. 26.

1 Reading comedy

1 If it is a second or subsequent reading, several influences – including a fuller awareness of the text as a whole; critical input received from media, friends or other sources; and reflection upon the previous reading(s) – may lead us to recalibrate our perception of the world or to become more aware of how the world 'works'.

2 John Frow, *Genre: The New Critical Idiom* (London: Routledge, 2006), p. 115.

3 Heather Dubrow, *Genre: The Critical Idiom* (London: Methuen, 1982), p. 2.

4 Frow, *Genre*, p. 18.

5 Tzetvan Todorov, *Genres in Discourse*, trans by Catherine Porter (Cambridge University Press, 1990) p. 19.

6 Frow, *Genre*, p. 84.

7 Alistair Fowler, *Kinds of Literature: An Introduction to the Therory of Genres and Modes* (Oxford : Clarendon, 1982), p. 74.

8 Fowler, *Kinds of Literature*, p. 169.

9 Rick Altman, *Film/Genre* (London: BFI, 1999), p. 207.

10 Altman, *Film/Genre*, p. 84.

11 Dubrow, *Genre*, p. 107.

12 Bert O. States, 'The phenomenological attitude' in J. G. Reinelt and J. R. Roach (eds.), pp. 26–36 in *Critical Theory and Performance*, new edn (Ann Arbor: University of Michigan, 2007), p. 27.

13 Spike Milligan, 'The great man', in *The Essential Spike Milligan* (London: Fourth Estate, 2003) pp: 67–8 (p. 67).

14 Jane Austen, *Pride and Prejudice* (New York: W. W. Norton, 2001), p. 3.

15 Susan Purdie, *Comedy: The Mastery of Discourse* (Toronto: University of Toronto Press, 1993), p. 49.

16 Molière, *Don Juan* trans. by George Graveley and Ian Maclean in *Don Juan and Other Plays* (Oxford University Press, 1989), pp. 31–91 (p. 33).

17 Molière, *Scapin the Schemer*, trans. by George Graveley and Ian Maclean in *Don Juan and Other Plays* (Oxford: Oxford University Press, 1989), pp. 337– 90 (p. 339).

18 Nikolai Erdman, *The Suicide*, adapted by Richard Nelson (New York: Broadway Play Publishing, 2000) pp. 1–2.

19 Neil Simon, *Chapter Two* (New York: Samuel French, 1979), p. 4.

20 Alan Ayckbourn, *Absurd Person Singular* in *Three Plays* (New York: Grove, 1975), pp. 11–93 (p. 15–16).

21 Potts, *Comedy*, p. 58.

22 Oscar Wilde, *The Importance of Being Earnest* in *The Importance of Being Earnest and Other Plays* (London: Penguin, 1986), pp. 247–313 (p. 313).

23 It should, of course, be acknowledged that any given production of this play might choose subtly or explicitly to subvert the idealistic ending by crafting an image suggesting something other than a perfectly 'happy ending'.

24 Ronald Gaskell, *Drama and Reality: The European theatre since Ibsen* (London: Routledge & Kegan Paul, 1972), p. 61.

25 William Shakespeare, *Twelfth Night or What You Will* (New York: New American Library, 1965), p. 135.

26 Shakespeare, *Twelfth Night*, p. 136.

27 J.M. Synge, *The Playboy of the Western World* in *J.M. Synge: The Complete Plays* (London: Methuen, 1995), pp. 173–229 (p. 229).

28 Synge, *The Playboy*, p. 229.

29 Joe Orton, *What the Butler Saw* in *The Complete Plays* (London: Methuen, 1997), pp. 361–448 (p. 448).

2 Comedy's foundations

1 Alan H. Sommerstein, *Greek Drama and Dramatists* (London: Routledge, 2002), p. 1.

2 Sommerstein, *Greek Drama and Dramatists* (2002), p. 25. However, Erich Segal, in Chapter 1 of *The Death of Comedy* (Cambridge: Harvard University Press, 2001), proposes two other 'related and legitimate' etymologies, with reference to dreaming and 'country matters'.

3 Rainer Schulte and John Biguenet, 'Introduction', in R. Schulte and J. Biguenet (eds.), *Theories of Translation: An Anthology of Essays from Dryden to Derrida* (University of Chicago Press, 1992), pp. 1–10.

4 Aristophanes, *The Wasps*, trans. by David Barrett in *Aristophanes: The Wasps, The Poet and the Women, The Frogs* (London: Penguin, 1964), pp. 33–94 (p. 75).

5 Aristophanes, *Lysistrata*, trans. by Kenneth McLeish (1993), p. 195.

6 Aristophanes, *Acharnians*, trans. by Kenneth McLeish in *Aristophanes Plays: One* (London: Methuen, 1993), pp. 1–60 (pp. 20–1).

7 MacDowell, *Aristophanes and Athens* pp. 16–26. In a subchapter titled 'The audience's expectations', MacDowell distinguishes five key features of 'the comic tradition' in Aristophanes' time: religion, form and structure, music and dancing, obscenity and personal ridicule.

8 Aristophanes, *The Wasps*, p. 87.

9 Aristophanes, *Lysistrata*, p. 232.

10 It should be said that, like other writers', Aristophanes' texts are sometimes notable for the ways they bend or break such 'rules'. MacDowell observes that *The Wasps* is the only extant play which includes all of these formal features.

11 David Wiles, *Greek Theatre Performance: An Introduction* (Cambridge University Press, 2000), p. 144.

12 Segal, *The Death of Comedy*, p. 154.

13 Segal, *The Death of Comedy*, p. 154.

14 R.L. Hunter, *The New Comedy of Greece and Rome* (Cambridge University Press, 1985), p. 12.

15 Menander, *The Malcontent*, trans. by J Michael Walton in *Aristophanes and Menander: New Comedy* (London: Methuen 1994), p. 127. When drawing upon the works of Menander and Plautus, I have cited the transliterated Ancient Greek or the Latin title, with a translation in parenthesis. Thereafter, I use the translated title. I have adopted this practice because one can find several different translations of a given title, which might cause confusion if the reader comes across a version and does not recognize it as the same play.

16 Menander, *The Malcontent*, p. 159.

17 Menander, *The Malcontent*, p. 160.

18 Menander, *The Malcontent*, p. 137.

19 Theophrastus, 'The characters' in P. Vellacott (trans.), *Theophrastus: The Characters / Menander: Plays and Fragments* (Harmondsworth: Penguin, 1973), pp. 31–61 (p. 38).

20 E. W. Handley, 'The conventions of the comic stage' in E. Segal (ed.), *Oxford Readings in Menander, Plautus, and Terence* (Oxford University Press, 2001), pp. 27–41 (p. 31).

21 Menander, *The Malcontent*, p. 158. It should be noted that, in most cases, a modern translator or editor has contributed a helping stage direction where none exists in the original manuscript. In this case, several later lines, like Knemon's 'Give me a hand, will you, girl? I want to get up', imply that the character has not been standing.

22 Menander, *The Malcontent*, pp. 130–1.

23 Menander, *The Malcontent*, p. 132.

24 Menander, *The Malcontent*, p. 151.

25 This number might have been much higher in any given year, as a festival might be repeated if it was deemed that there had been a breach of proper procedure.

26 George E. Duckworth calls this figure the *seruus* or 'Clever Trickster and Faithful Servant'. George E. Duckworth, *The Nature of Roman Comedy*, new edn (London: Bristol Classical, 1994), pp. 249–53.

27 Plautus, *The Braggart Soldier* trans. by Erich Segal in *Four Comedies* (Oxford University Press, 1996) pp. 1–74 (pp. 3–4).

28 Plautus, *The Braggart Soldier*, p. 6.

29 Terence, *The Girl From Andros*, trans. by Betty Radice in *The Comedies*, (London: Penguin, 1976), pp. 30–91 (p. 50).

3 Comedy's devices

1 Sean O'Casey, 'The power of laughter' in *The Green Crow* (London: Comet, 1987), p. 202.

2 Henri Bergson, 'Laughter' in W. Sypher (ed.), *Comedy* (Baltimore: Johns Hopkins University Press, 1980), pp. 58–180 (p. 64).

3 It is true that the social dynamics of an audience exert some influence upon the transaction, which makes it easier to discuss the notion of 'successful' humour in theory than in practice. An audience can be seen as an organism in its own right, though it is also inescapably composed of a collection of individuals. For any audience responding to a gag on stage or screen with a predominance of belly laughs, there are sure to be at least a few among them who react lukewarmly, if at all.

4 Simon Critchley, *On Humour* (London: Routledge, 2002), p. 1.

5 Arthur Koestler, *The Act of Creation* (London: Picador, 1978 [1964]), p. 35.

6 Arthur Schopenhauer, *The World as Will and Idea*, trans. by R. B. Haldane and John Kemp, excerpted in J. Morreal (ed.), *The Philosophy of Laughter and Humor* (Albany: SUNY, 1987), pp. 51–64 (p. 52).

7 This joke appeared in a newspaper advertisement for a comedy cabaret, and so turns up here as one aimed at a widest possible audience.

8 Norman Holland, *Laughing: A Psychology of Humor* (Ithaca: Cornell University Press, 1982), p. 198.

9 Mahadev L. Apte, *Humor and Laughter: An Anthropological Approach* (Ithaca: Cornell University Press, 1985), p. 261.

10 Jerry Palmer, *Taking Humour Seriously* (London: Routledge, 1994), p. 161.

11 Trevor Griffiths, *Comedians* (London: Faber and Faber, 1979), p. 19.

12 Susan Purdie, *Comedy*, p. 79.

13 Bergson, 'Laughter', p. 150.

14 Tom Stoppard, *On the Razzle* (London: Faber and Faber, 1982), p. 16.

15 Olson, *The Theory of Comedy*, p. 41.

16 Purdie, *Comedy*, p. 77.

17 Booker, *The Seven Basic Plots*, p. 107.

18 Plautus, *The Pot of Gold*, trans. by E.F. Watling in *The Pot of Gold and Other Plays* (London: Penguin, 1965), pp. 38–9.

19 Booker, *The Seven Basic Plots*, p. 150.

20 Booker, *The Seven Basic Plots*, p. 144.

21 Terry Johnson, *Hysteria* in *Plays: 2* (London: Methuen, 2003), p. 94.

22 Harry Levin, *Playboys & Killjoys* (Oxford University Press, 1987), p. 82.

23 William Shakespeare, *The Comedy of Errors* (London: Routledge, 1994), p. 32 (Act II, Scene ii, lines 110–12).

24 Shakespeare, *The Comedy of Errors*, p. 35 (Act II, Scene ii, lines 147–56).

25 Maurice Charney, *Comedy High and Low: An Introduction to the Experience of Comedy* (New York: Oxford University Press, 1978), p. 79.

26 Aristophanes, *Lysistrata*, p. 229. The translator McLeish gives these lines to Myrrhine, one of the principal characters, although in the Penguin translation, for example, the escapee is one of five unnamed women. Perhaps he does this to show her in a state of sexual hunger prior to the following scene in which she has to deny her husband satisfaction until he promises to make peace.

27 Johnson, *Hysteria*, pp. 130–1.

28 Shakespeare, *Twelfth Night*, Act III, Scene i, lines 1–7.

29 Walter Nash, *The Language of Humour: Style and technique in Comic Discourse* (London: Longman, 1985), p. 49.

30 Purdie, *Comedy*, p. 96.

31 Aristophanes, *Frogs*, trans. by Kenneth McLeish in *Six Greek Comedies* (London: Methuen, 2002), pp. 89–167 (p. 115).

32 Aristophanes, *Frogs*, p. 122.

33 Shakespeare, *Twelfth Night* Act II, Scene v, lines 65–70.

34 Richard Brinsley Sheridan, *The School for Scandal*, ed. by F. W. Bateson (London: A & C Black, 1995), pp. 102–3.

35 Aristophanes, *Frogs*, p. 91.

36 William Congreve, *The Way of the World* in *Four English Comedies* (London: Penguin, 1985), p. 226.

37 Johnson, *Hysteria*, p. 93.

38 Plautus, *The Braggart Soldier*, p. 69.

39 States, *Great Reckonings in Little Rooms: On the Phenomenology of Theater* (Berkeley: University of California Press, 1987), p. 171.

40 Plautus, *The Braggart Soldier*, p. 20.

41 Duckworth describes three types of *senex*, the second of which, the elderly lover, is a prime target for ridicule. He is portrayed as grotesque and decrepit, and is generally unkind to his wife and prone to be ill-tempered and unfaithful. Duckworth expresses great admiration for Euclio as a comic character, while acknowledging that his greater interest in protecting his 'pot of gold' than anything else makes him an unusual incarnation of the type. Duckworth, *The Nature of Roman Comedy*, pp. 242–9.

42 Plautus, *The Pot of Gold*, p. 18.

43 Terence, *The Eunuch*, trans. by Kenneth McLeish in M. Sargent (ed.) *Four Roman Comedies* (London: Methuen, 2003), p. 154.

44 J. L. Styan, *Restoration Comedy in Performance* (Cambridge University Press, 1986), p. 134.

45 Styan, *Restoration Comedy in Performance*, pp. 139–41. Styan details the 'series of tricks' by which Horner increases his pleasure (and the audience's) by escalating challenges to Mrs Pinchwife's disguise.

46 William Wycherley, *The Country Wife* (London: A & C Black, 1993), p. 78.

4 Comedy in the flesh

1 Voltaire, *Candide*, trans. by Robert M. Adams (New York: W. W. Norton, 1991), p. 2.

2 It is arguable that there are analytical operations which can be carried out on a dramatic text prior to performance considerations, but we should always be careful, for example, of how confidently we talk about what a play 'means' based solely upon an analysis of the script. The playwright's comic plans can be made, broken or transformed entirely in actual performance.

3 Georges Feydeau and Maurice Desvallières, *A Little Hotel on the Side*, trans. by John Mortimer (London: Samuel French, 1984), p. 1.

4 Roland Barthes, *Image-Music-Text*, trans. by Stephen Heath (London: Fontana, 1977), p. 182.

5 Simon Shepherd, *Theatre, Body and Pleasure* (London: Routledge, 2006), pp. 36–7.

6 In fact, I owe much of my approach to thinking about performance to Merleau-Ponty's writings, particularly *The Phenomenology of Perception* and his three essays on painting – 'Cézanne's doubt', 'Indirect language and the voices of Silence', and 'Eye and mind' – which refer his grasp of things to the realm of artistic expression.

7 Maurice Merleau-Ponty, 'Eye and mind' in G. A. Johnson (ed.) and M. B. Smith (trans.), *The Merleau-Ponty Aesthetics Reader: Philosophy and Painting* (Evanston: Northwestern University Press, 1993), pp. 121–49 (p. 143).

8 Shepherd, *Theatre, Body and Pleasure*, p. 18.

9 Ben Jonson, *Volpone* (London: Ernest Benn, 1968), pp. 25–6 (Act I, Scene iii, lines 27–33).

10 Molière, *Don Juan*, pp. 54–5.

11 Ayckbourn, *Absurd Person Singular*, p. 38.

12 William E. Gruber, *Comic Theaters: Studies in Performance and Audience Response* (Athens: University of Georgia Press, 1986), p. 1.

13 States, *Great Reckonings in Little Rooms*, p. 161.

14 Antonio Fava, *The Comic Mask in the Commedia dell'Arte* (Evanston: Northwestern University Press, 2007), p. 107.

15 Richard Andrews, *Scripts and Scenarios: The Performance of Comedy in Renaissance Italy* (Cambridge University Press, 1993), p. 199. Andrews traces this relationship forward to the English tradition of the Punch-and-Judy puppet show, and on to Tom-and-Jerry cartoons of the twentieth century.

16 McLeish, *The Theatre of Aristophanes* (London: Thames & Hudson, 1990), p. 53.

17 Frye, *Anatomy of Criticism*, p. 172.

18 W. Kenneth Little, 'Pitu's doubt: entrée clown self-fashioning in the circus tradition', *The Drama Review*, 30, 4 (1986), 51–64 (pp. 52–3).

19 Fava, *The Comic Mask*, p. 20.

20 Mel Gordon, *Lazzi: The Comic Routines of the Commedia dell'arte* (New York: Performing Arts Journal, 1983), p. 5.

21 Gordon, *Lazzi*, p. 18.

22 Andrews, *Scripts and Scenarios*, p. 176.

23 Andrews, *Scripts and Scenarios*, p. 181.

24 Wiles, *Shakespeare's Clown: Actor and Text in the Elizabethan Playhouse* (Cambridge University Press, 1987), p. 101.

25 Wolfgang Iser, 'Counter-sensical comedy and audience response in Beckett's *Waiting for Godot*' (1987) in S. Connor (ed.), *New Casebooks: Waiting for Godot and Endgame* (Houndmills: Macmillan, 1992), pp. 55–70 (p. 56).

26 Enid Welsford, *The Fool: His Social and Literary History* (London: Faber and Faber, 1968), p. 318.

27 Clifford Leech details the argument in his Introduction to the Arden Shakespeare edition of the play (1969), and Wiles concurs in his study of Kemp in *Shakespeare's Clown*.

28 Shakespeare, *The Two Gentlemen of Verona* (London: Methuen, 1986 [1969]), p. 32 (Act II, Scene iii, lines 4–11).

29 Shakespeare, *The Two Gentlemen of Verona*, pp. 32–3 (Act II, Scene iii, lines 13–23).

30 In another mode of writing, the all-time champion would have to be Laurence Sterne's novel, *The Life and Opinions of Tristram Shandy* (1759–67), whose perpetually distractable narrator fails to reach the point of his own birth for the first two-and-a-half volumes.

31 Shepherd, *Theatre, Body and Pleasure*, p. 64.

32 Ayckbourn, *Absurd Person Singular*, pp. 45–70.

33 Langer, *Feeling and Form*, p. 342.

34 Shepherd, *Theatre, Body and Pleasure*, p. 80.

35 Oscar Wilde, *An Ideal Husband* in *The Importance of Being Earnest and Other Plays* (London: Penguin, 1986), pp. 147–244 (pp. 192–3).

36 John Guare, *The House of Blue Leaves* (London: Methuen, 1993), p. 24.

37 Bergson, 'Laughter', p. 140.

38 Congreve, *The Way of the World*, p. 190 (Act IV, Scene i).

39 Styan, *Restoration Comedy in Performance*, p. 133.

40 Purdie, *Comedy*, p. 81.

41 Steve Seidman, 'Performance, enunciation and self-reference in Hollywood comedian comedy' in F. Krutnik (eds.) *Hollywood Comedians. The Film Reader*, (London: Routledge, 2003), pp. 21–41 (p. 22).

42 Sheridan, *The School for Scandal*, p. 106.

43 Katharine Worth, *Sheridan and Goldsmith* (Houndmills: Macmillan, 1992), p. 41.

44 Eric Bentley reminds us of Sir John Gielgud's advice about regulating the audience's laughter so that they don't tire themselves out too soon. The clever playwright helps out in this regard, by helping to orchestrate those brief hiatuses between comic peaks.

45 Sheridan, *The School for Scandal*, p. 106.

46 Sigmund Freud, 'Humour' (1927) in A. Dickson (ed.), *Art and Literature* (Harmondsworth: Penguin, 1990), pp. 425–33 (p. 427). It should be noted that I take humour in a wider sense than he does, but I believe the model to shed light on all joking situations.

47 Aristophanes, *Frogs*, pp. 124–5.

48 Shakespeare, *Much Ado About Nothing* (New York: New American Library, 1964), p. 37 (Act I, Scene i).

49 Wilde, *The Importance of Being Earnest*, p. 292.

50 Martin McDonagh, *The Lonesome West* in *The Beauty Queen of Leenane and Other Plays* (New York: Vintage, 1998), pp. 167–259 (pp. 172–3).

51 Peter L. Berger, *Redeeming Laughter: The Comic Dimension of Human Experience* (Berlin: de Gruyter, 1997), p. x.

52 Bergson, 'Laughter', p. 84.

53 Feydeau and Desvallières, *A Little Hotel on the Side*, p. 82.

54 Bentley, *The Life of the Drama*, p. 252.

55 Charney, *Comedy High and Low*, p. 45.

5 Comedy's range

1 Bentley, *The Life of the Drama*, p. 312.

2 Sophocles, *Antigone*, trans. by Don Taylor (London: Methuen, 1998), pp. 129–88 (pp. 141–2).

3 Sophocles, *Antigone*, p. 139.

4 Styan, *The Dark Comedy: The Development of Modern Comic Tragedy*, new edn (Cambridge University Press, 1968), p. 17.

5 Styan, *The Dark Comedy*, p. 17.

6 Anonymous, *Everyman* in *Three Late Medieval Morality Plays* (London: A & C Black, 1993), pp. 59–105 (p. 69, lines 122–3).

7 Anonymous, *Everyman*, p. 78 (lines 355–6).

8 Bergson, 'Laughter', p. 170.

9 Styan, *The Dark Comedy*, p. 11.

10 Marina Carr, *By the Bog of Cats*...in *Marina Carr: Plays* (London: Faber and Faber, 1999), pp. 257–341 (p. 265).

11 Carr, *By the Bog of Cats*..., p. 299.

12 Carr, *By the Bog of Cats*..., p. 311.

13 Carr, *By the Bog of Cats*..., p. 311.

14 Styan, *The Dark Comedy*, p. 283.

15 Bentley, *The Life of the Drama*, p. 319.

16 Styan, *The Dark Comedy*, p. 2.

17 His book is called *The Dark Voyage and the Golden Mean: A Philosophy of Comedy*.

18 Shakespeare, *Measure for Measure* (London: Methuen, 1979), p. 75 (Act III, Scene i, lines 132–9)

19 Styan, *The Dark Comedy*, pp. 22–3.

20 Styan, *The Dark Comedy*, p. 275.

21 Albert Bermel, *Comic Agony: Mixed Impressions in the Modern Theatre* (Evanston: Northwestern University Press, 1993), p. 7.

22 Freud, 'Humour', p. 433.

23 Ben Elton, *Popcorn* in *Plays: 1* (London: Methuen, 1998), pp. 173–255 (pp. 207–8).

24 Elton, *Popcorn*, pp. 185–6.

25 Nico Frijda, *The Emotions* (Cambridge University Press, 1986), p. 437.

26 Luigi Pirandello, *On Humor*, trans. by Antonio Illiano and Daniel P. Testa (Chapel Hill: University of North Carolina Press, 1960), pp. 117–18.

27 Theatre has found various conventions which allow a simplification of contextual representation, by urging the spectator to imagine much of the scenic environment, e.g., a forest represented by trees painted on a backdrop, or a kitchen suggested by a table and two chairs. The same space may serve for several settings, established by backdrop, set piece, dialogue or behaviour of the actors. Similarly, spectators are accustomed to accepting the passage of time between scenes with the help of lighting changes or references in the dialogue. It can still be argued, however, that these all remain theatrical strategies for filling in the blanks around a 'realistic', external correspondence to the world, even if convention readily exploits the spectator's imagination to supply much of the detail.

28 Antonin Artaud, *The Theater and its Double*, trans. by Mary Caroline Richards (New York: Grove Weidenfeld, 1958), p. 94.

29 Guillaume Apollinaire, *The Mammaries of Tiresias*, trans. by Maya Slater in *Three Pre-Surrealist Plays* (Oxford University Press, 1997), pp. 151–207 (pp. 169–70).

30 André Breton, 'Lightning rod' in *Anthology of Black Humor*, trans. by Mark Polizzotti (San Francisco: City Lights, 1997), pp. xiii–xix (p. xix).

31 Martin Esslin, *The Theatre of the Absurd*, new edn (New York: Vintage, 2004), pp. 23–4.

32 Esslin, *The Theatre of the Absurd*, p. 357.

33 Alfred Jarry, *Ubu the King*, trans. by Maya Slater in *Three Pre-Surrealist Plays* (Oxford University Press, 1997), pp. 49–147 (p. 65).

34 Jarry, *Ubu the King*, p. 81.

35 Maya Slater, 'Introduction' in *Three Pre-Surrealist Plays* (Oxford University Press, 1997), pp. ix–xlii (p. xxvi).

36 Jarry, *Ubu the King*, p. 120. The reference to Jarry's production notes is cited by Maya Slater, 'Introduction', p. xxxviii.

37 Philip Thomson, *The Grotesque* (London: Methuen, 1972), p. 27.

38 Thomson, *The Grotesque*, p. 59.

39 Esslin, *The Theatre of the Absurd*, pp. 335–6.

40 Jan Kott, *Shakespeare Our Contemporary*, trans. by Boleslaw Taborski (New York: W. W. Norton, 1974), p. 132.

41 Samuel Beckett, *Waiting for Godot* in *The Complete Dramatic Works* (London: Faber and Faber, 1990), pp. 7–88 (p. 88).

42 Eugène Ionesco, *The Bald Soprano*, trans. by Donald M. Allen in *The Bald Soprano and Other Plays* (New York: Grove, 1958), pp. 7–42 (p. 9).

43 Ionesco, *The Bald Soprano*, p. 14.

44 Ionesco, *The Bald Soprano*, p. 19.

45 Ionesco, *Rhinoceros*, trans. by Derek Prouse in *Rhinoceros, The Chairs, The Lesson* (London: Penguin, 1962), pp. 9–124 (p. 26).

46 Harold Pinter, *The Birthday Party* (London: Faber and Faber, 1991), p. 49.

47 Elin Diamond, *Pinter's Comic Play* (Lewisburg: Bucknell University Press, 1985), p. 64.

48 Diamond, *Pinter's Comic Play*, p. 64.

49 Pinter, *The Homecoming* (New York: Grove, 1978), p. 20.

50 Pinter, *The Homecoming*, p. 53.

51 John Orr, *Tragicomedy and Contemporary Culture* (Houndmills: Macmillan, 1991), p. 18.

52 Orr, *Tragicomedy and Contemporary Culture*, p. 8.

53 The delineation between the theatre characters and the six 'characters' (actually, seven, as an additional personage introduces the possibility of a third quality of being) presents a real challenge for any production. Outlining styles may serve to set apart the two registers of being. Pirandello suggests the possibility of masks for the 'characters', though I think the reverse is worth considering.

54 Luigi Pirandello, *Six Characters in Search of an Author*, trans. by Mark Musa, in *Six Characters in Search of an Author and other Plays* (London: Penguin, 1995), pp. 1–66 (p. 55).

55 Arthur Laurents, *West Side Story*, music by Leonard Bernstein and Iyrics by Stephen Sondheim in *Romeo and Juliet and West Side Story* (New York: Dell, 1965), pp. 131–224 (p. 208).

56 Jonathan Miller, *Subsequent Performances* (New York: Viking, 1986), pp. 34–5.

57 Molière, *Don Juan*, p. 91.

58 David Whitton, *Molière: Don Juan* (Cambridge University Press, 1995) p. 10.

59 Whitton, *Molière*, p. 25.

60 Whitton, *Molière*, p. 70.

61 Whitton, *Molière*, p. 76.

62 Whitton, *Molière*, p. 105.

63 Whitton, *Molière*, p. 135.

64 Anton Chekhov, *The Cherry Orchard*, trans. by Michael Frayn in *Chekhov: Plays* (London: Methuen, 1993), pp, 283–353 (p. 292).

65 Chekhov, *The Cherry Orchard*, p. 321.

66 Chekhov, *The Cherry Orchard*, p. 331.

67 James N. Loehlin, *Chekhov: The Cherry Orchard* (Cambridge University Press, 2006), p. 179.

68 Loehlin, *Chekhov*, p. 159.

69 Loehlin, *Chekhov*, p. 160.

70 David Bradby, *Beckett: Waiting for Godot* (Cambridge University Press, 2001), p. 80.

71 Bradby, *Beckett*, p. 94.

72 Bradby, *Beckett*, p. 94.

6 Comedy and society

1 D. C. Muecke, *Irony* (London: Methuen, 1970), p. 63.

2 Wilde, *The Importance of Being Earnest*, p. 313.

3 Claire Colebrook, *Irony: The New Critical Idiom* (London: Routledge, 2004), p. 14.

4 Pinter, *The Lover* in *Plays: Two* (London: Methuen, 1988), pp. 159–96 (p. 161).

5 Beckett, *Happy Days* in *The Complete Dramatic Works* (London: Faber and Faber, 1990), pp. 135–68 (p. 138).

6 Beckett, *Happy Days*, p. 156.

7 Beckett, *Happy Days*, p. 158.

8 Wycherley, *The Country Wife*, p. 54 (Act II, Scene i).

9 Peter Brooker, 'Key words in Brecht's theory and practice' in P. Thomson and G. Sacks (eds.), *Cambridge Companion to Brecht* (Cambridge University Press, 1994), pp. 185–200 (p. 181).

10 Bertolt Brecht, *Mother Courage and her Children*, in *Plays: Two*, trans. by John Willett (London: Methuen, 1987), pp. 95–182 (p. 99).

11 Brecht, *Brecht on Theatre*, p. 96.

12 Caryl Churchill, *Cloud Nine* in *Plays: One* (London: Methuen, 1985), pp. 243–320 (p. 265).

13 Wycherley, *The Country Wife*, p. 55.

14 Northrop Frye, 'The Argument of Comedy' (1949) in D. J. Palmer (ed.), *Comedy: Developments in Criticism* (Houndmills: Macmillan, 1984), pp. 74–84 (p. 76).

15 Bradby, *Beckett*, pp. 203–4.

16 Simon Dentith, *Parody* (London: Routledge, 2000), p. 37.

17 David Ives, *Speed-the-Play* in *All in the Timing: Fourteen Plays* (New York: Vintage, 1995), pp. 188–212 (p. 205).

18 David Mamet, *Speed-the-Plow* in *Plays: 3* (London: Methuen, 1996), pp. 118–84 (p. 175).

19 Shepherd, *Theatre, Body and Pleasure*, p. 32.

20 Shakespeare, *As You Like It* (London: Arden Shakespeare, 2006), p. 263 (Act III, Scene ii).

21 Erick Keown's review of the Stratford production for *Punch*, cited in Penny Gay, '*As You Like It*' in *Shakespeare's Comedies*, ed. by Emma Smith (Oxford: Blackwell, 2004), pp. 273–304 (p. 278).

22 Linda Hutcheon, *Irony's Edge: The Theory and Politics of Irony* (London: Routledge, 1994), p. 27.

23 Dentith, *Parody*, p. 20.

24 Matthew Hodgart, *Satire* (New York: McGraw-Hill, 1969), p. 11.

25 John Gay, *The Beggar's Opera* (London: Penguin, 1986). p. 121.

26 Aphra Behn, *The Rover* in *The Rover and Other Plays* (Oxford University Press, 1995), pp. 1–88 (p. 36).

27 This is one of a number of anecdotal quips for which Kaufman is famous.

28 George S. Kaufman and Moss Hart, *Once in a Lifetime* in *Six Plays by Kaufman and Hart* (New York: Random House, 1942), pp. 1–115 (p. 72).

29 Mikhail Bakhtin, *Rabelais and his World*, trans. by Hélène Iswolsky (Bloomington: Indiana University Press, 1984), p. 10.

30 Behn, *The Rover*, pp. 5–6.

31 Bakhtin, *Rabelais and his World*, pp. 19–20.

32 Julia Kristeva, 'Approaching abjection' in C. Cazeaux (ed.), *The Continental Aesthetics Reader* (London: Routledge, 2000), pp. 542–62 (p. 544).

33 Andrew Stott, *Comedy* (London: Routledge, 2005), pp. 86–7.

34 Mamet, *Glengarry Glen Ross* in *Plays: 3* (London: Methuen, 1996), pp. 1–66 (p. 26).

35 Mamet, *Glengarry Glen Ross*, p. 27.

36 Welsford, *The Fool*, pp. 319–20.

37 Welsford, *The Fool*, p. 76.

38 For a more thorough discussion of the time and trope, the reader is directed to Duncan Salkeld's *Madness and Drama in the Age of Shakespeare* (Manchester University Press, 1993).

39 Peter Barnes, *The Ruling Class* in *Plays: One* (London: Methuen, 1994), pp. 1–119 (p. 24).

40 Purdie, *Comedy*, p. 84.

41 Barnes, *The Ruling Class*, p. 69.

42 Barnes, *The Ruling Class*, p. 110.

43 Peter Buse, *Drama + Theory: Critical Approaches to Modern British Drama* (Manchester University Press, 2001), p. 104.

44 Ayckbourn *Conversations with Ayckbourn* (1981), cited in Christopher Innes, *Modern British Drama 1890–1990* (Cambridge University Press, 1992), p. 312.

45 Innes, *Modern British Drama*, p. 313.

46 For an extremely accessible introduction to materialist, Postmodern and post-colonial theory, see Mark Fortier's *Theory/Theatre: An Introduction,* new edn (London: Routledge, 2002), pp. 151–216.

47 Hélène Cixous, 'The laugh of the Medusa', trans. by Keith Cohen and Paula Cohen, in E. Marks and I. de Courtivron (eds.), *New French Feminisms* (New York: Schocken, 1981) pp. 245–64 (p. 245).

48 Ann-Marie MacDonald, *Goodnight Desdemona (Good Morning Juliet)* (New York: Grove, 1990), p. 14.

49 Orton, *What the Butler Saw*, p. 376.

50 Orton, *What the Butler Saw*, p. 413.

51 Buse, *Drama + Theory*, pp. 69–70.

52 C. W. E. Bigsby, *Modern American Drama, 1945–2000* (Cambridge University Press, 2000), p. 419.

53 Tony Kushner, *Angels in America, Part One: Millennium Approaches* (New York: Theatre Communications Group, 1993), p. 24.

54 Kushner, *Angels in America*, p. 25.

55 Bigsby, *Modern American Drama*, p. 421.

56 Kushner, *Angels in America*, p. 21.

57 Because this is a book about reading dramatic texts from the page and not about performance analysis, I am bypassing discussion of theatre practice and production with regard to postmodernism, interculturalism and postcolonialism. And it should be acknowledged that the concepts, choices and locations for actual production of existing texts have proved vastly fertile ground for these theoretical approaches.

58 Barnes, *The Ruling Class*, p. 26.

59 Churchill, *Top Girls* in *Plays: Two* (London: Methuen, 1990), pp. 75–6.

60 Chris Powell, 'A phenomenological analysis of humour in society' in C. Powell and G. E. C. Paton (eds.), *Humour in Society: Resistance and Control*, (Houndmills: Macmillan, 1988), pp. 86–105 (p. 88).

61 Ama Ata Aidoo, *The Dilemma of a Ghost* in *The Dilemma of a Ghost and Anowa* (Harlow: Longman, 1985) pp. 1–53 (p. 14).

62 I discuss this play and this issue in more depth in an essay titled 'Who's laughing now? Comic currents for a new Irish audience' in S. Brady and

F. Walsh (eds.), *Crossroads: Performance Studies and Irish Culture* (Basingstoke: Palgrave, 2009)

63 Fortier, *Theory/Theatre*, p. 193.

64 Helen Gilbert,'Introduction' to *The Rez Sisters* in H. Gilbert (ed.), *Postcolonial Plays: An Anthology* (London: Routledge, 2001), pp. 380–3 (p. 392).

65 George A. Test, *Satire: Spirit and Art* (Tampa: University of South Florida Press, 1991), p. 22.

66 Apte, *Humor and Laughter*, p. 227.

67 C. G. Jung, *Four Archetypes: Mother*Rebirth*Spirit*Trickster* (London: ARK, 1986), p. 143.

68 Ricki Stefanie Tannen, *The Female Trickster: The Mask That Reveals* (London: Routledge, 2007), p. 238.

69 Gilbert and Joanne Tompkins, *Post-Colonial Drama: Theory, Practice, Politics* (London: Routledge, 1996), p. 173.

70 Derek Walcott, *Pantomime* in *Postcolonial Plays: An Anthology* (London: Routledge, 2001), pp. 132–52 (p. 132).

71 Gilbert and Tompkins, *Post-colonial Drama*, p. 37.

72 George C. Wolfe, *The Colored Museum* (London: Methuen, 1987), pp. 1–2.

73 Wolfe, *The Colored Museum*, p. 24.

74 Edward Albee, *The Goat or Who is Sylvia?* (London: Methuen, 2004), p. 9.

75 Albee, *The Goat*, p. 12.

76 Albee, *The Goat*, p. 28.

77 Albee, *The Goat*, p. 43.

78 Albee, *The Goat*, p. 64.

79 John Storey, *Cultural Theory and Popular Culture: An Introduction*, new edn (Harlow: Pearson Education, 2001), p. 143. He cites Alexander Doty (italics in original).

Further reading

Comedy in general or overview:

W. D. Howarth, (ed.), *Comic Drama: The European Heritage* (London: Methuen, 1978). The 'Introduction' offers an engaging survey of comic theory through the ages, and contains the editor's own attempt at formally distinguishing the genre.

Erich Segal, *The Death of Comedy* (Cambridge, Mass.: Harvard University Press, 2001)

Andrew Stott, *Comedy* (London: Routledge, 2005)

The following volumes contain collections of essays or extracts on comedy, offering historical views on the subject:

Robert Corrigan (ed.), *Comedy: Meaning and Form* (Scranton: Chandler, 1965)

D.J. Palmer (ed.), *Comedy: Developments in Criticism* (Basingstoke: Macmillan, 1984)

Greek and Roman comedy:

Richard C. Beacham, *The Roman Theatre and its Audience* (London: Routledge, 1995)

R. L. Hunter, *The New Comedy of Greece and Rome* (Cambridge University Press, 1989)

Douglas MacDowell, *Aristophanes and Athens* (Oxford University Press, 1995)

Kenneth McLeish, *The Theatre of Aristophanes* (London: Thames & Hudson, 1980)

Alan H. Sommerstein, *Greek Drama and Dramatists* (London: Routledge, 2002)

J. Michael Walton and Peter D. Arnott, *Menander and the Making of Comedy* (Westport: Greenwood, 1996)

David Wiles, *Greek Theatre Performance: An Introduction* (Cambridge University Presss, 2000)

Humour and laughter:

Henri Bergson, 'Laughter' in W. Sypher (ed.), *Comedy* (Baltimore: Johns Hopkins University Press, 1980), pp. 59–180 remains an original point of reference for humour theory.

Simon Critchley, *On Humour* (London: Routledge, 2002), part of the Thinking in Action series, is a very readable treatment of humour across a range of disciplines.

William F. Fry, Jr., *Sweet Madness: A Study of Humor* (Palo Alto: Pacific, 1968), good especially for its discussion of the relationship between play and humour.

John Morreall, *The Philosophy of Laughter and Humour* (Albany: SUNY, 1987) supplies an historical collection of philosophers' views on humour and laughter.

Jerry Palmer, *Taking Humour Seriously* (London: Routledge, 1984) provides a comprehensive treatment of humour and society.

Robert R. Provine, *Laughter: A Scientific Investigation* (New York: Penguin, 2001), a scientific but entirely readable approach.

Comedy in performance:

Richard Andrews, *Scripts and Scenarios: The performance of Comedy in Renaissance Italy* (Cambridge University Press, 1993)

J. L. Styan, *Restoration Comedy in Performance* (Cambridge University Press, 1986)

David Wiles, *Shakespeare's Clown: Actor and Text in the Elizabethan Playhouse* (Cambridge University Press, 1987)

Commedia dell' arte:

Antonio Fava, *The Comic Mask in the Commedia dell'Arte* (Evanston: Northwestern University Press, 2007)

Barry Grantham, *Playing Commedia* (Portsmouth: Heinemann, 2000)

John Rudlin, *Commedia dell'Arte: An Actor's Handbook* (London: Routledge, 1994)

Other books of interest:

Albert Bermel, *Comic Agony: Mixed Impressions in the Modern Theatre* (Evanston: Northwestern University Press, 1993)

Mark Fortier, *Theory/Theatre: An Introduction*, new edn (London: Routledge, 2002). As noted in Chapter 6, this book offers extremely accessible introductions to the areas of gender studies, queer theory, Marxist theory, postcolonialism and more.

Alexander Leggatt, *English Stage Comedy 1490–1990* (London: Routledge, 1998)

J. L. Styan, *The Dark Comedy: The Development of Modern Comic Tragedy*, new edn (Cambridge University Press, 1968)

List of Texts

Aidoo, Ama Ata, *The Dilemma of a Ghost* in *The Dilemma of a Ghost and Anowa*
(Harlow: Longman, 1985), pp. 1–53
Albee, Edward, *The Goat or Who is Sylvia?* (London: Methuen, 2004)
Anonymous, *Everyman* in *Three Late Medieval Morality Plays* (London: A & C
Black, 1993), pp. 59–105
Apollinaire, Guillaume, *The Mammaries of Tiresias*, trans. by Maya Slater in
Three Pre-Surrealist Plays (Oxford University Press, 1997), pp. 151–207
Aristophanes, *Acharnians*, trans. by Kenneth McLeish in *Aristophanes Plays: One*
(London: Methuen, 1993), pp. 1–60
   Frogs, trans by Kenneth McLeish in *Six Greek Comedies* (London: Methuen,
2002), pp. 89–167
   Lysistrata, trans. by Kenneth McLeish in *Aristophanes Plays: One* (London:
Methuen, 1993), pp. 193–256
   The Wasps, trans. by David Barrett in *Aristophanes: The Wasps, The Poet
and the Women, The Frogs* (London: Penguin, 1964), pp. 33–94
Austen, Jane, *Pride and Prejudice* (New York: W. W. Norton, 2001)
Ayckbourn, Alan, *Absurd Person Singular* in *Three Plays* (New York: Grove,
1975), pp. 11–93
Barnes, Peter, *The Ruling Class* in *Plays: One* (London: Methuen, 1994),
pp. 1–119
Beckett, Samuel, *Happy Days* in *The Complete Dramatic Works* (London: Faber
and Faber, 1990), pp. 135–68
   Waiting for Godot in *The Complete Dramatic Works* (London: Faber and
Faber, 1990), pp. 7–88
Behn, Aphra, *The Rover* in *The Rover and Other Plays* (Oxford University Press,
1995), 1–88
Brecht, Bertolt, *Mother Courage and her Children*, trans. by John Willett in *Plays:
Two* (London: Methuen, 1987), pp. 95–182
Carr, Marina, *By the Bog of Cats...* in *Marina Carr: Plays* (London: Faber and
Faber, 1999), pp. 257–341
Chekhov, Anton, *The Cherry Orchard*, trans. by Michael Frayn in *Chekhov: Plays*
(London: Methuen, 1993), pp. 283–353
Churchill, Caryl, *Cloud Nine* in *Plays: One* (London: Methuen, 1985),
pp. 243–320

Top Girls in *Plays: Two* (London: Methuen, 1990)

Congreve, William, *The Way of the World* in *Four English Comedies* (London: Penguin, 1985), pp. 131–231

Elton, Ben, *Popcorn* in *Plays: 1* (London: Methuen, 1998), pp. 173–255

Erdman, Nikolai, *The Suicide* (New York: Broadway Play Publishing, 2000)

Feydeau, Georges and Maurice Desvallières, *A Little Hotel on the Side*, trans. by John Mortimer (London: Samuel French, 1984)

Griffiths, Trevor, *Comedians* (London: Faber and Faber, 1979)

Guare, John, *The House of Blue Leaves* (London: Methuen, 1993)

Ionesco, Eugène, *The Bald Soprano* trans. by Donald M. Allen in *The Bald Soprano and Other Plays* (New York: Grove, 1958), pp. 7–42

   Rhinoceros, trans. by Derek Prouse in *Rhinoceros, The Chairs, The Lesson* (London: Penguin, 1962), pp. 9–124

Ives, David, *Speed-the-Play* in *All in the Timing: Fourteen Plays* (New York: Vintage, 1995), pp. 199–212

Jarry, Alfred, *Ubu the King*, trans. by Maya Slater in *Three Pre-Surrealist Plays* (Oxford University Press, 1997), pp. 49–147

Johnson, Terry, *Hysteria* in *Plays: 2* (London: Methuen, 2003), pp. 89–190

Jonson, Ben, *Volpone* (London: Ernest Benn, 1968)

Kaufman, George S. and Moss Hart, *Once in a Lifetime* in *Six Plays by Kaufman and Hart* (New York: Random House, 1942), pp. 1–115

Kushner, Tony, *Angels in America, Part One: Millennium Approaches* (New York: Theatre Communications Group, 1993)

Laurents, Arthur, *West Side Story*, music by Leonard Bernstein and Lyrics by Stephen Sondheim in *Romeo and Juliet and West Side Story* (New York: Dell, 1965), pp. 131–224

McDonagh, Martin, *The Lonesome West* in *The Beauty Queen of Leenane and Other Plays* (New York: Vintage, 1998), pp. 167–259.

Mamet, David, *Glengarry Glen Ross* in *Plays: 3* (London: Methuen, 1996), pp. 1–66

Mamet, David, *Speed-the-Plow* in *Plays: 3* (London: Methuen, 1996), pp. 119–84

   Goodnight Desdemona (Good Morning Juliet) (New York: Grove, 1990)

Menander, *The Malcontent*, trans. by J. Michael Walton in *Aristophanes and Menander: New Comedy* (London: Methuen, 1994)

Milligan, Spike, 'The great man' in *The Essential Spike Milligan* (London: Fourth Estate, 2003), pp. 67–8

Molière, *Don Juan*, trans. by George Graveley and Ian Maclean in *Don Juan and Other Plays* (Oxford University press, 1989), pp. 31–91

   Scapin the Schemer, trans. by George Graveley and Ian Maclean in *Don Juan and Other Plays* (Oxford University Press, 1989), pp. 337–90

Orton, Joe, *What the Butler Saw* in *The Complete Plays* (London: Methuen, 1997), pp. 361–448

Pinter, Harold, *The Birthday Party* (London: Faber and Faber, 1991)

   The Homecoming (New York: Grove, 1978)

   The Lover in *Plays: Two* (London: Methuen, 1988), pp. 159–96

Pirandello, Luigi, *Six Characters in Search of an Author*, trans. by Mark Musa in *Six Characters in Search of an Author and Other Plays* (London: Penguin, 1995), pp. 1–66

Plautus, *The Braggart Soldier*, trans. by Erich Segal in *Four Comedies* (Oxford University Press, 1996), pp. 1–74

   The Pot of Gold, trans. by E.F. Watling in *The Pot of Gold and Other Plays* (London: Penguin, 1965), pp. 7–49

Shakespeare, William, *As You Like It* (London: Arden Shakespeare, 2006)

   The Comedy of Errors (London: Routledge, 1994)

   Measure for Measure (London: Methuen, 1979)

   Much Ado About Nothing (New York: New American Library, 1964)

   Twelfth Night or What You Will (New York: New American Library, 1965)

   The Two Gentlemen of Verona (London: Methuen, 1986)

Sheridan, Richard Brinsley, *The School for Scandal* (London: A & C Black, 1995)

Simon, Neil, *Chapter Two* (New York: Samuel French, 1979)

Sophocles, *Antigone*, trans. by Don Taylor (London: Methuen, 1998), pp. 129–88

Stoppard, Tom, *On the Razzle* (London: Faber and Faber, 1982)

Synge, J. M., *The Playboy of the Western World* in *J. M. Synge: The Complete Plays* (London: Methuen, 1995), pp. 173–229

Terence, *The Eunuch*, trans. by Kenneth McLeish in *Four Roman Comedies* (London: Methuen, 2003), pp. 139–216

   The Girl From Andros, trans. by Betty Radice in *The Comedies* (London: Penguin, 1976), pp. 30–91

Voltaire, *Candide*, trans. by Robert M. Adams (New York: W. W. Norton, 1991)

Walcott, Derek, *Pantomime* in *Postcolonial Plays: An Anthology* (London: Routledge, 2001), pp. 132–52

Wilde, Oscar, *An Ideal Husband* in *The Importance of Being Earnest and other Plays* (London: Penguin, 1986), pp. 147–244

   The Importance of Being Earnest in *The Importance of Being Earnest and Other Plays* (London: Penguin, 1986), pp. 247–313

Wolfe, George C., *The Colored Museum* (London: Methuen, 1987)

Wycherley, William, *The Country Wife* (London: A & C Black, 1993)

Bibliography

Altman, Rick, *Film/Genre* (London: BFI, 1999)

Andrews, Richard, 'Scripted theatre and the *commedia dell'arte*' in J. R. Mulryne and M. Shewing (eds.), *Theatre of the English and Italian Renaissance* (London: Macmillan, 1991), pp. 21–54

   Scripts and Scenarios: The Performance of Comedy in Renaissance Italy (Cambridge University Press, 1993)

Apte, Mahadev L., *Humor and Laughter: An Anthropological Approach* (Ithaca: Cornell University Press, 1985)

Apter, Michael J., *The Experience of Motivation: The Theory of Psychological Reversals* (London: Academic, 1982)

Aristotle, *Poetics*, trans. by Malcolm Heath (London: Penguin, 1996)

Artaud, Antonin, *The Theater and its Double*, trans. by Mary Caroline Richards (New York: Grove Weidenfeld, 1958)

Bakhtin, Mikhail, *Rabelais and his World*, trans. by Hélène Iswolsky (Bloomington: Indiana University Press, 1984)

Bakhtin, Mikhail and P. N. Medvedev, 'Genres as ideological forms', trans. by A. J. Wehrle in P. Morris (ed.), in *The Bakhtin Reader* (London: Edward Arnold, 1994), pp. 174–82

Barthes, Roland, *Image-Music-Text*, trans by Stephen Heath (London: Fontana, 1977)

Beacham, Richard C., *The Roman Theatre and its Audience* (London: Routledge, 1995)

Belsey, Catherine, *Critical Practice* (London: Routledge, 1980)

Bennett, Andrew and Nicholas Royle, *Introduction to Literature, Criticism and Theory*, new edn (Harlow: Prentice Hall, 1999)

Bentley, Eric, *The Life of the Drama* (New York: Applause, 1991)

Berger, Peter L., *Redeeming Laughter: The Comic Dimension of Human Experience* (Berlin: de Gruyter, 1997)

Bergson, Henri, 'Laughter' in W. Sypher (ed.), *Comedy* (Baltimore: Johns Hopkins University Press, 1980), pp. 59–190

Berlyne, Daniel, *Conflict, Arousal, and Curiosity* (New York: McGraw-Hill, 1960)

Bermel, Albert, *Comic Agony: Mixed Impressions in the Modern Theatre* (Evanston: Northwestern University Press, 1993)

Bigsby, C. W. E., *Modern American Drama, 1945–2000* (Cambridge: Cambridge University Press, 2000)

Booker, Christopher, *The Seven Basic Plots: Why We Tell Stories* (London: Continuum, 2004)

Booth, Wayne, *A Rhetoric of Irony* (University of Chicago Press, 1974)

Bradby, David, *Beckett: Waiting for Godot* (Cambridge: Cambridge University Press, 2001)

Brecht, Bertolt, *Brecht on Theatre: The Development of an Aesthetic*, ed. and trans. by John Willett (London: Methuen, 1993)

Breton, André, 'Lightning rod' in *Anthology of Black Humor*, trans. by Mark Polizzotti (San Francisco: City Lights, 1997), pp. xiii–xix

Bristol, Michael D., *Carnival and Theater: Plebeian Culture and the Structure of Authority in Renaissance England* (New York: Routledge, 1985)

Brooker, Peter, 'Key words in Brecht's theory and practice' in P. Thomson and G. Sacks (eds.), *The Cambridge Companion to Brecht* (Cambridge University Press, 1994), pp. 185–200

Buse, Peter, *Drama + Theory: Critical Approaches to Modern British Drama* (Manchester University Press, 2001)

Calderwood, James L., & Harold E. Toliver, 'Introduction to comedy' in J. L. Calderwood and H. E. Toliver (eds.) *Perspectives on Drama* (New York: Oxford, 1968), pp. 163–76.

Charney, Maurice, *Comedy High and Low: An Introduction to the Experience of Comedy* (New York: Oxford University Press, 1978)

Cixous, Hélène, 'The Laugh of the Medusa', trans. by Keith Cohen and Paula Cohen, in E. Marks and I. de Courtivron (eds.) *New French Feminisms*, (New York: Schocken, 1981), 245–64

Colebrook, Claire, *Irony: The New Critical Idiom* (London: Routledge, 2004)

Connery, Brian A. and Kirk Combe, 'Theorizing satire: a retrospective and introduction' in B. A. Connery and K. Combe (eds.), *Theorizing Satire: Essays in Literary Criticism* (Basingstoke: Macmillan, 1995), pp. 1–15

Cook, Albert, *The Dark Voyage and the Golden Mean: A Philosophy of Comedy* (New York: W. W. Norton, 1966)

Cooper, Lane, *An Aristotelian Theory of Comedy* (Oxford: Blackwell, 1924)

Cordner, Michael, Peter Holland and John Kerrigan, 'Introduction' in M. Cordner, P. Holland and J. Kerrigan (eds.), *English Comedy* (Cambridge University Press, 1994), pp. 1–11

Cornford, Francis Macdonald, *The Origin of Attic Comedy* (Garden City: Anchor, 1967)

Cornwell, Neil, *The Absurd in Literature* (Manchester University Press, 2006)

Corrigan, Robert W., 'Introduction: comedy and the comic spirit' in R. W. Corrigan (ed.), *Comedy: Meaning and Form* (Scranton: Chandler, 1965), pp. 1–11

Critchley, Simon, *On Humour* (London: Routledge, 2002)

Dane, Joseph A., *Parody: Critical Concepts Versus Literary Practices, Aristophanes to Sterne* (Norman: University of Oklahoma Press, 1988)

Dentith, Simon, *Parody* (London: Routledge, 2000)

Diamond, Elin, *Pinter's Comic Play* (Lewisburg: Bucknell University Press, 1985)

Donaldson, Ian, 'Justice in the stocks' (1970) in D. J. Palmer (ed.),
     Comedy: Developments in Criticism (Basingstoke: Macmillan, 1984),
     pp. 103–14
Douglas, Mary, *Implicit Meanings* (London: Routledge and Kegan Paul, 1975)
Dubrow, Heather, *Genre: The Critical Idiom* (London: Methuen, 1982)
Duckworth, George E., *The Nature of Roman Comedy*, new edn (London: Bristol
     Classical, 1994)
Dürrenmatt, Friedrich, 'Comedy and the modern world' (1958) in D. J. Palmer
     (ed.), *Comedy: Developments in Criticism* (Basingstoke: Macmillan,
     1984), 131–4
     'Postscript' in *The Visit*, trans. by Patrick Bowles (New York: Grove, 1962),
     pp. 105–8
Dutton, Richard, *Modern Tragicomedy and the British Tradition: Beckett, Pinter,
     Stoppard, Albee and Storey* (Brighton: Harvester, 1986)
Eco, Umberto, 'Frames of comic freedom' in T. Sebeok (ed.), *Carnival!* (Berlin:
     Mouton, 1984), pp. 1–9
Elliott, Robert C., *The Power of Satire: Magic, Ritual, Art* (Princeton University
     Press, 1972)
Ellis, M. J., *Why People Play* (Englewood Cliffs: Prentice Hall, 1973)
Enright, D. J., *The Alluring Problem: An Essay on Irony* (Oxford University
     Press, 1988)
Esslin, Martin, *The Theatre of the Absurd*, new edn (New York: Vintage, 2004)
     'Introduction' in M. Esslin (ed.), *Absurd Drama* (London: Penguin, 1965),
     pp. 7–23
Fava, Antonio, *The Comic Mask in the Commedia dell'arte* (Evanston:
     Northwestern University Press, 2007)
Fortier, Mark, *Theory/Theatre: An Introduction*, new edn (London: Routledge,
     2002)
Foucault, Michel, *Madness and Civilization: A History of Insanity in the Age of
     Reason*, trans. by Richard Howard (New York: Vintage, 1988)
Fowler, Alistair, *Kinds of Literature: An Introduction to the Theory of Genres and
     Modes* (Oxford: Clarendon, 1982)
Freud, Sigmund, 'Humour' (1927) in A. Dickson (ed.), *Art and Literature*
     (Harmondsworth: Penguin, 1990), pp. 425–33
     Jokes and their Relation to the Unconscious, trans. by James Strachey, ed. by
     Angela Richards (London: Penguin, 1991)
Frijda, Nico, *The Emotions* (Cambridge University Press, 1986)
Frow, John, *Genre: The New Critical Idiom* (London: Routledge, 2006)
Fry, Christopher, *An Experience of Critics and the Approach to Dramatic Criticism*
     (London: Perpetua, 1952)
Frye, Northrop, *Anatomy of Criticism* (London: Penguin, 1990)
     'The Argument of comedy' (1949) in D. J. Palmer (ed.), *Comedy:
     Developments in Criticism* (Basingstoke: Macmillan, 1984), pp. 74–84
Gaskell, Ronald, *Drama and Reality : The European Theatre since Ibsen* (London:
     Routledge & Kegan Paul, 1972)

Gay, Penny, '*As You Like It*' in *Shakespeare's Comedies*, ed. by Emma Smith (Oxford: Blackwell, 2004), pp. 273–304

Genette, Gérard, *Paratexts: Thresholds of Interpretation*, trans. by Jane E. Lewin (Cambridge University Press, 1987)

George, David J., 'Introduction' in D. J. George and C. J. Gossip (eds.), *Studies in the Commedia dell'Arte* (Cardiff: University of Wales Press, 1993), pp. 1–11

Gilbert, Helen, 'Introduction' to *Pantomime* in H. Gilbert (ed.) *Postcolonial Plays: An anthology* (London: Routledge, 2001), pp. 128–31

   'Introduction' to *The Rez Sisters* in H. Gilbert (ed.) *Postcolonial Plays: An anthology* (London: Routledge, 2001), pp. 390–3

Gilbert, Helen and Joanne Tompkins, *Post-Colonial Drama: Theory, Practice, Politics* (London: Routledge, 1996)

Glasgow, R. D. V., *Madness, Masks, and Laughter: An Essay on Comedy* (Madison: Fairleigh Dickinson University Press, 1995)

Goffman, Erving, *Frame Analysis: An Essay on the Organization of Experience*, new edn (Boston: Northeastern University Press, 1986)

Gordon, Mel, *Lazzi: The Comic Routines of the Commedia dell'arte* (New York: Performing Arts Journal, 1983)

Grantham, Barry, *Playing Commedia* (Portsmouth: Heinemann, 2000)

Gray, Frances, *Women and Laughter* (Basingstoke: Macmillan, 1994)

Grene, Nicholas, *Shakespeare, Jonson, Molière: The Comic Contract* (London: Macmillan, 1980)

Grice, Paul, 'Logic and conversation (1967, 1987)' in P. Grice, *Studies in the Way of Words* (Cambridge, Mass.: Harvard University Press, 1989), pp. 1–143

Gruber, William E., *Comic Theaters: Studies in Performance and Audience Response* (Athens, Ga.: University of Georgia Press, 1986)

Gurewitch, Martin, *Comedy: The Irrational Vision* (Ithaca: Cornell University Press, 1975)

Handley, E. W., 'The conventions of the comic stage' in E. Segal (ed.), *Oxford Readings in Menander, Plautus, and Terence* (Oxford University Press, 2002), pp. 27–41

Henke, Robert, *Performance and Literature in the Commedia dell'Arte* (Cambridge University Press, 2002)

Herr, Christopher J., 'Satire in Modern and Contemporary Theater' in R. Quintero (ed.), *A Companion to Satire* (Oxford: Blackwell, 2007), pp. 460–75

Hinchliffe, Arnold P., *The Absurd* (London: Methuen, 1969)

Hobbes, Thomas, *Leviathan*, excerpted in J. Morreall (ed.), *The Philosophy of Laughter and Humor* (Albany: SUNY, 1987), p. 19

Hodgart, Matthew, *Satire* (New York: McGraw-Hill, 1969)

Hodgdon, Barbara, 'Sexual disguise and the theatre of gender' in A. Leggatt (ed.), *The Cambridge Companion to Shakespearean Comedy* (Cambridge: Cambridge University, 2002), pp. 179–97

Holland, Norman, *Laughing: A Psychology of Humor* (Ithaca: Cornell University Press, 1982)

Holub, Robert C., *Reception Theory: A Critical Introduction* (London: Methuen, 1984)

Howard, Jean E., 'Cross-dressing, the theatre and gender struggle in early modern England' in L. Goodman (ed.), *The Routledge Reader in Gender and Performance* (London: Routledge, 1998), pp. 47–51

Huizinga, Johan, *Homo Ludens: A Study of the Play-Element in Culture* (Boston: Beacon, 1955)

Hunter, R. L., *The New Comedy of Greece and Rome* (Cambridge University Press, 1989)

Hutcheon, Linda, *Irony's Edge: The Theory and Politics of Irony* (London: Routledge, 1994)

Ingarden, Roman, *The Litetrary Work of Art*, trans. by George G. Grabowicz (Evanston: Northwestern University Press, 1973)

Innes, Christopher, *Avant Garde Theatre 1892–1992* (London: Routledge, 1993)
Modern British Drama 1890–1990 (Cambridge University Press, 1992)

Iser, Wolfgang, 'Counter-sensical Comedy and audience response in Beckett's *Waiting for Godot*' (1987) in S. Connor (ed.), *New Casebooks: Waiting for Godot and Endgame* (Basingstoke: Macmillan, 1992), pp. 55–72
The Implied Reader: Patterns of Communication in Prose Fiction from Bunyan to Beckett (Baltimore: Johns Hopkins University Press, 1974)

Janko, Richard, *Aristotle on Comedy: Towards a Reconstruction of Poetics II* (London: Duckworth, 2002 [1984])

Jung, C. G., *Four Archetypes: Mother*Rebirth*Spirit*Trickster* (London: ARK, 1986)

Kairoff, Claudia Thomas, 'Gendering satire: Behn to Burney' in R. Quintero (ed.) *A Companion to Satire* (Oxford: Blackwell, 2007), pp. 276–92

Katritzky, M. A., *The Art of Commedia: A Study in the Commedia dell'Arte 1560–1620 with Special Reference to the Visual Records* (Amsterdam: Rodopi, 2006)

Kempe, Andy, 'Reading plays for performance' in D. Hornbrook (ed.), *On the Subject of Drama* (London: Routledge, 1998), pp. 92–111

Kern, Edith, *The Absolute Comic* (New York: Columbia University Press, 1980)

Kerr, Walter, *Tragedy and Comedy* (New York: Da Capo, 1985)

Knight, Charles A., *The Literature of Satire* (Cambridge University Press, 2004)

Knight, G. Wilson, *The Wheel of Fire: Interpretations of Shakespearian Tragedy* (London: Routledge, 1993)

Knowlson, James, 'Tradition and Innovation in Ionesco's *La Cantatrice chauve*' in E. Brater and R. Cohn (eds.), *Around the Absurd: Essays on Modern and Postmodern Drama* (Ann Arbor: University of Michigan Press, 1990), pp. 57–71

Knox, Bernard, 'Euripidean Comedy' in E. Segal (ed.), *Oxford Readings in Menander, Plautus, and Terence* (Oxford University Press, 2001), pp. 3–24

Ko, Yu Jin, 'Shakespeare's Rosalind: *charactor* of contingency' in S. Hengen (ed.), *Performing Gender and Comedy: Theories, Texts and Contexts* (Amsterdam: Gordon and Beach, 1998), pp. 21–34

Koestler, Arthur, *The Act of Creation* (London: Picador, 1978)

Konstan, David, *Roman Comedy* (Ithaca: Cornell University Press, 1983)

Kott, Jan, *Shakespeare Our Contemporary*, trans. by Boleslaw Taborski (New York: W. W. Norton, 1974)

Kristeva, Julia, 'Approaching abjection' in C. Cazeaux (ed.), *The Continental Aesthetics Reader* (London: Routledge, 2000), pp. 542–62

Krutnik, Frank, 'Conforming passions?: contemporary romantic comedy' in S. Neal (ed.), *Genre and Contemporary Hollywood* (London: BFI, 2002), pp. 130–47

    'General introduction' in F. Krutnik (ed.), *Hollywood Comedians: The Film Reader* (London: Routledge, 2003), pp. 1–18

Kundera, Milan, *Testaments Betrayed*, trans. by Linda Asher (New York: Perennial, 2001)

Langer, Susanne, *Feeling and Form* (New York: Charles Scribner's Sons, 1953)

Leggatt, Alexander, *English Stage Comedy 1490–1990* (London: Routledge, 1998)

Levin, Harry, *Playboys & Killjoys* (Oxford University Press, 1987)

Little, W. Kenneth, 'Pitu's doubt: entrée clown self-fashioning in the circus tradition', *The Drama Review*, 30, 4(1986), 51–64

Loehlin, James N., *Chekhov: The Cherry Orchard* (Cambridge University Press, 2006)

Lowenfeld, Margaret, *Play in Childhood*, new edn (London: Mac Keith, 1991)

MacDowell, Douglas, *Aristophanes and Athens* (Oxford University Press, 1995)

McLeish, Kenneth, *Roman Comedy* (Bristol: Macmillan Education, 1994)

    The Theatre of Aristophanes (London: Thames & Hudson, 1980)

Mast, Gerald, *The Comic Mind: Comedy and the Movies* (London: New English Library, 1974)

Meredith, George, 'An essay on comedy' in W. Sypher (ed.), *Comedy* (Baltimore: Johns Hopkins University Press, 1980), pp. 1–57

Merleau-Ponty, Maurice, 'Cézanne's doubt' (1945) in G. A. Johnson (ed.) and M. B. Smith (trans.), *The Merleau-Ponty Aesthetics Reader: Philosophy and Painting* (Evanston: Norhthwestern University Press, 1993), pp. 59–75

    'Eye and mind' in G. A. Johnson (ed.) and M. B. Smith (trans.), *The Merleau-Ponty Aesthetics Reader: Philosophy and Painting* (Evanston: Northwestern University Press, 1993), pp 121–49

    'Indirect language and the voices of silence' (1952) in G. A. Johnson (ed.) and M. B. Smith (trans.), *The Merleau-Ponty Aesthetics Reader: Philosophy and Painting* (Evanston: Northwestern University Press, 1993), pp. 76–120

    The Phenomenology of Perception, trans. by Colin Smith (London: Routledge, 1996)

Miller, Jonathan, 'Jokes and joking: a serious laughing matter' in J. Durant (ed.), *Laughing Matters: A Serious Look at Humour* (Burnt Mill: Longman Scientific & Technical, 1988), pp. 5–16
  Subsequent Performances (New York: Viking, 1986)
Miller, Scott, *Strike Up the Band: A New History of Musical Theatre* (Portsmouth: Heinemann, 2007)
Morreall, John, *The Philosophy of Laughter and Humour* (Albany: State University of New York Press, 1987)
Muecke, D. C. *Irony* (London: Methuen, 1970)
Nash, Walter, *The Language of Humour: Style and technique in Comic Discourse* (London: Longman, 1985)
Nelson, Y. G. A., Comedy: *An Introduction to Comedy in Literature, Drama, and Cinema* (Oxford University Press, 1990)
O'Casey, Sean, 'The power of laughter' in *The Green Crow* (London: Comet, 1987)
O'Connor, Frank, *The Art of the Theatre* (Dublin: Maurice Fridberg, 1947)
Olson, Elder, *The Theory of Comedy* (Bloomington: Indiana University Press, 1968)
Orr, John, *Tragicomedy and Contemporary Culture* (Basingstoke: Macmillan, 1991)
Palmer, D. J., 'Introduction' in D. J. Palmer (ed.), *Comedy: Developments in Criticism* (Basingstoke: Macmillan, 1984), pp. 8–22
Palmer, Jerry, *The Logic of the Absurd: On Film and Television Comedy* (London: BFI, 1987)
  Taking Humour Seriously (London: Routledge, 1994)
Paul, William, 'The impossibility of romance: Hollywood comedy, 1978–1999' in S. Neal (ed.), *Genre and Contemporary Hollywood* (London: BFI, 2002), pp. 117–29
Pickering, Jerry V., *Theatre: A Contemporary Introduction*, new edn (St. Paul: West, 1981)
Pirandello, Luigi, *On Humor*, trans. by Antonio Illiano and Daniel P. Testa (Chapel Hill: University of North Carolina Press, 1960)
Potts, L. Y., *Comedy* (London: Hutchinson & Co., 1957)
Powell, Chris, 'A phenomenological analysis of humour in society' in C. Powell and G. E. C. Paton (eds.), *Humour in Society: Resistance and Control* (Basingstoke: Macmillan, 1988), pp. 86–105
Provine, Robert R., *Laughter: A Scientific Investigation* (New York: Penguin, 2001)
Purdie, Susan, *Comedy: The Mastery of Discourse* (University of Toronto Press, 1993)
Quintero, Ruben, 'Introduction: understanding satire' in R. Quintero (ed.), *A Companion to Satire* (Oxford: Blackwell, 2007), pp. 1–11
Richards, Kenneth and Laura Richards, *The Commedia dell'arte: A Documentary History* (Oxford: Blackwell, 1990)
Salkeld, Duncan, *Madness and Drama in the Age of Shakespeare* (Manchester University Press, 1993)

Sartre, Jean-Paul, 'Play' in R. Denoon Cumming (ed.), *The Philosophy of Jean-Paul Sartre* (New York: Vintage, 1965), pp. 310–16

Schechner, Richard, *The Future of Ritual* (London: Routledge, 1993)
    Performance Studies: An Introduction (London: Routledge, 2002)

Schopenhauer, Arthur, *The World as Will and Idea*, trans. by R. B. Haldane and John Kemp, excerpted in J. Morreall (ed.), *The Philosophy of Laughter and Humor* (Albany: SUNY, 1987), pp. 51–64

Schulte, Rainer and John Biguenet 'Introduction' in R. Schulte and J. Biguenet (eds.), *Theories of Translation : An Anthlogy of Essays from Dryden to Derrida* (University of Chicago Press, 1992), pp. 1–10

Schutz, Alfred, *Collected Papers I* (The Hague: Martinus Nijhoff, 1971)

Segal, Erich, *The Death of Comedy* (Cambridge: Harvard University Press, 2001)

Segal, Erich (ed.), *Oxford Readings in Menander, Plautus, and Terence* (Oxford University Press, 2001)

Seidman, Steve, 'Performance, enunciation and self-reference in Hollywood comedian comedy' in F. Krutnik (ed.), *Hollywood Comedians: The Film Reader* (London: Routledge, 2003), pp. 21–41

Shepherd, Simon, *Theatre, Body and Pleasure* (London: Routledge, 2006)

Silk, M. S., *Aristophanes and the Definition of Comedy* (Oxford University Press, 2000)

Slater, Maya, 'Introduction' in M. Slater (trans.), *Three Pre-Surrealist Plays* (Oxford University Press, 1997), pp. ix-xlii

Slater, Niall W., *Plautus in Performance: The Theatre of the Mind* (Amsterdam: Harwood Academic, 2000)

Sommerstein, Alan H., *Greek Drama and Dramatists* (London: Routledge, 2002)

Spencer, Herbert, 'The physiology of laughter' in J. Morreall (ed.), *The Philosophy of Laughter and Humor* (Albany: SUNY, 1987), pp. 99–110

States, Bert O., *Great Reckonings in Little Rooms: On the Phenomenology of Theater* (Berkeley: University of California Press, 1987)
    'The phenomenological attitude' in J. G. Reinelt and J. R. Roach (eds.), *Critical Theory and Performance* (Ann Arbor: University of Michigan Press, 2007), pp. 26–36

Storey, John, *Cultural Theory and Popular Culture: An Introduction*, new edn (Harlow: Pearson Education, 2001)

Stott, Andrew, *Comedy* (London: Routledge, 2005)

Styan, J. L., *The Dark Comedy: The Development of Modern Comic Tragedy*, new edn (Cambridge University Press, 1968)
    The English Stage: A History of Drama and Performance (Cambridge University Press, 1996)
    Modern Drama in Theory and Practice 1: Realism and Naturalism (Cambridge University Press, 1991)
    Restoration Comedy in Performance (Cambridge University Press, 1986)

Taaffe, Lauren K. *Aristophanes and Women* (London: Routledge, 1993)

Tannen, Ricki Stefanie, *The Female Trickster: The Mask that Reveals* (London: Routledge, 2007)

Test, George A., *Satire: Spirit and Art* (Tampa: University of South Florida Press, 1991)

Theophrastus, 'The characters' in P. Vellacott (trans.), *Theophrastus: The Characters / Menander: Plays and Fragments* (Harmondsworth: Penguin, 1973), pp. 31–61

Thomson, Philip, *The Grotesque* (London: Methuen, 1972)

Todorov, Tzetvan, *Genres in Discourse*, trans. by Catherine Porter (Cambridge University Press, 1990)

Traub, Valerie, 'The Homoerotics of Shakespearian comedy' in E. Smith (ed.) *Shakespeare's Comedies* (Oxford: Blackwell, 2004), pp. 164–91

Turner, Victor, *The Anthropology of Performance* (New York: PAJ, 1988) *From Ritual to Theatre* (New York: PAJ, 1982)

Ubersfeld, Anne, 'The pleasure of the spectator', trans. by Pierre Bouillaguet and Charles Jose, *Modern Drama*, 25, 1 (1982), 128–33

Walton, J. Michael and Peter D. Arnott, *Menander and the Making of Comedy* (Westport: Greenwood, 1996)

Weinbrot, Howard D., *Menippean Satire Reconsidered: From Antiquity to the Eighteenth Century* (Baltimore: Johns Hopkins University Press, 2005)

Weitz, Eric, 'Comic patterns in *Kevin's Bed* and *Twenty Grand*', in E. Weitz (ed.), *The Power of Laughter: Comedy and Contemporary Irish Theatre* (Dublin: Carysfort, 2004), pp. 103–17
'Who's Laughing now? Comic currents for a new Irish audience' in S. Brady and F. Walsh (eds.), *Crossroads: Performance Studies and Irish Culture* (Basingstoke: Palgrave, 2009)

Welsford, Enid, *The Fool: His Social and Literary History* (London: Faber and Faber, 1968)

Whitton, David, '*Dom Juan* the director's play' in D. Bradby and A. Calder (eds.), *The Cambridge Companion to Molière*, (Cambridge University Press, 2006), pp. 201–13
Molière: Don Juan (Cambridge University Press, 1995)

Wickham, Glynne, *A History of the Theatre*, new edn (Cambridge University Press, 1992)

Wiles, David, *Greek Theatre Performance: An Introduction* (Cambridge University Press, 2000)
Shakespeare's Clown: Actor and text in the Elizabethan Playhouse (Cambridge University Press, 1987)

Willeford, William, *The Fool and His Scepter* (Evanston: Northwestern University Press, 1969)

Wilshire, Bruce, *Role Playing and Identity: The Limits of Theatre as Metaphor* (Bloomington: Indiana University Press, 1982)

Winnicott, D. W., *Playing and Reality* (London: Routledge, 1991)

Worrall, Nick, *Nikolai Gogol and Ivan Turgenev* (London: Macmillan, 1982)

Worth, Katharine, *Sheridan and Goldsmith* (Houndmills: Macmillan, 1992)

Index

Cambridge Introductions to . . .